Long As I Hope to Live

CLAUDIA CARLI
Translated by Laura Watkinson

The true story of the Jewish girl
ALIDA LOPES DIAS (1929–1943),
her friendship album and all the girls
who wrote in it

HODDER &
STOUGHTON

First published in Great Britain in 2021 by Hodder & Stoughton
An Hachette UK company

This paperback edition published in 2022

1

First published in Dutch as *Zoo lang ik hoop te leven* by
Meulenhoff Boekerij in 2020
Translation from Dutch by Laura Watkinson

This publication has been made possible with financial support
from the Dutch Foundation for Literature.

A CIP catalogue record for this title is available from the British Library

Paperback ISBN 978 1 529 38596 0
eBook ISBN 978 1 529 38594 6

Typeset in Quadraat by Palimpsest Book Production Limited, Falkirk, Stirlingshire

Printed and bound in Great Britain by Clays Ltd, Elcograf S.p.A.

Hodder & Stoughton policy is to use papers that are natural, renewable
and recyclable products and made from wood grown in sustainable forests.
The logging and manufacturing processes are expected to conform to the
environmental regulations of the country of origin.

Hodder & Stoughton Ltd
Carmelite House
50 Victoria Embankment
London EC4Y 0DZ

www.hodder.co.uk

As
Long
As I
Hope
to
Live

CONTENTS

In 1945 Gretha Lopes Dias returned to the Netherlands, the only one of her family to do so. She survived Auschwitz. When she arrived home, she found the friendship album that had belonged to Alie, her younger sister. Among those who wrote poems in her book were nineteen of Alie's young girlfriends. Gretha was the last to write in the album, not a poem, but a promise: that she would keep the book for as long as she lives.

When I first saw the album, it was Gretha's promise that really touched me. Gretha had left it to my stepfather. He was a good friend of Gretha and her second husband, Ari. If it hadn't been for his friendship with them, I couldn't have written this book. In the final years of her life, Gretha told more and more stories about her sister, their parents, the camp at Vught and how the family was torn apart.

After her death, I realised there was no one left to tell the story of Gretha and her little sister. I wanted to know all those stories, I wanted to find out what Alie's life was like and who those friends were who had written in her album. I was fascinated by the beautiful handwriting of those young girls and their sweet, moving and sometimes amusing poems for Alie.

I began my research into the girls in 2011. Sometimes months would pass before I came across new information. However, as more archives have been digitised, the project really gained momentum in recent years. I was aware that another of the girls, Tirtsa, had survived the war and was still alive. After an extensive search, I finally managed to locate her in May 2019, and so hers is the most recent story to have been included here.

During my research, I made many fascinating discoveries, and I talked to relatives of the girls, including a son and a daughter, and also a woman who lived next door to Alie as a child. However, the dearest to me are the four girls I found who survived the war. They are now ladies in their eighties: Adele Zimmer, Rosa Snijders, Mimi de Leeuw and Tirtsa Steinberg. Their stories and the black-and-white photograph of Class 4A that Rosa gave me helped me bring life and colour to the girls who wrote in the friendship album.

The events in this book actually happened. Sometimes the people I spoke to could still remember their conversations word for word, but that was not usually the case, so most of the dialogue is fictionalised. At the back of the book, there are some examples of how I went about my research. The chapters are named after the people who wrote in the album, as a tribute to them, and the book follows the same order as the friendship album.

Only six of the nineteen girls survived the war. Through these stories, I hope to present a picture of the world these girls lived in, so that no one will forget they were here.

An entire world in one small album.

Claudia Carli,
Amsterdam 2019

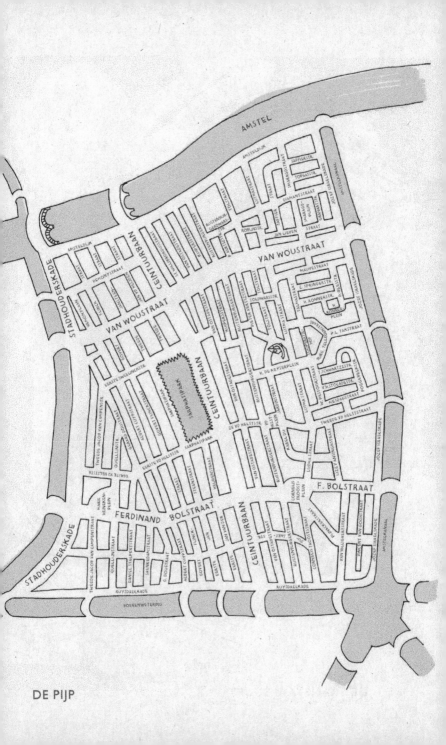

DE PIJP

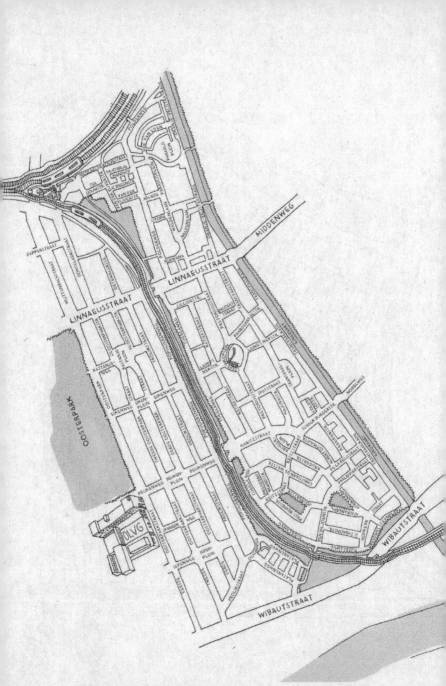

DE TRANSVAALBUURT

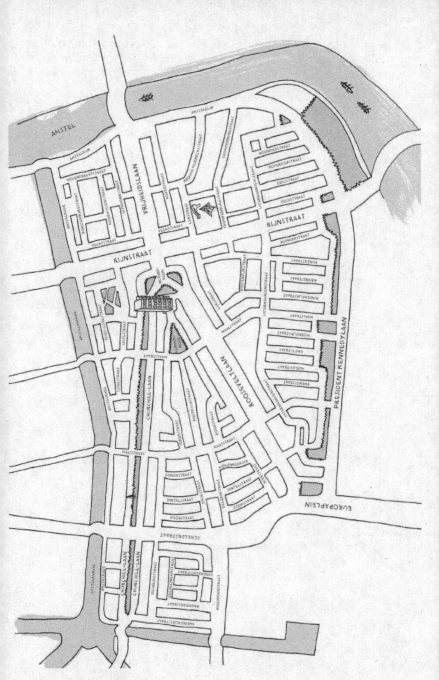

DE RIVIERENBUURT

Alida Lopes Dias

1941

It makes no difference if Alie has her eyes open or shut: it is still pitch dark.

Judging by the sound of the rattling carts out on the street, it is early in the morning. The carts are going to the Albert Cuyp market. She is not allowed to go there anymore, or to any other markets for that matter. She hears the front door of the building quietly close and then paws pattering on the stairs: Roosje, following Father. Father no longer has his regular market pitch, so now he walks the streets with a basket of flowers. Her father is optimistic. 'If this is all, then we're lucky,' he keeps saying.

Alie smells a familiar scent, so warm and sweet. Her stomach starts to rumble.

Feeling her way in the darkness, she carefully removes the black-out paper from the window. It is still not quite light outside. She puts on her socks and follows the scent of baking to the kitchen. Her mother is wearing her oven gloves and is struggling with a baking tin. She has her woollen cardigan over her nightdress. Her feet are bare – she gets too hot if she covers her feet. Mother brushes a dark curl out of her eyes. About six months ago, grey hairs began to show among the brown. Alie's mother is not as optimistic as her father. She worries, but never when Alie is around – only when she thinks Alie cannot see.

Three cakes are lined up on the counter. A fourth is stuck inside the baking tin.

'Are you alright?' asks Alie.

Mother jumps, almost dropping the baking tin. She looks round at Alie.

'Oh, now it's not a surprise!' she says.

'The smell already gave it away,' replies Alie.

Mother puts down the tin, gives her daughter a hug and a kiss and wishes her a life that is one hundred years long.

'A hundred years?' says Alie, doing the sum in her head. 'It'll be 2029 then. I wonder if I'll still be able to remember what this birthday was like.'

She goes into the living room, where Roosje jumps up on her.

'Alida Lopes Dias, Govert Flinckstraat 265, first floor,' Father reads from an envelope. 'Is that you? That's a fancy name. I thought you were called Alie Dias.' He peers at her over his glasses.

She tries to take the letter out of his hand, but he pulls it away and taps his cheek.

'First a kiss.'

She gives him a big smacker on the cheek and snatches the envelope.

'Happy birthday, *sjeintje*,' he says, giving her a kiss back. 'You're twelve now.'

It is a birthday card from Aunt Kitty, with a picture of Shirley Temple on the front. Aunt Kitty and Alie are both mad about films, but the cinema is off limits too.

'Aunt Kitty's coming next week,' Alie tells her mother, who has just come through from the kitchen with the breakfast tray.

'That's nice,' says Mother, placing a brown parcel with a white ribbon around it on Alie's plate. Roosje jumps up onto a chair, but Mother pushes her off again.

Father sits down at the table and acts very surprised. 'What's all this?' he says, pointing at the parcel. 'Is it your birthday or something?'

Alie laughs and pulls the ribbon off the parcel. There is a dark-brown book inside, with a crocodile leather print.

'A friendship album!' She opens the book. The pages are still pressed crisply together. The snow-white paper smells new. Alie loves books and paper. She used to be able to spend hours browsing around stationery shops. But that was before the war. Now it is a luxury she can no longer enjoy.

'It's beautiful!' She thanks her mother and father, fetches a pen from her bedroom and opens the book to the first page.

'You have to go to school, Aaltje. Finish your bread,' says Mother.

'Just a second,' says Alie, trying to write as neatly as possible. This is something she can do only once.

Als dit album vuns wordt
verzoek ik het terug te brengen
naar M'des Goodtflinksta
(Adam Nurd)   P 654

febra 50 1932

21-3-18

Dit album behoort aan mij
hoe lang ik hoop te leven
Als ik nga naar ik bij mij geboorte zijn
Dies is mijn naam ik en mijn vaders Adam
Amsterdam is plaats waar ik ter
wereld kwam.

Whoever finds this album
is requested to return it to
Alie Dias
Govertflinkstr 265-I
(A'dam Zuid)

•

received in 1942

•

21–9–19
This album belongs to me
As long as I hope to live
Alie is my name given to me at birth
Dias is my name from my father's line
Amsterdam the place where I came into this world.

Annie Fransman

26 January 1930
11 December 1942

for get me not
•
Z & M
•
19–9–1941
Dear Alie,

I'm not a born poet,
And I'm no good at rhyme.
But I don't want to
parrot anyone else either,
So no word or song from me,
Just the wish: forget me not.

Your friend,
Annie Fransman.
•
Ip, dip, dup,
the date's the wrong way up.

SEPTEMBER

Alie is hurrying to school. Roosje is trying to keep up with her little legs.

'I'm in a hurry, Roos. You're going to have to take yourself into the park.'

She walks past the Sarphatipark, but Roosje keeps following her.

'Go on. Off you go,' she says, pushing the dog towards the park entrance.

Roosje stops and stares at Alie with a dopy look on her face.

'Fine. I'll go with you.' Alie walks to the entrance, where two men are hanging a sign on the fence. One of them is up a ladder. She recognises him: he is the father of one of the girls in her street. She is about to go into the park with Roosje, but the man at the foot of the ladder stops her.

'Read the sign, please.' He points up at the words, written in thick black letters.

Alie cannot see very clearly, because the man up the ladder is blocking her view.

She reads: NO . . . ALLOWED.

'Is that new?' she asks. 'Aren't dogs allowed in the park anymore?'

The men look at each other in surprise.

'Your dog can go into the park, but . . .'

Alie takes a closer look at the sign.

NO JEWS ALLOWED.

'So you'll have to go around the outside,' says the man at the bottom of the ladder.

For a second, Alie has no idea what to do. She reads the sign again. That really is what it says.

'Leave the girl alone,' says the man up the ladder.

'She'd better get used to it,' the other man replies.

Her cheeks flushing, Alie hurries past the park and heads for her school. She feels so ashamed for thinking it was dogs that were forbidden to enter the park. Roosje follows her. Alie snaps at her to go and take herself for a walk in the park. Startled by Alie's loud voice, Roosje comes to a stop. Alie looks up at the big trees in the park, which are all the colours of the autumn. She waits while Roosje squeezes her way through the fence, and then Alie walks on to Ceintuurbaan. Roosje trots alongside her: Roosje in the park, Alie out on the street.

'A friendship album? Nice. Is it pretty?' asks Jenny.

Alie is walking home at lunchtime with Annie and Jenny.

There is a crowd at the entrance to the park. Everyone is looking at the sign.

'Look, it's over there,' says Alie.

Jenny and Annie stare at the sign.

Some boys from their school are reading the words out loud and making jokes. One of the boys shouts the order in a German accent and does a salute.

Jenny and Annie laugh. Alie wants to join in, but she can see that a few of the older people there do not seem to find it very funny. They are Jewish too. When a couple of the boys push another boy into the park, a man grabs them by their collars.

'Stop that,' he says. His accent is German. 'Stop and think about what this means.' The man becomes emotional and his wife leads him away.

The fun is over, and everyone goes their own way.

When the girls walk into the living room, Roosje jumps up at them.

'Is that cake I can smell? I haven't had cake for ages!' Jenny exclaims.

Alie fetches the friendship album and shows it to her friends.

'It's beautiful. Is it crocodile leather?' Jenny says, running her hand over the cover.

'No, I think it's paper, but it's just like the real thing, isn't it?' Alie replies.

'Can I write something in it?' asks Annie.

'Can I too?' says Jenny.

'Me first,' says Annie.

Alie is amused that they are fighting to be the first to write in her album.

'It's still completely empty. You can both write in it,' she says with a smile.

Mother brings in some sandwiches for them. The girls look disappointed.

'Oh, alright then.' Mother goes back into the kitchen and returns with three slices of cake.

'Thank you, Mrs Dias.' Annie and Jenny pounce on the cake. Roosje jumps up onto a chair, trying to join in. Alie secretly gives her a bit.

'Can I write in your album now?' asks Annie when she has finished her cake.

'Are your hands clean?' says Alie. She brushes the crumbs off the tablecloth and opens the album.

'What are you going to write?' asks Jenny, standing right up close to Annie.

Annie holds the pen over the paper. She thinks about it. She leans forward and begins to write.

'You will write neatly, won't you? It's Alie's birthday present,' says Jenny.

'Hey, I can't do it with you standing there.' Annie moves the album away from Jenny.

'Do you have any pictures to stick in, or do you want some of mine?' says Alie.

She fetches a book from the cupboard and takes out a few cut-out pictures for Jenny and Annie to look at.

'Have you written anything yet?' Jenny says, trying to peek.

'Don't look.' Annie turns away and sighs. 'I don't know what to put.'

'Then why don't you do "Roses wilt" or something like that?'

Alie hands her a pretty picture of some roses.

'No, I'll think of something,' she says, leafing through the empty album.

Alie gives her all of the pictures for inspiration. Annie studies them and then starts writing.

'Shall I write my real name? Marianne?' she asks when she has finished.

'No, when she's older, she won't remember who Marianne was,' says Jenny.

'Just put Annie,' says Alie.

'Your friend Annie Fransman.' Annie signs the poem and shows it to them.

'Z & M,' reads Alie. 'Who's Z?'

Mimi Mok

5 February 1930
21 July 1994

21-3-13.

Lieve Alie.

Rozen verwelken.
Bloemen vergaan.
Maar onze liefde.
Blijft eeuwig bestaan.

Je Vriendin
Mien Mok.

21-9-19.
Dear Alie,

Roses wilt.
Flowers wither.
But our love
Will last forever.

Your Friend
Mimi Mok

SEPTEMBER

Alie is helping Mother with the food for the holidays. The Jewish new year 5702 is about to begin. They have saved up food coupons for the celebrations. Although the family is not really religious, they do take part in Jewish holidays. They have fresh fruit and vegetables on the kitchen counter, and chicken soup is bubbling away on the small gas stove. There are no eggs available though, and little meat. Mother is making fishcakes. She has a very small amount of fish and is padding out the fishcakes with potato and crumbs. The whole house smells of food.

The *Joodsche Weekblad* has tips for what to cook in spite of the food shortages. Alie is leafing through the newspaper.

'We're not allowed to do any sports or exercise outside now either,' says Alie, looking at the list. 'Does roller skating count as doing sports outside?' she wonders out loud.

'No, that's playing. And they can never take that away from you,' says Mother firmly.

'Unless you do it in the park – then it's not allowed,' Alie replies wryly.

'Why don't you go out and skate for a while? And take the dog with you,' says Mother. 'I'm nearly finished here anyway.'

Alie skates along with the wind in her hair.

'Come on, Roosje, faster!' Roosje tries to keep up with Alie, running as quickly as she can.

Alie bends down and grabs Roosje by her scruff, so the little dog can pull her along. Roosje struggles to run with Alie holding on to her, and she soon gives up. Alie lets go and glides to a stop.

'Good girl.' She pats the dog's back. The two of them head together towards the park. The colours of the trees go from yellow to deep red. There are not many people around. Everything smells so fresh and wet. Alie fights the temptation to enter the park. They walk to the entrance. She looks around: still no one in sight.

She stretches out her right foot until it is hovering above the soil of the park. Then she sees a group of children coming. Quickly, Alie pulls her foot back. Albertine, who lives across the road from her, just saw what she was doing. She always sees everything. No secret is safe from her. Her parents are members of the NSB, the Dutch National Socialist Movement.

'Come on, Roosje, let's go.' Alie quickly skates home.

On the corner, she meets Mimi. Mimi and Alie have been in the same class since they started school. Her parents used to have a cigar shop, but Jews are no longer allowed to run their own businesses.

'Where are you going? Can I come roller skating too?' asks Mimi.

'Albertine and her gang are over there,' says Alie, glancing back over her shoulder.

Mimi isn't listening. 'Wait there and I'll go and fetch my skates,' she says, running inside.

Albertine and her friends turn onto the street.

'Hey, Alie,' Albertine shouts.

Alie ignores her.

Albertine walks up to Alie, followed by her friends.

'Hey, were you in the park just now?' asks Albertine, standing right in front of Alie.

'Of course not,' says Alie.

'Of course not,' says Albertine, mimicking her in a silly voice. The other girls giggle.

Alie turns around, trying to ignore them.

'I'm going to tell my mum and dad,' says Albertine, and she pulls Alie's hair.

Alie is startled. Albertine's going to tell her parents? She wants to say something, but because of the pain she can only give a little yelp. That makes the girls laugh even more.

When Mimi comes back out, Alie is standing there with tears in her eyes.

'What happened?' she asks.

'Albertine and her friends,' growls Alie, rubbing the sore spot on her head. Mimi understands.

'I'm going home. I don't feel like playing outside anymore,' says Alie. 'Do you want to come with me?'

As they are taking off their skates at the foot of the steps, the upstairs neighbour comes out.

'Hello, girls. Having fun?' she asks.

'We're going back in. Albertine from across the road is out with her gang and she's being really annoying,' says Alie.

'I can imagine. They're such mean little girls. Would you two like some sweets?'

'Thank you, Mrs . . .' Alie is still rubbing the painful spot on her scalp.

'Call me Luise. We're friends, aren't we, Alie?' She gently strokes Alie's head. Alie feels a bit awkward. She does not know the woman very well, but she does not want to be rude, and the tin of sweets that the neighbour is offering her is full of all kinds of goodies: butterscotch and acid drops and liquorice comfits.

'Take what you like. There's too much for me to eat all by myself.'

'Thank you . . . Luise,' says Alie.

Roosje patters along after them and struggles up the steep stairs.

Mother comes out of the kitchen.

'Albertine pulled my hair,' says Alie.

'And? Did you give her a slap?' asks Mother.

'As if! She'd only go and tell her mum and dad,' Alie says anxiously.

Mother gives her a kiss. And another and another. There have been a lot of kisses and cuddles lately.

Then Mother sniffs. 'Have you been eating sweets?' Alie feels as if she has been caught out, but she does not really know why.

'The neighbour gave them to me.'

'Which neighbour?'

'The lady upstairs. She's quite nice. She said I can call her Luise.'

'Did she want anything else?'

'No.' Alie thinks it is a strange question. 'What would she want from me?'

'I want you to steer clear of her,' says Mother, sounding worried.

'But not Albertine?' Alie exclaims.

Mother goes into the kitchen and comes back with a dish of sliced apple and honey.

'Look,' Alie says to Mimi. 'It's my friendship album. Will you write something in it?'

Benjamin Roeg

2 June 1903
4 June 1943

Alie, bij alles wat je doet
Laat het Kwade ? handel goed
In tegenslag ? bij voorspoed
En spreekt rechtvaardig ? blij gemoed

2-10-'41

B. Kies

Alie, in everything you do,
Avoid evil and do what's good.
In both fortune and misfortune
Keep good faith and a happy mood.

2.10.41

B. Roeg

SEPTEMBER

Alie smells the flowers that are in a vase on the dining table. It is just like the old days, when Father used to bring home the flowers he had been unable to sell. Mother always joked that she had the most romantic husband in the Netherlands.

'How are things at school, Aaltje?' asks Alie's brother-in-law, Berry. 'Which school are you at again?'

'The Herman Elteschool,' she replies. 'You know that.'

'Oh yes, run by the Know Less and Chutzpah Society.' He gives her a big grin. He has such lovely white teeth. Gretha and Alie both laugh.

'Knowledge and Godliness,' Mother corrects him.

The room is full. Grandpa is there, and Aunt Sara and Uncle Eli. Aunt Kitty and her cousin Sammie.

Gretha is sitting on Berry's lap – and not because the room is so packed. They keep touching each other and laughing about nothing. Alie can see why, though. Berry is so handsome, with his thick brown hair. And that laugh! He roars when Gretha whispers something in his ear. He kisses the back of her neck and chuckles as a lock of her dark-brown curls slips into his mouth. They kiss each other on the lips.

'Hey, stop messing about, you two. You're not alone now,' says Mother.

'Oh, let the young people have their fun,' says Aunt Sara. 'I remember what it's like to be a newlywed,' she says with a sigh, looking at Uncle Eli, who is reading the newspaper and does not hear her.

'Sorry, Mrs Dias. Would you like a little help?' says Berry, standing up and taking the tray full of cups from Mother.

'What a *sjnokkeltje*, eh?' says Gretha, coming to sit by Alie.

Alie gives her a shy smile.

'That boy of Maurits's has died too,' Grandpa says, showing Father a page in the *Joodsche Weekblad*. 'They say it's more than a hundred already.' Grandpa shakes his head. 'This is not good. This is not good at all.'

'And all because those troublemakers in the WA wanted a fight,' Grandpa says bitterly.

'Stop it, Pa,' says Father, taking the newspaper from his hands. He looks at Alie and sees that she has been following the conversation.

'We're celebrating Aaltje's birthday. Is it time for the song?' he asks the room in general.

He is trying to keep it light for her, but Alie knows what happened to all those men and boys who got picked up during the raid. They were sent to Mauthausen and half of them are dead now. Mauthausen is a prison camp, they say, but it is more like a death camp. Those who end up there don't survive. No one knows what really happened. People say they had to do hard labour and that there was a disease. They all got infected and only a few pulled through. But the survivors were not allowed to go home.

'Aal, why don't you show us what you got for your birthday?' says Father, sounding bright and cheery.

Alie fetches the album and shows it to Grandpa.

'What's that?' Grandpa peers at the book with his glasses on. '*Poesie?*' he reads. 'Is it a book about cats? But you've got a dog.'

Alie laughs. 'No, Grandpa. It's a friendship album. Your friends are supposed to write poems in it.'

'Oh, that's lovely,' he says, handing it back.

'Can I see your present?' says Berry, coming out of the kitchen. She hands it to him.

'My goodness, what a nice book. What's it for?' He looks at it as if he's never seen a friendship album before.

'For writing in,' she says.

'For writing what in? Shopping lists? Very handy!'

He gives her another big grin.

'Would you like to write in it?' asks Alie.

He takes a slip of paper from his pocket. 'Will you write something for me too?'

'What am I supposed to write on that?' asks Alie. She knows he is just being silly, but she takes the paper and writes: 'Thank you for writing in my album.'

Berry turns to an empty page and starts thinking. Then Father calls him and he puts the album down.

Alie goes and sits next to Grandpa and gives him a cuddle. He has looked so thin since Grandma is no longer here. Her death seems recent, but she has been gone a year now. Without Grandma, Grandpa does not seem like Grandpa anymore.

OCTOBER

Mr Roeg tries to maintain order in the classroom. The children are still in high spirits after the holidays. He has to raise his voice, almost shouting to get their attention. Some new children have joined the class. He counts them, notes their names on a sheet of paper and then picks up his chalk. He writes on the board: 'Arithmetic, national history, nature studies.' That is the plan for this morning. He puts some sums on the board, and the children get to work. After arithmetic, they move on to history. They are starting the Eighty Years' War.

Mr Roeg tells them about Philip II and his oppression of the Netherlands. The children listen attentively as he explains how the Protestants were persecuted as heretics. Then he whistles the Wilhelmus, the national anthem of the Kingdom of the Netherlands, and tells the children that this song is about the revolt against the Spanish and about its leader, William of Orange.

He asks if anyone in the class has a Portuguese name. Alie and a number of other children raise their hands. Then he tells them that most of the Jews were expelled from Spain and went to Portugal during that period. Later – when they were no longer wanted in Portugal either – most fled to the north, many to Amsterdam, where they were welcomed. He asks if anyone in the class knows who was the first person in their family to come to Amsterdam.

Alie does not really like history, but she knows the answer to this question, because her father is always talking about it. She puts up her hand: the first Lopes Dias came to Amsterdam in the seventeenth century, but the first Lopes Dias she knows by name is Jacob, who was born in 1750. He lived with lots of brothers and sisters on a street called Hartjessteeg in the old Jewish neighbourhood. They were followed by another six generations of the Lopes Dias family before Alie's father was born.

She adds that it is a pity that he will be the last Lopes Dias, as he has only two daughters. She does have uncles who have sons, though, so they will continue the line. Mr Roeg agrees with her and says that he thinks many more generations will follow.

After history, the children go out into the playground for their nature lesson.

Across the road are the gardens of the houses beside the Sarphatipark. Alie sits leaning against the fence and tries to draw one of the trees.

The tree has dark leaves, almost black. She notices that a lot of people are at home. A little girl with a bow in her hair is standing at a window. In another house, a young woman is shaking out a duster on the balcony. There is a man with an easel on another balcony, brushing paint onto his canvas.

Mr Roeg talks to them about autumn. Their teacher is good at telling all kinds of stories, not just about nature. The autumn sun shines down as they sit on the ground without their coats.

As the children collect leaves that have fallen from the trees, they hear shouting from the other part of the playground. The children from the Christian school have their playtime now. They share the same building, but there is a large partition across the middle of the playground. A few children peep over the fence. They smile. Alie smiles back at them.

'Keep your eyes to yourself, Jew!' one of the children shouts.

Alie feels so ashamed.

Agatha jumps up on the fence, hitting out at the children with a stick.

'Say that again! I dare you!'

Jenny goes to join her.

Mr Roeg comes over to see what all the noise is about.

'They are being mean and calling us Jews, sir,' says Agatha, panting.

Mr Roeg strides back into the school. The children all try to look over the fence when they hear him talking over there. He has walked through the inside of the building and out into the other half of the playground.

Alie hates it when anyone calls her a Jew like that, as if it is an insult. But if she objected every time someone called her a Jew, she would be pretty busy. People sometimes used to say it before the war too – mainly to her parents when they thought the flowers were too expensive. They used to say they were cheating people because they were Jewish.

The teacher comes back.

'If they start shouting things at you again, report it to me. The headmistress of the other school says she'll keep an eye on them. They're to stop calling you names. We respect one another here.'

Mr Roeg tries to start the lesson again, but the sun has gone in and a cold breeze is blowing across the playground. He looks at his pocket watch.

'Time to get changed for gym, boys. Girls, go back to the classroom and take out your language books.'

Alie gives the album to Agatha and asks her to write in it. Some other girls stand around, admiring the book. They want to write in it too.

'Is there some kind of meeting I don't know about?' Mr Roeg comes and stands by them. Alie quickly tries to grab back her album, but Mr Roeg is too fast.

'I'm confiscating this for now, Alie.'

'You're not going to get that back without a long lecture,' says Jenny, and she pretends to be really sad about it, sobbing silently. She pulls such a funny face that Alie bursts out laughing.

'Miss Lopes Dias, do you want your album back or would you rather lose it for good? Because that's always an option. I could give it to some poor, needy child.'

The rest of the class laughs. Alie does not find it funny, and she remains silent.

After the lesson, she has to go and see the teacher. She is prepared for a lecture, but he simply returns the album.

'It was no fun when they called you names, was it?' he says quietly.

Surprised, Alie nods.

'I just can't get used to the way it happens so easily these days. The way it seems so normal.'

Alie does not know how to respond.

'Well, we'll have to learn how to deal with it one way or another. Here at school I can help you, but outside of school you're going to have to develop a thicker skin. They're just words, Alie. Remember that.'

She nods again. 'Yes, sir.'

'Speaking of words, I've added a few to your album. I hope you don't mind.' He smiles.

Out in the corridor she opens the album and sees the pages, now filled with a picture and a poem.

Agatha van Schaik

1 April 1930
9 July 1943

gt wond

Lieve Alida

Ik heb je leeren kennen,
't Geen mijn hart niet spijt
Ik heb het ondervonden,
Je bent een keurige meid.

Je liefh. vriendinnetje
Agatha v. Schaik

Ip Dip Dup,
the date's the wrong way up.

.

2–10–'41
Dear Alida
I have come to know you,
Which I don't regret at all,
And I've found out,
That you're a really nice girl.

Your nice friend,
Agatha v. Schaik

OCTOBER

Alie is walking past the Sint-Willibrorduskerk, across the bridge over the Amstel to Weesperzijde. The sun is shining. It is not cold, and Alie's coat is open. On the bridge, she stops for a moment. She looks down the river to the Amstel Hotel and, further on, she can see the theatre, the Carré. She went there once, with her father. He wanted her to listen to some real music. It was an opera, and Alie and her father sat all the way up in the gods. The people on the stage were tiny. It was beautiful music, but Alie still prefers real songs.

She hums a tune as she walks on. The leaves are falling from the trees beside the water. A gentle breeze blows them on to the river-bank. She breathes in the fresh air, which already smells of autumn. Alie is on her way to the girls' home where Agatha lives.

'There's a reason she's in there, the poor girl,' Alie's mother had said. 'It's for problem children.' She gave Alie a basket of food for the girls at the home. 'I'm sure they don't have much.'

Alie rings the doorbell of the house in Gijsbrecht van Aemstelstraat. A slim young woman answers.

'Is Agatha in?' Alie shakes the woman's hand. 'I'm Alie. I'm at school with Agatha.' She peeps past the woman and wonders if she has the right place. It looks like any normal house.

'This is the home, isn't it?' She says the word as if it is something very scary.

The woman smiles. 'Come on in, Alie. We've been expecting you. I'm Miss Vega. I run the home. Agatha is in the living room. Why don't you give me your coat?'

Alie sees Miss Vega's office as she walks down the hallway to the living room, which is large and airy and looks really cosy.

'Alie, you're here!' says Agatha, jumping up off the cushion-covered sofa. 'Come on, I'll show you my room,' Agatha says, pulling her along.

Miss Vega holds up Alie's basket. 'Where shall I put this?'

'It's for you. From my mother. She . . .' Alie does not dare to repeat what her mother said about the home. But Miss Vega is pleasantly surprised when she takes the tea towel off the basket.

'Your mother really shouldn't have. Not with all these food shortages!' says Miss Vega.

Agatha takes Alie by the hand.

'And now my room.' Alie and Agatha climb the stairs to the first floor, where six small rooms have been created inside one big space. Each of the rooms has been decorated by the girls themselves.

Alie drops down onto Agatha's bed and looks at the drawings and photos of film stars hanging on the wall.

'Are you allowed to hang things on the wall?'

'Why wouldn't we be?' Agatha says, arranging the pillows on her bed.

'You're not going to live here forever, are you?' Alie gets up off the bed and looks out of the window.

'No, but Miss Vega says I can make it as cosy as I like.'

'She's really nice. Maybe even nicer than my mother,' says Alie with a smile.

'My mother's kind too,' says Agatha sadly.

'Actually . . . where is your mother? Why do you live here?' Alie asks curiously.

'Oh, you know. My mother's having problems. That's why.' Agatha falls silent.

'Here's your album. I've almost finished writing, and I just need to put in some pictures. I'll do it later,' says Agatha, handing Alie her friendship album.

There is a quiet meow, and a grey-striped kitten wanders into the room.

'Oh, it's so cute.' Alie strokes the little animal. 'Was it a stray?'

'We got him off someone in the street whose cat had a litter. We weren't allowed to keep him at first, but some of the girls sulked until Miss Vega gave in.'

Alie picks up the cat and puts him on her lap, but he jumps onto the bed.

'Miss Vega says he's not allowed on the beds. It's not hygienic,' says Agatha, putting the kitten on the floor. 'Do you want to play a game?'

They head back downstairs to the living room, where more girls are now sitting. They are all older than Agatha.

'Who's your friend?' A girl holds out her hand to shake Alie's.

'This is Alie. She's in my class at school.'

'I'm Anna Aalsvel. So you're the one who brought all that lovely food?'

Alie nods. 'My mother thought . . .' She stops. She can't say that Mother thinks everyone here is a problem child, can she? 'She thought you could maybe do with a little extra.'

'That was kind of her.' Anna picks up a deck of cards from the bookshelf. 'Fancy a game of thirty-one?'

Alie nods. The three of them sit down at the dining table. The two other girls in the room come and join them.

'Alie, this is Greta and Esther.'

Alie shakes the girls' hands. Anna shuffles the cards.

'Esther is an assistant at a playschool, and Greta works as a maid.'

'Do you have a job too?' Alie asks Anna.

'Yes, I'm a seamstress.'

Anna starts dealing the cards. 'Who's in?'

Esther sits down. Miss Vega comes in with a big dish full of food. Greta follows her with a pot of tea.

'Clear a bit of space for the goodies.'

She does not have to ask them twice. The girls immediately put down their card game and pounce on the food.

'No, wait a second. You're like a pack of wild animals!' Miss Vega pulls the dish away. 'Let's show Alie that we're young ladies.'

Agatha puts back a handful of nuts. 'But it looks so good.'

'Fetch the side plates and then you can eat,' says Miss Vega, looking sternly at Agatha.

Agatha gets up and walks over to the sideboard. Alie helps her. When everything is on the table, Alie is reluctant to help herself.

'Take something, Alie,' says Anna, offering the dish to her.

'If you don't fancy it, I'll take it,' says Agatha, grabbing a stuffed tomato. Miss Vega gives her another stern look. Agatha quickly puts it on Alie's plate. 'Um, I'll take it . . . and put it on your plate for you.' Alie bursts out laughing. Miss Vega and the other girls can't help joining in.

'Is she this cheeky at school too?' Esther asks.

'She wouldn't dare. Our teacher has a bit of a temper.'

Alie takes a bite of her tomato.

'Ah, I can handle Roegie,' says Agatha in a tough voice.

The girls giggle. 'Roegie? Don't let Mr Roeg hear you calling him that.' Miss Vega offers the dish to Agatha now, who eagerly puts a few things on her plate.

'So, are there any nice boys in your class?' Anna says, looking at Alie, who blushes, taken by surprise.

'Everyone likes Jopie,' says Agatha with her mouth full.

'I don't!' Alie says defensively.

'You can be honest with us. We know how to keep a secret,' Greta says conspiratorially.

'Ladies, shall we stop bothering Alie now? I don't think she came here to reveal her innermost secrets,' says Miss Vega, pouring more tea for Alie, much to her relief.

'I'm engaged,' says Esther. 'To Ies. We're getting married this year. He's so handsome. Do you want to see a picture of him?' She goes to fetch the photograph.

Greta and Agatha lean over to Alie. 'When she shows you the photo, try to be a bit enthusiastic. He's not much of a looker!'

Before Alie can reply, Esther pushes the photo of Ies under her nose.

Ies has crooked teeth and one of his eyelids droops. He does have nice hair though.

'Well?' Esther is waiting for her reaction. 'He's handsome, eh?'

'He . . . ,' Alie does not look at Agatha and Greta, who are trying not to laugh, '. . . has lovely hair.'

Esther lets out an enamoured sigh. 'He does, doesn't he?' She looks at the photo as if he is standing beside her.

'He's so kind and helpful,' Miss Vega says, trying to support Esther, because Agatha and Greta are giggling. 'He always helps out with jobs around the house. He's such a good handyman.'

'We're just teasing,' says Greta. 'Ies is a like a big brother to us.'

Agatha hums a tune.

'When you look at me with those peepers,' Greta sings along quietly. 'I'll forgive you anything . . .'

The rest of the girls join in, and even Miss Vega starts singing.

After the food, Agatha finishes her poem. She chooses a couple of pictures to go with it.

'So, are we friends now?'

'Of course we are!' says Alie. 'Only my friends write in my album.'

Agatha signs her poem and gives the album back to Alie.

Alie bursts out laughing.

'I know it's not 2 October today, but I did start it before,' Agatha says apologetically.

'That's not what I'm laughing at,' says Alie. 'I think you're a nice friend too.'

Inge Frankenstein

23 April 1932
7 July 1944

1861   geet

muy   Lieve Ria   2-10-41.

Een goede daad is soms meer
waard. Dan alle schatten,
hier op aard.

Je vriendinnetje
Inge Frankenstein

tip
tap
top
de datum staat er op.

for
get
me
not

•

2–10–41
Dear Alie

A good deed sometimes has more worth.
Than all the treasures here on Earth.

Your friend,
Inge Frankenstein

•

bip
bap
bop
the date is at the top.

Berry Waterman

8 April 1920
24 January 1944

Ver   get

mij

Lieve Alie,
Al ben je nou de jongste spruit,
Borden moet je wasschen,
en daarmee uit.
Al huil je nou tranen met
tuiten. Eerst je werk en
dan naar buiten

Bert

For
Get
Me
Not

•

2–10 –'41

Dear Alie,

Even though you're the youngest.
You have to wash the dishes – and that's that!
Even if you cry your eyes out.
First do your work – and then you can go out.

Berry

1942

6 Jan 1915

Beste Alie

Iemand kwam mij vragen
Om ook mijn steentje bij te dragen
Dus stiek ik er maar gewoon wat
Wat er maar op dan komt het al

Ik hoop dat je gezond mag blijven,
Je toekomst veel geluk mag zijn.
En als je ouder bent geworden,
Je haartje altijd maar mag zien

Vaal   Je vriendinnetje
maal
staal   Roos Dave
weide
...... Vaal

Rosa Levie

30 April 1929
15 December 1942

6 Jan 1942

Dear Alie,

Someone came and asked me
If I would chip in too
So here I go,
Watch out, here it comes.

I hope you will stay healthy,
That your future is lots of happiness.
And when you are older,
That your heart will always be pure.

Your friend,
Rosa Levie

.

Lena de Rood

1 August 1930
2 July 1943

lieve mie
Ek heb een aardig diertje
op het plaat op goed en klein
het plaat nich altijd horen
Alles goed wees braaf en rein

Je vriendin nicht
Lena de Rood

for
get
me
not
•

10–1–42

Dear Alie.

There is a good clock.
In the hearts of big and small.
Its sound can always be heard.
Be good, be honest and pure.

Your friend
Lena de Rood
•

Do re mi fa sol
Another page is full
•

Ip bip bop
the date is at the top

Jenny Cohen

7 April 1929
12 October 1942

Het lieve vogel blaast us onze
vriendschap uit

When this bird sings,
our friendship will be over.

•

12–1–42
Dear Alie,

I lay sleeping in my garden
When an angel came along and called:
Jenny, you have to wake up
To write a poem for Alie

Your friend, Jenny Cohen.

JANUARY

When Alie walks into the classroom, she sees some children talking in a corner. Jenny is with them, and she looks unhappy. Alie goes over to her.

'Sam's gone. And Henri.'

Alie looks at their empty seats.

'Where to?' she asks.

Jenny shrugs.

'Do you want to come to mine for lunch today?' Jenny asks, just before the teacher comes in and tells everyone to sit down.

Mr Roeg looks around the classroom and sees the empty seats. He picks up a list and writes something down.

When the morning classes are over and the children are allowed to go home, Alie walks with Jenny.

'I'm going home, after all. I don't feel very well,' says Alie, when they are almost at the corner of the street. Jenny has to walk straight on. She lives on Van Woustraat. Jenny looks disappointed.

'Shall I call round for you after lunch?' They both know it's a bit of a detour.

'Or you could eat at mine instead,' says Alie. She's not keen on the idea of going home on her own either.

'My mother's expecting me. She'll get worried otherwise.'

Jenny walks on. They glance back at each other.

At home, Alie's mother has made her a jam sandwich, but Alie is not enjoying it. Her mother can tell something is wrong.

'What's up?'

Alie points at her stomach.

'You're not getting ill, are you?' her mother says, sounding worried.

She puts her hand on Alie's forehead. 'Hmm, you don't have a temperature.' She takes a good look at Alie's pale face. 'Did something happen at school?'

Alie hesitates, but she knows there is no point in remaining silent. Her mother always keeps on asking questions until Alie tells her the truth.

'Henri and two others are gone.'

Mother looks surprised. 'Gone? What do you mean?'

Alie looks sadly at her mother. 'There are empty seats in the classroom.'

Now Mother understands what she means. She pulls Alie close. Then she remembers something. 'Didn't those children come from Germany?' she says.

'Yes, but they've been living here all their lives.'

'I read that Jews from Germany had to report to the authorities for emigration, so that's what they'll have done,' says Mother.

'Jenny's father comes from Germany too, doesn't he?' says Alie. She goes to her room and fetches her album.

'Can I go round to Jenny's? Then we can walk back to school together.'

'Jenny won't have to report for emigration. Her father comes from The Hague,' her mother says, trying to reassure Alie.

'I want to go and see her anyway. Can I?' asks Alie.

'I'll walk round there with you,' says Mother, fetching her coat.

They walk down the street, around the corner and onto Van Woustraat. Everyone is walking quickly because of the rain.

They go across the busy Ceintuurbaan, where a police officer and a German soldier are directing the traffic. When a cyclist tries to cross the road, the soldier gives him a threatening look. He orders the cyclist to dismount and show his identity card. Alie links arms with her mother.

When they get to Jenny's, Mother does not go upstairs with Alie.

'Come straight home after school, eh?' She gives Alie a kiss. Then she fastens her coat up all the way and walks on to the greengrocer's.

'Jenny's still eating. Would you like a slice of bread?' asks Betsie, Jenny's mother, already cutting a slice of the tough bread.

'Go on, tuck in. Or you won't have enough energy to learn anything.' Betsie puts a slice of cheese on the bread.

Alie sits down and takes a bite. She is actually a bit peckish. Jenny puts her arm around Alie. She is glad that her friend is there. When they have finished eating, they go to Jenny's room. Alie almost trips over a play kitchen on the floor.

'Do you still play with that?' Alie thinks it is a bit childish.

'I'm giving it to my cousin Riet in The Hague. She doesn't have a father now, and she's always enjoyed playing with it. She's coming to pick it up with her mother.'

'Is that still allowed?' Alie is surprised. 'Jews can't travel anymore, can they?'

'Riet's mother isn't Jewish, so she isn't either.' Jenny moves the little kitchen aside and flops down onto her bed.

'So your father doesn't come from Germany then?'

'No. Do I look German? I can't even speak the language. Can you?'

'Nein,' says Alie and they both laugh.

'I can count in German. Listen. *Eins, zwei, drei, vier, foompf,*' says Jenny.

Alie smiles. 'It's *fünf,* not *foompf.*'

'*Foompf, foompf, foompf,*' says Jenny, pretending to be a rabbit.

'Foompf little bunnies hopping in the meadow,' jokes Alie.

'Do you have a bunny boy-*Freund*?' says Jenny, in her bad German accent.

'*Ja,* Barend the bunny,' says Alie, and they both scream with laughter when Jenny imitates him. Barend is the only boy in the class with buck teeth.

Jenny picks up a fashion catalogue off her bedside table. She opens it and starts gazing at the beautiful clothes.

'I really want this one,' she says, showing Alie an evening dress.

Alie points at a pair of gloves. 'They're nice.'

'All from De Bonneterie,' says Jenny. 'My father used to sell supplies to their sewing workshop.' She turns the pages. 'When the war's over, I want to be a model.'

Alie looks at her in surprise. 'I thought you wanted to work in an office?'

'I think it'd be a bit dull. When you're a model, you get to wear all those beautiful dresses,' says Jenny, heading to her wardrobe. 'If I work in an office, I'll never earn enough money to afford clothes like that.' She takes out her very best dress, which she is allowed to wear only on holidays, and holds it up against herself.

'And what do you want to be when you grow up?' she asks Alie.

'A seamstress, like Greet. In a sewing workshop or something like that,' Alie replies. 'Hey, do you know what we'll do? I'll make beautiful dresses and you can model them for rich customers.'

'That's not a bad idea,' says Jenny, going to sit beside Alie.

'Do you think you could make this one?' Jenny shows Alie the blue dress again.

'I'll need a few sewing lessons first,' says Alie with a grin. They both look longingly at the beautiful dress.

'Jenny, Alie, time to go back to school!' Jenny's mother calls from the kitchen.

'Oh, here. You were going to do this for me.' Alie gives her the friendship album. 'Will you write in it?'

Jenny eagerly takes the book and runs her hand gently over the cover. Then she opens it and is about to start writing.

'Keep it for a while. You can give it back to me when you're finished.'

Lientje de Jong

3 April 1930
28 May 1943

You in look
every corner
must

•

12–2–42
Dear Alie,

A little *nikkertje* walked along the beach.
cleaning his teeth with bright-white sand
Alie, be as pure
As white as the teeth
of the *nikkertje*.

Your classmate,
Lientje de Jong

•

Bish, bosh, beauty,
Alie is a cutie.

AUTHOR'S NOTE:
Sadly there were a lot of standard poems of this kind in circulation at that
time, partly because there was little to no education about racism. I did not
wish to omit this poem about the 'nikkertje' (the little n*gger boy), however.
Firstly, because I do not want to rewrite history. Secondly, because I want to
keep alive the memory of all the girls who wrote in the album, and that
includes the memory of Lientje. And also because it offers an opportunity to
reflect on the bitter fact that a girl who was murdered because she was Jewish
could write a racist poem in a friendship album.

FEBRUARY

There is an excited buzz in the classroom. Alie walks over to her seat and sees that there is a new girl sitting in front of her. The other children are clearly talking about her.

Jenny comes in and sits down next to Alie.

'Hello, I'm Lientje.' The new girl reaches out and warmly shakes first Alie's hand and then Jenny's.

'Have you two been at this school for long? Is it nice here? I'm from Wormerveer, but we weren't allowed to live there anymore.' Lientje chatters away. Alie and Jenny can't help smiling – and Lientje notices.

'Sorry, I always talk too much when I'm a bit nervous.' She looks at the other children in the class. 'Do you think they're gossiping about me?'

Alie looks at their classmates, and then at Jenny.

'Some children left our school not that long ago, and you're sitting in one of their places,' says Jenny.

'I had to leave my school too,' says Lientje with a sigh. 'And my house.'

Alie feels a pang of sympathy for her. 'There are lots of new children. I wouldn't worry about it,' she says.

'But anyway, we live in Amsterdam now. And that's nice too. It's a bit busy though. I live across the river. Where do you two live?'

Alie is about to reply, but the teacher tells the class to be silent.

'Boys and girls, you'll have noticed that we have a new student in the class. Lientje, would you please stand up for a moment?'

Lientje looks shyly around the classroom.

'Lientje comes from Wormerveer and, as you've probably heard, all Jews from the *mediene* have to come to Amsterdam.' Mr Roeg enthusiastically shakes Lientje by the hand. 'We're glad to have you here, Lientje. Welcome to the class.'

Lientje blushes because of all the attention and quickly sits down as the teacher starts the lesson.

'Now, who can explain to me what "mediene" means?'

'It's the Dutch Jewish communities outside of Amsterdam,' someone says in a bored voice.

'Well, you're enthusiastic, aren't you?'

When Alie opens up her desk, Lientje spots her album.

'Is that a friendship album?' asks Lientje.

'Yes, do you have them in Wormerveer too?' Alie asks in surprise.

The teacher claps his hands for silence.

After the lesson, Alie takes out her album and shows it to Lientje.

'Look what Jenny wrote for me. Funny, huh?'

When this bird sings,
our friendship will be over.

Lientje thinks about it. 'Oh, I get it. It can't ever sing, can it? Because it's made out of paper.' She looks sad. 'You two are really good friends, aren't you?'

'We're best friends,' says Jenny.

'Do you have a best friend too?' asks Alie.

'Yes, but I don't think I'll see her again any time soon. She's not Jewish,' she says miserably.

'Here.' Alie holds out the album. 'Will you write in my book?'

Lientje looks surprised – and pleased. 'But we've only just met.'

'You can never have too many friends.'

Lientje takes the album with both hands. 'I'll write something nice in it for you.'

After school, Alie walks some of the way home with Jenny and Lientje. They drop Jenny off at her house and continue to the corner of Ceintuurbaan. 'I have to go to President Brandstraat,' says Lientje.

'That's where Annie Fransman lives too. That's tough. It's a long walk.'

'I wish I could go on the tram. Then I'd get home faster.' Lientje looks at the tram that is just passing. 'Do you want to come and play at my house tomorrow?' she asks hopefully.

'I don't know if I'm allowed. My mother likes me to go straight home after school.'

'Mine too. She thinks the city's scary.'

Alie can see that Lientje is disappointed. 'I'll ask her. My father works at the market near there.'

'I hope she lets you. And you can have your album back.'

'I'll let you know tomorrow!' she shouts after Lientje, who is walking quickly through the cold towards the River Amstel. Lientje nods and gives her a little wave. It starts snowing. Wet snow.

Alie buttons up her coat and quickly heads home.

In the middle of the night, Alie is woken by the loud roar of an aeroplane.

The British, flying to Germany. Sounds like three of them.

Alie recognises the different planes by the sound of their engines. She gets out of bed and carefully opens the blackout curtain. She sees the lights of the anti-aircraft guns searching the sky for the planes. Then there is the sound of gunfire. Alie listens. She can still hear the planes. Thank goodness – no one got hit.

Feeling cold, she climbs back into bed. Then she hears someone bumping about in the living room.

'Aaltje, are you still awake?' Father comes into her bedroom carrying a mechanical flashlight.

'They didn't get them, eh?' Father opens the curtain a bit and peers up at the sky. 'Let's hope they get to drop their load, and then the sooner all this will be over.' He closes the curtain and comes over to tuck Alie in, nice and snug.

'Do you think we'll have to move house too?' Alie asks in a worried voice.

'Move house? Where to?' Father asks.

'Lientje had to come to Amsterdam. She left everything behind. All she was allowed to bring was her clothes and a few little bits and pieces.'

'All the Jews in the rest of the country had to come to Amsterdam, but we already live here.' Father kisses her on the forehead. 'I just wonder where all these people are supposed to live.'

'Can I come and see you at the market tomorrow? Then I can visit Lientje.'

'It's fine by me, but we'll walk back together. I don't want you out on the streets on your own that late.'

Father leaves the room. 'Sleep tight, *sjeintje*.'

The anti-aircraft guns roar outside again. A plane flies over, this time in the opposite direction. She hopes they are bombing the whole of Germany. Then the war will be over soon.

Alie and Lientje are walking from school to the market. They walk along Weesperzijde to Tweede Oosterparkstraat and then along Beukenweg to Tugelaweg.

Alie stops. 'Do we have far to go?' she asks wearily.

'No, we're nearly there,' says Lientje.

'Do you have to walk all this way every day?'

Lientje shrugs. 'It's not that bad.'

The market is on the playground in Joubertstraat. There is a big fence around it, with a policeman guarding the entrance. He lets them in when Alie says her father is at the market. It's very busy, with people jostling one another to get to the food stalls. Father is there with a handcart selling nuts and dried fruit. It is almost impossible to get hold of flowers these days.

'Hello there, girls,' he says to Alie and Lientje. 'You're late. I'm almost finished here.'

'It's quite a long way,' says Alie, and then she smells something really good. She looks around and sees a man roasting chestnuts on a fire. He is praising his wares in a singsong voice: 'Roast chestnuts. So good to eat! Get them here! Lovely and sweet! Hot chestnuts!'

'Can we have a bag, Father?'

Father looks at the money in his apron. He has not earned much today. 'Another time.'

'How often do I come here? Oh, go on, please?' Alie nags.

'Lientje!' A woman hurries over and gives Lientje a hug.

'Mum, this is Alie, my new friend.'

'Hello,' Alie says with a polite smile.

Lientje's mother looks thin and a bit grey.

'It's so nice that Lientje has already made a new friend.' Lientje's mother gives Alie a hug too.

'Well, if I'd known everyone gets such a warm welcome in Wormerveer, I'd have made sure to visit,' says Father.

Lientje's mother laughs and shakes his hand. 'Saar de Jong, nice to meet you.'

'Leendert, Alie's father.'

'Can we have some chestnuts, Mum?' asks Lientje.

'Do you know, I was just thinking of getting something nice to eat,' says Lientje's mother.

'Lucky you,' Father says to Alie.

He takes some change out of his apron and gives it to her. 'My treat, Mrs De Jong.'

Lientje's mother and Alie's father chat for a while.

Alie and Lientje buy a big paper cone of roasted chestnuts and take turns carrying it to warm their hands. Alie's father gives them some dried dates from his handcart too.

'I'll come and fetch you in a bit, Aaltje. Stay inside. Don't go wandering the streets.' He plants a kiss on her head.

Alie and Lientje walk across the market to Lientje's house. Her father opens the door for them and sees the cone of chestnuts.

'Where did you get those from?' he asks.

'Alie's father bought them for us.'

He shakes Alie's hand. 'That's nice. What does your father do, Alie?'

'He works a few days at the Joubert market, sir,' Alie says. 'He's really a flower seller, but he can't do that anymore. So now he helps my aunt with her nuts and fruit.'

'He's lucky to have work,' says Lientje's father with a sigh.

Lientje takes Alie to her room. 'Do you want to see my doll?'

Lientje does not have a bedroom to herself. There are two beds in the room and a mattress leaning against the wall.

'How many of you sleep in here?' exclaims Alie, when she sees all the bedding.

'Four of us. Me, my brother Hartog and my two big sisters. My brother Ies sleeps on the sofa. My father and mother have the little side room. And my uncle and aunt have their own bedroom.'

Lientje picks up the doll that is lying on the bed.

'She's a cutie, isn't she?' she says, stroking the doll's beautiful curly hair. 'I had more dolls at home, but I was only allowed to bring one.' Lientje looks sadly around the room. 'Otherwise this place would have been really packed. Hey, do you want to play Monopoly?'

Alie nods. They go into the living room and sit down at the dining table. Hartog comes out of the kitchen. 'Can I play too?'

Lientje looks at Alie. 'Of course.' They lay out all the cards neatly.

'Dad, will you be the bank?' Lientje asks her father.

'Another time. I'm just going round to see if your uncle needs any help.' As her father leaves, Lientje's aunt and one of her big sisters come in.

'Who's your friend?' asks Lientje's sister.

'This is Alie, my friend from school.'

The two women say hello to Alie.

'Want me to play too?' asks the sister.

Lientje shares out the money. They share the last few chestnuts too.

Just as they start playing, the doorbell rings. Alie is disappointed that her father has come to pick her up.

'We've only just started!'

'Sorry, Aaltje, we have to be back home before the curfew. It wasn't my idea,' Father says with a shrug.

Alie reluctantly puts on her coat.

'Lientje hasn't even written in my album yet,' says Alie, hoping to stretch it out a little.

'She can do that tonight,' says Lientje's aunt, who knows that they need to leave before dark.

Alie waves through the window at everyone inside.

'Pretty crowded in there, eh?' asks Father.

Alie nods. 'Yes, but good fun.'

Alie's father takes her arm, and they walk home together along the Amstel, as the setting sun colours the sky pink.

The table is laid, and Alie is playing on the floor with Roosje, who starts barking as soon as she hears Father and Berry on the stairs.

'Alie, will you come and get the food?' Mother calls from the kitchen.

Alie stands up and heads into the kitchen. She picks up a steaming dish of fried potatoes and Gretha carries through a pan of peas. When Berry comes in, she quickly puts down the pan on the table and throws her arms around him. They kiss. Alie watches and smiles when Gretha's lipstick leaves a mark on Berry's cheek.

When Alie goes back into the kitchen to fetch something else, she walks in on what looks like a serious conversation between her parents. She doesn't hear exactly what they're saying, but Mother's face is pale.

'I'm sure it'll all be fine,' says Father quietly.

'What will be fine?' asks Alie.

Father and Mother look as if they have been caught out.

'Nothing that you need to worry about, *sjeintje*,' says Father. 'Let's go and eat. It smells delicious.'

Alie stares at her mother, who is busy wiping the kitchen counter and clearly trying to avoid her gaze.

'Why are you standing there? Take the jug of water through. Then we can eat.'

'I'll ask Greet then,' says Alie, picking up the jug.

As she steps into the living room, the conversation stops. Alie pours water for everyone.

'Shall I serve?' asks Father. 'What are we having?' He takes the lids off the dishes.

'Fried potatoes, peas and . . . more peas. That's all there is,' says Mother.

'No meat?' asks Berry, sounding disappointed.

'Most of the kosher butchers are closed now. The one on Van Woustraat sold out within an hour,' says Gretha.

Berry takes a big helping of the potatoes and peas.

'Mmm, tasty! Potatoes and peas. And I'll just imagine the steak for myself.'

'How was your day, Dad?' asks Alie.

'Oh, fine. I helped Uncle Eli at the market today. We had a batch of pickles to sell.'

'And how was the medical examination?' asks Gretha.

Mother gives her a nudge.

'What?' says Gretha.

'Maybe your parents don't want to talk about it over dinner. Because . . .' Berry does not finish his sentence, but looks meaningfully at Alie.

'What nonsense. I want to know how it went. There's no reason Alie shouldn't know too,' says Gretha.

'Know what?' Alie looks at Father expectantly. Now he is going to have to say something.

'Do you remember that letter I got the other day? The one about reporting for a medical examination?'

Alie nods. Yes, she remembers.

'It was for the labour service.'

'Do you have to go away?' she asks anxiously.

'No, I don't. I just had to go in for an examination. I still have a permit for this year, but they might need men in the future.'

'But when? Where will you have to go? What do they want you to do?' Alie and Gretha are both worried.

'And that's why I don't want to discuss this at the dinner table,' says Mother.

They eat in silence for a while.

'Did you know I had a medical too?' says Berry.

'For the labour service?' asks Gretha.

'For military service.'

'Were you in the army?' asks Alie.

'I didn't want to go and my parents certainly didn't want me to, because then they'd have had to do without my pay. So I wanted to be declared unfit.'

Gretha laughs. 'But you're perfectly healthy.'

'I do have one flaw: the little finger on my right hand. From sewing hats.' He mimes sewing with his little finger sticking out.

Everyone laughs.

'No, seriously. I have constant cramp in the damn thing.'

'So they declared you unfit?' asks Alie.

'No, I was told to report to the Fifth Infantry Regiment. I'd kept insisting that I was the breadwinner for my parents and all my brothers and sisters, so they were kind enough to give me the evening shift. So I could do it in the evening after my day at work.'

'I had an examination for military service too. That was in 1915,' says Father.

'There was a war then as well, wasn't there?' asks Alie.

'Yes, in the rest of the world, but not in the Netherlands. There was military service though. Luckily I had a disability too.'

Mother laughs. 'Your eyes. You're as blind as a bat,' she says.

'Only my right eye. There was nothing wrong with the other one,' Father protests.

'So they'll declare you unfit for that reason again, won't they, Dad?' asks Alie.

'I think so. They'll make me do alternative service instead, like I did back then, administrative work.'

Alie feels a little reassured.

When they have finished eating, they clear the table. Berry picks up a dish to take to the kitchen.

'No, you sit there, lad. We wouldn't want you to strain that little finger of yours,' Father jokes.

Lea Janowitz

11 April 1931
8 May 2010

for	me
in	joy
and	sorrow
not	get

•

Dear Alie,

When you see the rain flowing outside
Then you mustn't think,
Why won't the sun come?
For when you see the sun again
Then you'll think happily, ah,
now the forget-me-not is flowering.

From your friend Lea

•

When this branch withers
Our friendship will be broken

LEA'S STORY
1942

Lea walks into the sewing workshop, where a number of staff are busy at work, bent over their sewing machines. The rattling of the machines echoes off the low beams of the basement ceiling. The room smells of leather.

She heads to the back and watches as her mother, Blanka, stitches two pieces of leather together. Blanka takes her work from under the needle and cuts the thread. She studies the stitching and gives it a pull to see if it is strong enough.

'Can I go and play at Riekje's?' asks Lea.

'Have you done the shopping?' her mother asks, without looking up from her work.

'It's Saturday.'

'We don't bother with Shabbat, do we? You only have a couple of chores.'

'Can't Harry do it?'

'Your brother's already helping your father. You can play when you're finished.' Her mother takes a packet of cigarettes out of her apron and peers into it. She pulls out the last one and lights it.

'Would you be a sweetheart and pop upstairs for another packet?' She crumples up the empty one and throws it into the bin.

Lea goes upstairs and takes a new packet of cigarettes from the carton. She clips some coupons from the ration books in the kitchen drawer, grabs a shopping bag and heads back downstairs.

'Do you have everyone's coupons?' her mother asks.

Lea counts the coupons and nods.

Leaving the workshop, she walks up Prinsengracht. She feels at home in Amsterdam. It is so different from Zagreb, where she lived for a few years with her aunt and uncle. It feels like home, because she is with her father and mother again.

Her basket full of food, Lea walks into the high-ceilinged hallway. In the back room, she sets the table for several people. One or two of the staff always stay to eat with them.

When she is ready, she goes downstairs to the workshop.

'The table's laid,' she says. Her mother does not look up from her work.

'I'll be there in a minute. I just need to finish this.'

Lea watches her mother's slender hands carefully cutting the leather, so as not to waste any valuable material.

She loves her mother, but it took a while. They were reunited only three years ago now.

'Come on, let's go upstairs,' says her mother, laying out some work for later. Lea smells a mixture of Chanel and cigarette smoke as her mother walks past close to her.

Harry and Father are back. Everyone at the table is chatting away. Leentje and Ben from the workshop are staying for lunch. One of her father's business associates is also eating with them. Her parents speak mainly German, interspersed with Dutch with a strong German accent. The adults smoke and drink coffee. Lea listens to their conversations. Her father's business associate takes him aside and speaks to him for a moment.

'Shouldn't you be making plans for when things here get too hard to handle?' he asks. 'Given your experiences in Germany, I think it would be wise.'

Her father shrugs. 'Where would we go?'

'I might be able to arrange something.'

Father raises his eyebrows. 'I'll bear that in mind. Thank you.'

'My fiancé's family have decided to leave,' says Leentje in a quiet voice. 'His brother wants us to go as well.'

'It's dangerous – and it's risky for anyone who helps you too,' says Ben. 'If the Krauts find out, they . . .'

Lea's father looks pointedly at Lea. Ben quickly changes the subject.

'I'd better get back to work. The De Haans are collecting their suitcase tomorrow.'

Leentje goes with him.

Harry picks up a ball that was in the corner. He bounces it on the floor.

'Why don't you take your ball and go and play somewhere else for a while?' their father says.

Harry leaves the room.

'Was Leentje talking about going into hiding?' asks Lea.

'I don't know,' her father replies. 'But it's nothing you need to concern yourself with.'

Lea understands that her parents want to protect her, but she is already well aware of what is going on.

'Lea, will you do the washing up?' asks her mother, who is clearing the dining table.

Harry is bouncing the ball around the hallway now.

'Is that what we're going to do too?' asks Lea. 'Go into hiding?'

'I told you. You don't have to worry about that,' says her father.

'But are you thinking about it?'

Annoyed, her father opens the door. 'Didn't I tell you to go and play somewhere else with that ball, Harry? Go outside.'

'There's nowhere I can play football outside,' shouts Harry. 'I'm not allowed in the Vondelpark, and, if I play by the canal outside, the ball will go into the water.' Harry hurls the ball down the hallway and storms upstairs.

'Harry! You need to help with the drying-up,' their father yells, going after him.

'Oh, just leave him,' their mother shouts.

'So we're not going to talk about it?' says Lea.

'Where would we go?' her mother replies. 'With my accent and Harry who can't sit still? Let's just be glad that we're here and that we're building up the business again.'

She takes her cigarettes and lights one.

'Why don't you make a start on the dishes? Harry will come and help you in a minute.'

Lea stacks the dirty dishes and makes some soapy water.

A little later, Harry comes into the kitchen. He picks up a tea towel and starts drying.

'Do you want to play catch afterwards?' asks Lea.

'Where's the fun in that?'

'Well, then you could go outside with the ball.'

'I want to play football.'

'Alright then, let's not.'

Lea rinses a cup, and bubbles of foam fly into the air. Harry tries to catch them.

'Give that here.' He grabs the brush and tries to make more foam.

'Give it back. I'm not finished.'

Then he splashes in the water and gets it all over Lea.

'Hey!' she says, splashing back at Harry.

Harry does see the fun in that, and he throws a load of water over Lea.

'Stop it!'

Harry laughs and tries to splash her again, but Lea grabs the brush out of his hands. He is still laughing, so Lea shakes the brush, spraying water at him. He closes his eyes and screws up his face. Lea feels guilty.

'Did the soap get in your eyes?'

Harry opens his eyes wide, roaring with laughter. He grabs the brush and completely soaks Lea's face. He does it more roughly than she did too.

'Stop it! That's not nice.'

Harry tosses the brush into the soapy water.

'Sorry,' he says.

They look at each other. They are both dripping wet. Harry gently wipes Lea's face with the tea towel.

'Hey, I'll finish this,' he says, giving Lea a peck on the cheek. 'You wanted to go to Riekje's, didn't you?'

Lea finishes drying her face. As she leaves the room, she glances back at Harry, who is playing with the dishes. She can see why he is bored. Harry always wants to be doing something. He is constantly busy and running around.

'Are you in bed yet?' her father asks from the hallway.

He walks into the bedroom and checks that the curtain is shut properly.

'Is that man going to help us?' asks Lea.

'Help us? What with?'

'Not getting caught and taken away.'

'Go to sleep,' says her father, stroking her hair.

'But the Nazis already put you in prison once,' she says in a worried voice. 'They could come and take you again.'

'That only happened because they wanted my suitcase factory. Do you remember what it was like there?'

Lea shakes her head. She can't remember anything about their time in Germany.

Her father sits down on her bed.

'The factory was in a strategically important location, close to a train station. And it had a concrete basement. And that was why they wanted it.'

'Why didn't you sell it to them?'

'They didn't want to pay me anything for it, and I didn't want to give it away. So they made up a reason for throwing me into prison.'

'I'm glad you're back.' Lea gives her father a cuddle.

'Thanks to your mother. She was the one who got me out.'

He breaks away from her hug.

'Go on. Close your eyes now. I'm just going to go and help your mother in the workshop.'

'Will you ask Mum to come and say goodnight to me?'

Lea waits for her mother to come, but it is a long wait, and she falls asleep.

It is quiet on the street as Lea and Harry walk to school. They walk along the canal towards the Rijksmuseum. In the passageway through the museum, they can hear their own footsteps.

Harry stamps extra hard.

'Oooh! Waaah!' he shouts. There is an echo. He repeats it, louder and louder.

'Shh, or someone will hear you.' Lea is walking a few steps ahead of him.

'There's no one around. It's Sunday.'

Lea walks on, feeling embarrassed. Harry catches up with her.

'I'll go ahead,' he says. 'I'll see you at school.'

As she walks around the corner, she just catches sight of him turning right at Hobbemakade.

In the corridor, a bunch of girls is standing around a girl from the third-year class. She is wearing a really pretty dress and has a big bow in her hair. Lea is surprised to see her looking so smart. Today's not the day for the school photograph, is it? As the girl spins in a circle, the bottom of her dress swirls out.

'It's beautiful,' says Jenny from her class. Lea admires the dress too.

'It was made specially. I've got new shoes too.' She stretches out her leg.

'Happy birthday,' says another girl.

'It's not my birthday,' she replies.

'Then why are you wearing such nice clothes?' asks Lea.

'For when we go to Poland.'

Feeling really upset, Lea walks away from the girl and goes to sit in her classroom, next to Annie.

'It's strange that she's wearing such nice clothes,' says Annie. 'It's warm clothes you should be taking, isn't it?'

They are interrupted by Mr Roeg tapping his desk.

'Silence, everyone.'

Annie raises her hand.

'Yes, Annie?'

'Sir, if you're going to Poland, you should take warm clothes, shouldn't you?'

Mr Roeg hesitates. 'I think that's probably something you should discuss with your parents. I'd rather talk to you about Shavuot, which we'll be celebrating again soon. Now who can explain exactly what it is that we celebrate at Shavuot?'

No one puts up their hand.

'Everyone knows that,' says one boy.

'You're forgetting that there are some children who haven't had a Jewish education right from the start. Children who never have Jewish holidays at home,' says the teacher.

'We celebrate receiving the Torah on Mount Sinai seven weeks after the exodus from Egypt,' says Lea.

'That's right. Good, Lea.'

They do not celebrate Jewish holidays at home either, but Lea still knows about them.

After school, Lea walks into the workshop and says hello to everyone – loudly, to make herself heard above the sound of the sewing machines.

'Where's Harry?' asks her mother.

'He wanted to play football for a bit in the school playground. He'll be home soon.'

Her mother pins together two pieces of fabric and lays them out beside the sewing machine.

'Come on. Let's go upstairs for a cup of tea and a little break.'

Lea boils the water and puts some tea in the pot.

Her mother gets out the cups and lights a cigarette.

They hear footsteps above. Tock, tock, tock. Someone is coming down the stairs.

'Ah, it's Gerard. I hope he's brought us some goodies,' says her mother.

Gerard opens the kitchen door and deposits a heavy sack on the floor.

'What's that you've brought for us?' asks her mother. 'Give the neighbour a cup of tea, Lea.'

Her mother peers inside the sack and takes out potatoes, onions, carrots and kale.

'I'll mash that up and make a good old Dutch *stamppot*. Thank you.'

She gives the neighbour a cigarette.

'I might have a nice fish for you next week. I'm off fishing with my brother-in-law.'

'Then I'll cook it and you can come and eat with us. How does that sound?' says her mother.

97

'I'd better be off then,' the neighbour says later, finishing his tea.

Lea notices that he has forgotten the sack, so she runs after him. She goes upstairs to the attic. The neighbour is already on the steps and about to head out through the window.

'You forgot the sack,' she says.

He takes it and says goodbye. Then he goes through the window, gently closing it from the outside. It clicks shut. It now looks like any normal window, except that it has no handle allowing it to be opened from the inside.

She goes to her bedroom. Her suitcase is in the corner, with her best clothes inside. Warm jumpers and cardigans. She opens it for a moment. It is ready for when they leave. She is not going to wear them to school.

In the kitchen, her mother is putting the vegetables in the sink.

'Shall we start making dinner now?' she says to Lea.

Lea washes and chops the vegetables.

'Why is it that we don't celebrate any Jewish holidays?' she asks.

'We don't have time for holidays,' says her mother, peeling potatoes and pausing for the occasional puff of her cigarette. 'And I went to a Catholic school in Poland, remember? Don't try bringing up your Jewish holidays there.'

Her mother looks at the clock.

'Are you sure he'll be home soon? Is that what he said?'

'As soon as the school playground closes,' says Lea.

Her mother carries on preparing the meal. 'So which holiday is coming up?'

'Shavuot.'

'And what is it that we eat then? Dairy?'

Lea nods.

'I'll cook something nice for you. Alright? I'll just go and take a look out of the window to see if he's coming.'

Lea can tell she is worried. In Germany, when Harry was little, he often used to be completely red in the face when he got home from school. When their mother asked him why, he said he had been running. Until one day, she stood at the window and saw Harry coming round the corner with a gang of boys chasing after him and shouting, 'Jude, Jude!'

The front door slams shut and a flushed-looking Harry comes into the kitchen. He pours himself a big glass of water and gulps it down.

Mother touches his face, which is bright red.

'What have you been doing?' she asks.

'Football and then ran home,' he says, looking for something to eat.

'And was everything alright? Nothing bad happened?' she asks.

Harry brushes her hand away and goes into the living room. 'I'm fine.'

Their mother takes a long drag on her cigarette.

'It's not like Germany,' says Lea.

'I certainly hope not,' her mother replies.

It is the handicrafts lesson. Lea and the others in her class are doing embroidery with the girls from the other fourth-year class, while 'their' boys are having Hebrew lessons with the boys from the other class.

Lea is not enjoying it. She likes sewing, but with a machine like in the workshop.

She looks at the clock. The lesson is almost over. They are all sitting together around a big table: Alie is there, Jenny, Rosa, Tirtsa. She does not know the girls from the other class very well. Everyone is concentrating on their work.

'Did you hear about Betty?' someone whispers. 'They came for her last night.'

'Then why is she here today?' asks Lea.

'She screamed so loud that they left her and her family at home. She wouldn't stop screaming. I suppose it was too much trouble for them.'

They look at Betty. She seems quite calm now.

The bell goes and the girls tidy away their things. As they are about to leave the classroom, Mr Roeg comes in.

'Return to your classroom, everyone,' he says.

'But the bell's gone, sir,' says Jenny.

'Just go back to your classroom.'

Reluctantly, the girls do as they are told. The weather is lovely today, and they really want to head straight outside.

'Some of the streets have been blocked off. It's not safe to go home now,' says Mr Roeg.

'Again?' a boy exclaims.

'Do you know which neighbourhoods?' asks Lea.

'No, not exactly, but definitely Zuid and the Rivierenbuurt.'

The children are alarmed. Nearly everyone lives in those areas.

'For the children who don't live there, we have arranged escorts. Put your hand up if you live somewhere else.'

Lea raises her hand. So do Rosa and Lientje.

'Lientje, you can't leave either. We're not sure what's going on in the Transvaalbuurt.'

Disappointed, Lientje lowers her hand.

The few children who are allowed to go stand in the corridor. One by one, they leave with an escort.

'You can come with me,' says a big man.

Lea feels uncomfortable. The man does not look at all trustworthy. He is wearing a grubby coat and a faded cap. She does not want to go with him.

'What's your name?'

'Lea,' she says. She does not tell him her last name. You never know.

'Okay. Where do you live, Lea?'

Lea hesitates. 'I think I'll just stay here.'

'Are you sure? This could go on all evening,' says the man. 'Tell me where you live, and I'll take you there.'

She is annoyed that he is being so pushy.

'Lea, are you still here?' says Mr Roeg, coming out into the corridor. 'You have to go. Other children need to be escorted.'

'So I have to know where you live,' says the man in a friendly voice.

'Prinsengracht,' she says.

'Prinsengracht is pretty long. What number?'

'Near Leidseplein.'

Lea goes with the man. They walk part of the way down Van Ostadestraat. Lea goes to turn the corner, but the man stops her.

'We'll go straight on. That's better.'

They walk on.

'Give me your arm,' he says, tucking her arm through his.

They go on walking. Then the man takes her hand. She tries to hold his hand as loosely as possible. She pulls her arm back a little too, so that she can run away if necessary. She looks at him. She can tell he is not Jewish. He is not wearing a star. He is quite unremarkable, the kind of man she would not notice in a crowd.

At Ferdinand Bolstraat, they turn off. They walk all the way down Ceintuurbaan, Van Baerlestraat. Lea looks around. She hardly ever comes here.

'Where are we going?' she asks.

'Prinsengracht, right?' says the man.

She tries to protest. There are lots of people around, but no one pays any attention. It's just a man with a child.

As they approach the Vondelpark, the man looks at her star and then walks past the park.

She could always run into the park if she has to.

Leidseplein is really busy. There are policemen directing the traffic. He pulls Lea a little closer, so that his arm covers her star.

'Are you going to tell me what number you live at now?' The man gives her a nice smile, and Lea gives in.

'488,' she says. She finally believes that he is going to take her home.

When they get there, she runs into the workshop. Her parents are surprised to see the stranger.

'Good afternoon,' he says. 'We were asked to escort the children home. There are raids in Zuid.'

Her parents do not look at all surprised to hear this news, and her father gives the man a firm handshake.

'You're doing good work. Thank you,' he says.

Before he leaves, the man strokes Lea's head.

'Did you know someone was going to bring me home?' she asks when the man has gone.

'We heard people had volunteered to help,' her father says.

'But why? It's dangerous, isn't it?'

'And that's why you should have thanked him,' her mother says.

.

Lea is playing outside with Riekje, a little further along Prinsengracht. The weather is good, so they are wearing their summer dresses and sandals. They draw hopscotch squares on the pavement with chalk, but people keep walking by and interrupting them. The constant stopping and starting starts to annoy them after a while.

'Do you want to play upstairs instead?' asks Riekje.

'But it's such a nice day,' says Lea. 'What do you want to do if we go inside?'

'Play with dolls?'

'No, that's boring.'

'Maybe Mum will let us bake something. Biscuits?'

'No, I bet we won't be allowed. Everything's rationed,' says Lea.

'Or . . . we could practise handstands and cartwheels up in the attic,' says Riekje enthusiastically.

'Yes, great idea.'

They go inside, but then Lea looks at her dress and has second thoughts.

'I'm going to pop home and fetch my gym shorts.'

She walks home and is about to let herself in when, to her bewilderment, a German police officer opens the door and pulls her inside. Before she can say anything, the man pushes her down the hallway and into the living room, where her parents are sitting on the sofa.

'Are you alright? Did he hurt you?' her mother asks, when she sees that Lea has tears in her eyes.

'He pulled me inside and he was really rough.'

'Was that really necessary?' her mother says in German. 'She's just a child.'

'Then the other one shouldn't have run off,' snarls the German.

Lea sits close to her mother.

'Harry got away?'

Her mother nods.

'He'll be back. They can't cope without their mummies,' scoffs a Dutch man who comes into the room.

The man piles up lots of their belongings on the table. He is a giant of a man with a huge head. His nose is flat, and there is a sneer on his face. Lea is scared of him.

'We'll wait for the brat, and then you're all coming with us,' he says.

Lea looks at her parents, who seem to have given up. Will they really have to go with the men? They can't, can they? Surely they're not just going to let this happen.

'What's in there?' the man asks, pointing at a locked cupboard.

'Nothing special,' says her mother.

'I'll be the judge of that. Take everything out and bring it over here.'

Lea follows her mother to the cupboard. 'Should I scream?' she whispers.

Her mother looks at her.

'Then maybe we'll be allowed to stay.'

Her mother looks at the big man and shakes her head.

'But we have to do something, don't we?' Lea does not understand. These men can't take them away, can they?

Lea puts her hand on her stomach.

'I've got a really bad stomach ache. I don't feel well,' she says in a feeble voice. She gives the man her most pitiful look. She hopes it will work and he will let them go.

'Then go to the toilet,' he says, pointing into the hall. 'But leave the door open.'

Disappointed, Lea goes to the toilet and stays in there for ages. She flushes a few times to make it seem genuine, while she tries to come up with another bright idea.

After a while, when she returns, she hears her father trying to persuade the man to let them go. But he refuses to budge.

Lea remembers the suitcase with her best clothes inside. The men mustn't take that away with them.

'I'm cold,' she says. 'Can I put on something warm?'

Her mother quickly says, 'Go upstairs and get changed.'

But the man looks at her suspiciously. 'It's a really warm day. So how can you be cold? You're staying here.'

'She doesn't feel well. She just said that. That dress is so thin,' her mother says.

The man stands up. 'Then we'll all go.'

Everyone troops upstairs. Her parents take some warmer clothes out of their suitcases too.

They could try to escape through the attic window, but she knows that the two men are keeping a close eye on them. Lea has no idea what to do. She does not have a plan. She goes to her room, where she puts on a jumper and grabs her coat.

Tock, tock, tock – the sound of footsteps on the attic stairs.

It's the neighbour! Lea hurries into her parents' bedroom, but there is no time to warn him, and the neighbour walks straight into the clutches of the two men, who are just as surprised as he is. He tries to go back up the stairs, but it is no good. They grab the neighbour, push him onto a chair and start questioning him.

'Who are you?' asks the big man. 'Do you live here?' He looks at Lea's parents. 'You said there was no one else in the house.'

'I live next door. I just popped round.'

'Your papers,' the man orders.

'I don't have them on me. They're at home.'

The man takes a good look at the neighbour. 'Are you Jewish?'

'No.'

'You're coming with us too. Associating with Jews is forbidden. You know that.'

'I just come in through the back, so it doesn't cause any trouble.'

'Show me,' says the man.

The neighbour goes upstairs with him.

The German takes Lea and her parents back downstairs.

'He just brings something round now and then, for the children,' her father says, trying to help, when the man and the neighbour come downstairs.

Then the neighbour stops and looks at the man.

'Wait a second. Aren't you that boxer? Sam Olij?' he asks. 'The champion from Landsmeer?'

The man looks flattered and confirms that he is indeed Sam Olij.

Then the door opens, and Harry is standing there in the hallway. Olij just laughs at him.

'What did I tell you? Good, we're all here. Time to go.'

'Do I really have to go too?' the neighbour pleads.

'You can go home and report to the police station on Leidseplein tomorrow,' says Olij.

The neighbour hurries out of the room.

Lea's mother stands up. 'I'm just going to get something for the boy. Lea, will you help me?'

They head into the kitchen.

Her mother packs bread, cheese and something to drink. Then she dashes through to the back room, where she takes a carton of cigarettes and her bottle of Chanel out of the cupboard. Lea looks at her in surprise. What good will that do her?

The four of them walk along Prinsengracht, escorted by the two men. As they pass Riekje's house, Lea nervously glances up. She sees Riekje, with her mother beside her. Riekje starts to wave, but her mother quickly pulls her away by the hair.

They are dropped off at the police station on Leidseplein. Olij and the German do not return for them until seven o'clock that evening. They take them to Euterpestraat, to the headquarters of the SD, the Sichersheitsdienst.

When they get there, it is quiet. There are guards and they see some senior German officers walking around.

Her parents have to register.

'Your papers, please,' says the man behind the desk.

Her father hands over all the documents. The man studies them carefully.

'So you were born in Russia?' he asks.

'Yes, but I lived in Germany for a long time,' says her father.

'And you were expelled from Germany?'

'We've been in the Netherlands since 1936.'

The man picks up the papers and takes them to one of the German officers. They discuss the situation and look at Lea and her family.

The German officer writes a big S on their form in red pencil.

'What does that mean?' asks her father.

The man does not answer his question. 'Find somewhere to sit and wait until you're called. Next!'

Her parents do as the man says.

Harry has already made some friends, and they are playing a game together.

Over the course of the evening, more people are brought in and the place becomes busier and busier. Lea sees that some of them are still in their pyjamas.

Lea wakes up when her mother calls her. They have to leave.

The long line of people is led through the dark streets to the trams that will take them to Centraal Station.

On the tram in the middle of the night, Lea sits on the edge of her seat, staring intently at her father. Any minute now he could give her the signal – she will be ready when he tells her they have to jump off the tram.

But as they pull up in front of the railway station, her father has not given her a signal. And when they get off the tram in the dark, there is still no signal. Lea does not understand. This would be a good moment to make a run for it, wouldn't it?

They are herded into the station's big hall. Four German soldiers are waiting there, and the whole line of people has to pass between them.

'They're damn well counting us,' her mother curses. 'Like *Schweine*.'

A woman behind them hears her and repeats what Lea's mother said. 'Yes, like *Schweine*,' she shouts, pointing at the Germans. '*Schweinehunde* – that's what you are!'

Before the Germans can hear her, two men behind her grab hold of her, one of them putting his hand over her mouth so she cannot say anything else. The flow of people carries them to the trains.

Lea is shocked. Why did the men stop her? The woman's right, isn't she?

Her parents are looking out of the train window. Harry is still asleep, and Lea is snuggled up close to her mother. Mist is hanging over the landscape, and a watery sun is trying to break through. The empty countryside is such a contrast with the busy Prinsengracht.

'I don't like the look of that S on our form,' her mother says, folding the form and handing it to Lea. 'When we get to Westerbork, say you have a stomach ache and that you need to go to the toilet. Take the form with you, rip it up and flush it down the toilet.'

Lea hides the form under her jumper.

In the early morning, they stop at the railway station at Hooghalen. From there, they are transported to the camp at Westerbork.

As they walk into the camp, her father sees some people he knows, German refugees who were in the camp even before the war. An old acquaintance comes over to them.

'Make sure not to get sent away on the first train that leaves.'

Father looks at Harry and Lea. 'Remember that.'

They are taken to a large building, where lots of people are sitting at desks with typewriters and registering the newcomers. They are from the Joodsche Raad. There are a few German guards too.

Before their turn comes, Lea asks where the toilets are. She is directed to a wooden hut, which has a sort of frame with holes in. There are no separate toilets for men and women. Lea waits for a woman to leave before tearing the form into tiny pieces. She looks to see how to flush them away, but there is no way to flush the toilet. So she throws the bits of paper into the muck at the bottom. They stay on the top, but she leaves them there.

When she gets back to the registration desk, her parents are having a heated discussion with the man who is registering them.

'That's impossible. You must have a form with your name on it.'

'We were never given one,' her mother says, lying with a straight face.

'We really don't know anything about that form. Here are our other papers though.' Her father hands them over. 'This is all we got back after the last registration.'

The man discusses the situation with one of his colleagues, who makes a dismissive gesture.

'Alright, just go with that OD man. He'll take you to your barracks.'

The Jewish supervisor from the *Ordedienst*, known as the OD and which keeps day-to-day order in the camp, is a long-time resident and knows her parents. He leads them to the barracks. It is a large building, with the entrance in the middle. Her father and brother go to one side, to the men's section. Lea and her mother are sent the other way, to the women's section.

A young woman comes over to them and offers to show them around. She points at the big tables in the middle of the entrance area. 'This is the kitchen. Not because there's any cooking done here, but that's where the mess tins go and where we get our food. This is the women's area, and the men are on the other side. At the end, behind the screen, there are taps and a toilet.'

'Is it a normal toilet? One you can flush?' asks Lea.

'Unfortunately all the toilets here are the same.'

Lea and her mother thank the woman. As she turns to go, Lea's mother stops her.

'When we were registering, there were some people who had a red S on their forms,' she says casually. 'Do you know what that means?'

'It means "Strafgeval". If you have that, you get sent to the punishment block. It's guarded by the SS. You don't want to end up there.'

In the barracks, there are rows of bunk beds, three bunks high. Lea takes the top bed. Her mother puts her belongings on the middle one.

'Shall we go and look for your father and Harry? And see if we can get something to eat?'

Outside, the sun is shining, and people are walking about on the sandy ground. There are lots of other children there too. Lea looks along the line of barracks. For now, this is her home.

Alie is lying on the bed and looking at Gretha, who is brushing her dark curls in front of the mirror. Alie has loved watching Gretha do that ever since she was a little girl. She thinks Gretha is beautiful. The shorter hairdo she has had since she married Berry suits her.

'The school photographer is coming tomorrow. What should I do with my hair?' asks Alie.

Gretha sits down beside Alie on the bed and runs her fingers through Alie's hair. 'How about giving it a wash first? If it's clean, you won't have to do much to it.'

Alie stands up and looks in the mirror. Gretha is right – her hair is a bit greasy. 'But it'll take ages to dry.'

'You could go to bed with wet hair.'

'No, then it'll be all over the place when I wake up.' She lifts her long brown curls and shakes them around.

Gretha brushes Alie's hair. She takes a length of hair at the front and twists it.

'Hand me those grips.' Alie takes four hairgrips from the shelf under the mirror. Gretha holds three of them between her teeth and opens the other one. She gives the brush to Alie and slides the first grip into the roll of hair.

'Your hair is so thick,' she says admiringly, slipping in the other grips around the hair and checking to see if it will hold. 'Give it a shake.'

Alie shakes her head around. The hairdo stays in place.

'Perfect.' Gretha kisses her on the cheek.

Alie looks at her hair in the mirror.

Gretha takes her lipstick from the drawer and puts some on herself. Then she dabs it with her finger and pouts at her reflection.

'I'm the tallest in the class, and with this roll in my hair I'll stick up above everyone else.'

Alie takes out the grips, and the length of hair falls down in front of her eyes in a thick curl. Gretha tries again, fixing Alie's hair in a high ponytail this time.

Mother puts her head around the corner. She is wearing an apron, and her face is flushed. 'Will you girls lay the table? Berry and your father will be home soon.' She looks at Alie's hair. 'Doesn't that look a bit too old for you?'

'Well, I am the oldest in the class. What do you think I should do with my hair?'

'Put it in a nice bow. I still have that white one lying around somewhere,' says Mother, heading back into the living room.

'No, Mum! I'm not ten anymore!'

Mother comes back with a piece of white satin cloth, the size of a man's handkerchief. She folds it in two.

'Let's just see what it looks like.' Mother turns Alie toward the mirror. She takes a strand of hair and expertly wraps the cloth around it before tying the ends in a big bow, almost as big as Alie's head.

'Beautiful.' Mother looks fondly at Alie. 'Just like when you were little.'

Alie is not impressed.

'What do you think, Greet? It looks nice, doesn't it?'

'I see what Aaltje means. It is a bit childish.'

Mother looks disappointed. 'Oh, alright.'

'Why don't you try it?' Alie takes the bow out of her hair and sits her mother down on the bed.

Mother laughs. 'Don't be silly,' she says.

'Here. I'll help.' Gretha picks up the brush and runs it through her mother's hair. 'What have you been doing? Your hair's all fluffy at the front.' Gretha tries to smooth it.

'I've been frying potatoes. Got myself all hot and bothered.' Mother shuts her eyes as the brush strokes her scalp.

As Alie gathers her mother's hair and lifts it, she notices that she is starting to go grey. She nudges Gretha, and the two girls start whispering.

'Hey, I can hear you. You know who gave me those grey hairs? You two!'

Alie gives Mother a kiss. Then she ties up the bow, and they look at the result in the mirror.

'What a mess.' Alie and Gretha burst out laughing.

'Maybe with a bit of make-up?' says Gretha, picking up her red lipstick.

'Me too,' says Alie. Gretha puts just a dab of lipstick on Alie. The dark red stands out brightly against her pale skin.

'Now you, Mum,' says Gretha.

'Can I do it?' says Alie, grabbing the lipstick.

'I have to finish the dinner. They'll be home any minute,' Mother protests.

'Then they can lay the table themselves,' Alie says, putting lipstick on her mother's lips. She tries to do it as neatly as possible. And because she is trying so hard, she starts shaking. Gretha giggles.

Alie loses concentration and slips. A red streak runs from her mother's lip and onto her cheek. Mother looks in the mirror. 'No! What are you doing?' she snaps.

But when Alie and Gretha burst out laughing, she can't help joining in.

'You're a fine pair, you two. Making fun of your poor old mother.'

'Come here.' Gretha takes a cloth and removes the lipstick from her mother's cheek. They stand next to each other in front of the mirror, all three of them wearing red lipstick.

'Ah, me and my beautiful daughters. We could go on the stage.'

Alie leaves the lock of hair in front of her eye. She likes the way it looks.

'Can I wear lipstick for the photo tomorrow?'

'Are you completely *meshuggah*? You're only twelve,' says Mother.

'A second ago you said I could go on the stage, didn't you?'

'Go and lay the table. Before you get any other strange notions in your head.' Mother goes back to the kitchen.

Gretha removes the lipstick from Alie's lips.

'I would go with that roll in your hair tomorrow.'

Alie walks into the classroom. Some of the other girls have bows in their hair. She sits down beside Jenny.

'Phew. I'm glad you don't have a bow either,' says Alie.

'I stopped at the corner and took it out,' says Jenny.

Mr Roeg comes into the classroom. He has a list, and he calls out the names. Everyone is present today. Before long, the children start talking. They are all buzzing with anticipation.

'The photographer hasn't arrived yet, so we'll do some work first,' says Mr Roeg.

The children sigh.

'So, who was Rabbi Akiva?' he asks, writing the name on the board.

No one answers.

'We've talked about him before. Come on!' he urges them.

'He was an important scholar, sir,' someone shouts.

'That's right. He lived in Roman times and . . .' Then the headmaster comes into the classroom, interrupting Mr Roeg. A man with a big camera is following him.

Jenny nudges Alie. 'It's the photographer!' she says, running her fingers through her hair.

Alie pats her hair. 'Is it still straight?' she asks Jenny.

Mr Roeg shakes the photographer's hand. 'Where do you want them?'

The photographer looks outside. It is starting to rain a little.

'Wherever you like,' says the photographer. He starts setting up his camera. The boys stand around him, asking him about the camera. The photographer peers through his fingers, using them as a frame to work out the best shot. The boys copy him.

'Hey, Johnny! Click!'

'Alie! Give me a cute smile. Click!'

Mr Roeg gathers the children in front of the window.

'Will this side of the classroom work?'

'Let's put them in front of the blackboard. Otherwise I'll have too much backlight.' The photographer moves some of the children to the other side of the classroom.

'The tall children at the back, please.'

'He means you, sir!'

The children laugh.

'Keep the jokes for when we need to smile for the photograph,' says Mr Roeg with a grin.

The children are now lined up in four rows, but some of them are hidden behind the person in front. People are pushing and pulling. The children in the front row sit on tables. The four boys at the back climb up onto a desk, almost knocking one another off. Alie is right at the back, just behind the teacher. She checks to see if her hair is sticking up too high.

The photographer focuses his lens. Some of the boys start practising funny faces.

'I can only take one photograph. So think carefully about what you want to look like,' the photographer says sternly. 'And you need to stay very still too, or the picture will be blurred and you'll look like a ghost.'

Mr Roeg eyes the boys on the desk, who keep nudging one another.

'Even if you're smiling?' Lientje asks in a worried voice.

'Smiling's fine, but you'll have to keep your face like that for a while,' says the photographer. Are you all ready?' The photographer peers through the camera with a look of concentration on his face.

The children try to gaze into the camera, but not all of them manage it. Alie smiles as she looks past Mr Roeg and at the photographer.

'Stand still, everyone.'

'Aye aye, Cap'n!' One of the boys on the table salutes.

The photographer presses the button: click!

APRIL

It is quiet in the house this early in the morning. Alie gets out of bed, but there is no one else around. Then the doorbell rings, startling her. Roosje barks. Alie peers cautiously down from the window.

'Aaltje, open the door. Quick!' Father is standing out on the street, hiding something under his coat.

Alie pulls the rope to open the building's front door downstairs. Father comes up the stairs, carrying a light-brown wooden box.

Roosje sniffs at it when Father puts it on the table. He opens the lid. There is a record player inside, with 'AGA' written on it.

'Where did you get that from?' asks Alie.

'Borrowed it from a pal,' he says, opening a cupboard. 'I bumped into him when I dropped your mother off at the market.' He throws everything in the cupboard onto the floor. Right at the back, there is a package wrapped in brown paper. He takes it out carefully, blows off some dust. He sits down on the floor and Alie sits beside him.

'What's that?' she asks.

'I can't get it out of my head,' says Father, taking a gramophone record out of the brown paper.

'Caruso.'

Alie peers at the words on the record: 'Luca . . . van Letelle? Who's that?' she reads out loud.

Father laughs out loud. '"E lucevan le stelle." It's an aria from Puccini's *Tosca*.' Humming the tune, he stands up. He puts the record on the player and plugs it in. He presses a button and the record begins to turn. Then he lifts the arm with the needle and carefully places it on the record. A quiet crackling sound comes from the holes at the back of the record player. Roosje looks up. Then a piano starts playing. It sounds hollow, as if it is being played in a cellar somewhere. The singer's voice is muffled. He is singing slowly.

Father closes his eyes and quietly sings along. He goes and sits in his chair. Roosje sits at his feet, resting her head on his legs.

'Hey, I know this,' Alie says. 'You used to play this a lot, didn't you?' she asks, but Father does not reply. He is listening.

The man belts out some long notes. Father holds his breath, his whole body singing along in silence, his face in a painful grimace.

Alie wants to giggle, but she sees that her father has tears in his eyes. When the song is finished, Father stands up and heads into the kitchen.

His clothes are neatly folded on the living-room table. His heavy work shoes are by the door.

Alie feels a pang in her stomach. She follows Father into the kitchen and finds him staring out of the window. When he hears Alie, he sighs and takes a sip of water.

Alie puts her arms around his waist. She presses her cheek to his back and does not say a word. She can feel his irregular breathing and the occasional deep sigh.

'What's he singing about?' asks Alie.

'About how much he loves life,' says Father quietly. He turns round. His eyes are sad, but he is smiling. 'And so do I,' he says, sounding full of hope. He gives Alie a kiss. 'Shall we listen to it again? I have to take the record player back this afternoon.'

Alie goes back into the living room with Father. He places the needle on the record one more time and sits down in his chair. Alie sits on his lap, and Roosje drops onto the floor in front of them. They listen together.

Early the next morning, Alie opens her bedroom door and sees her father sitting in his chair. He is writing something.

Alie gives him a kiss. She sees that he was writing in her album. Father quickly closes the book and puts it down.

'Read it after I've gone,' he says.

He puts Alie on his lap, and she starts crying. Roosje climbs out of her basket and jumps up at them.

'You said they'd declare you unfit,' Alie says.

'I have to go. I'm unemployed, and there's work for me there.' Father wipes the tears from her cheeks.

'But I'm going to miss you so much,' says Alie.

'Overijssel isn't that far. And I'll be allowed to go on leave.' Father puts on his cheery voice. 'Before you know it, the war will be over. It can't go on much longer now.'

'Do you really think so?'

'Absolutely. And this means that at least you'll have food until then. They'll send my pay to you.'

'What about you?' asks Alie.

'They'll feed me well at the camp. If I work hard, I might even get a bit of meat.'

'Can you do that though? Work hard?'

'Hey, have you seen these muscles of mine?' he jokes, posing for her. Alie does not laugh.

'But all you're used to is selling flowers and things.'

'Oh, they'll make me do the paperwork or something like that,' says Father. 'The others can do the hard labour.'

That makes Alie feel better.

Father looks up as Mother comes into the room and silently strokes his hair.

'Gretha's made some coffee.' She puts the coffeepot down on the table. Father breathes in the aroma.

'It's the real thing,' he says. 'Got it from an old friend of mine.'

Father, Mother and Gretha savour the real coffee.

'Can I have some?' asks Alie.

'If you go and fetch the milk,' says Father.

'I'll help you,' says Gretha.

When they come back, Father and Mother are hugging. Mother quickly dries her tears and drinks her coffee.

Father pours a small amount of coffee into Alie's cup. He adds some milk and hands it to her. Alie takes a sip – and winces.

'Oh . . . ugh!'

Father, Mother and Gretha burst out laughing.

'Real coffee. Delicious, eh?' says Father.

Alie washes it down with the last of the milk. But the taste stays in her mouth. Her eyes fill with tears.

'Hey, it's not that bad, is it?' Father says.

'I just wanted to drink what you're drinking, Dad. It's the last thing we'll do together,' says Alie.

'Don't say that. I'll be back on leave. And then we'll have another coffee together. Deal?'

Alie nods through her tears.

'Promise me you'll keep doing your best at school when I'm gone. Alright?'

Alie nods again.

'Shouldn't you be taking this jumper, Dad?' Gretha shouts through from their parents' bedroom.

Father gives Alie a big kiss on the top of her head and goes to join Gretha.

'Come on. We're taking your father to the train. Go and get dressed,' says Mother.

Father puts on his warm winter coat and gives Roosje one last hug. 'Hold the fort for me, eh, Roosje? My little wolf.'

Roosje rests her paw on Father's arm. He picks up his suitcase and heads downstairs, with Alie, Gretha and Mother following him.

Outside, Father stops to look up at their home.

'Well, so long for now.' He turns around and they walk down the street. A few people come out to wish Father good luck. A few houses along, a young man with a suitcase in his hand comes out of a house. A young woman carrying a baby waves him goodbye. She is trying to be cheerful for the baby's sake. The man walks away alone.

There are special trams to take the men and their families to Amstel Station. The trams are soon full.

They have to walk the last part of the way. It is cold and Alie wraps her scarf more tightly around her neck and holds Father's hand. Mother is wearing a headscarf to protect herself from the chilly wind. She links arms with her husband.

A long procession of men and boys, all wrapped up warm and wearing sturdy shoes, walk with their families to the entrance of the station. Outside the station, it is busy. Inside, it is even busier. There is a man with a sign saying MOLENGOOT.

'That's where I'm going,' says Father.

Under police guard, everyone says goodbye to one another: men with suitcases, crying mothers, women kissing their husbands. Fathers smoking one cigarette after another. Women still making up bags of food for the journey. Children playing tag.

Alie holds on to Father's hand the whole time. There is so much noise that they have to shout to make themselves heard.

'I'm just going to ask what time we're leaving.' Father is about to walk away, but Mother pulls him back.

'You'll see when you have to go. Stay with us a little longer.'

'I'll go and find out,' says Gretha, walking towards the departure board.

'Have you put everything you'll need for the journey in a place that will be easy to get to?' asks Mother.

Father checks his suitcase again.

'Will you be allowed to keep that with you?' asks Mother. Father does not reply, just looks around.

'How about I wrap it up in a cloth? Like those people over there.' Mother points at a woman who is wrapping things up in a tea towel for her husband.

Mother takes a tea towel out of the suitcase and neatly wraps up Father's sandwiches.

'How long is the journey?' asks Alie.

'Two or three hours, I think,' says Father.

'There's nothing up on the board yet,' says Gretha, coming back.

'Stop going on about the departure board,' snaps Mother. 'They're the only ones who are leaving the station.'

Alie looks around and sees that her mother is right. It really is only men and their families. Jewish men. Jewish families.

When the announcement is made, Alie feels a cold shiver. All the men have to go to the platform. She grips her father's hand.

'Hey, Aaltje. I need that hand for work.'

She looks up at her father, who is trying to smile. Alie's eyes fill with tears. Gretha's crying too and is unusually quiet.

'Don't cry,' says Father, with a lump in his throat. 'Give me a smile – and I'll take it with me.'

Alie forces herself to smile. She gives her father a big hug.

'Now I really do have to go.' He hugs Mother and takes her hand. They walk to the platform. Father hesitates for a moment and then puts his suitcase on the train.

'Let's not drag this out any longer,' he says, turning to Alie, Gretha and Mother. 'You'll take good care of one another, won't you?'

He gives them all one last kiss and boards the train.

The train is packed. Everyone is quickly trying to say one last thing at the window or the door. Women are weeping, men are putting on a brave face and making jokes. Mothers are crying for their sons.

The doors close. Father manages to get a seat by the open window. He leans out as the train slowly starts moving.

'Keep your chins up!' he shouts. 'See you soon!'

'Bye, Daddy. Love you. Bye!' Alie tries to shout above the noise. She waves until it feels as if her arm is about to fall off.

Like a snake, the train curves around the bend. Alie sees Father wave one last time. Then he disappears from sight.

29 APRIL

'To whom it may concern. As of next Sunday, all Jews will have to wear the Star of David on their clothing. These badges will be distributed by the Joodsche Raad.'

Mother lowers the piece of paper and looks in alarm at Gretha.

'What does that mean?' asks Alie.

'That it's going to be the same as Germany,' Mother says, angrily throwing the paper onto the table. 'Your father has just left – and now this!'

Gretha picks up the paper and reads it for herself. Mother walks to the window and stares outside.

'Within three days, we need to have paid for the damn things and have them attached to us.'

'You can get them from the shul round the corner, on Gerard Doustraat,' says Gretha.

'I don't want to get them at all,' replies Mother, pulling a face.

Alie sits quietly on a chair. She has curled up her legs and is hugging Roosje.

'Roosje doesn't need to wear a star, does she?' she asks.

'You get four per person. They cost four cents each. Oh, and one textile point,' says Gretha, looking at Mother.

'Is that each?' asks Mother. 'Then we'll have to hand over three times four textile points. It's daylight robbery!'

'That's twenty-four plus twenty-four makes forty-eight cents, plus forty-eight textile points,' Alie says.

'Do Dad and Berry need them too?' she asks.

'Then we don't have enough points,' says Mother with a sigh. 'That can't be right, can it?'

Gretha takes another look at the paper. 'Oh. No, it's one textile point for four stars.'

'Which we also have to pay for. That's outrageous,' says Mother.

'What date is it on Sunday?' Gretha puts down the piece of paper and starts counting. 'Friday's the first . . . so Sunday is the third. We'd better go and fetch them now, because everyone will want to get it done before Shabbat, of course.' She stands up and puts her arm around her mother. 'We have to do it. We have no choice.'

'We have to do this. We have to do that . . .' Mother pushes Gretha's arm away. 'Why can't they just leave us in peace?' She stomps angrily into the kitchen, where Alie hears her banging pans and crockery around.

'But why do we have to do it, Gretha?' asks Alie.

'They keep coming up with new ideas to keep us down. They did it in Germany. And now they're doing it here.'

Gretha goes and sits next to Alie on the arm of the chair.

'But then everyone can see that you're Jewish.'

'That's exactly the point,' Mother shouts through from the kitchen.

'Is every Jew in the Netherlands getting one?' asks Alie.

Gretha nods. 'Everyone's getting four.'

'How many stars does that make?' asks Alie.

'A whole sky full,' says Gretha with a sigh.

'Guess what I've got!' says Gretha, walking in through the door, a little out of breath.

'A nice cream cake for your mother?' says Mother, coming out of the kitchen.

Gretha unwraps the brown paper from around the parcel she is carrying and places the contents on the table: a pile of pieces of yellow fabric printed with stars, with a dotted line around them. In the middle of the star, in letters that look a bit like Hebrew, the word JOOD is written very clearly: JEW. 'I thought I might as well go and get them right away.'

Alie hands a piece of cloth to her mother, who looks at it before tossing it onto the table. She returns to the kitchen.

'It's just fabric, Mother,' Gretha shouts after her.

Gretha takes a pair of scissors from Mother's sewing basket and starts cutting.

'Can I help?' Alie picks up a pair of nail scissors and a piece of cloth. She cuts very carefully along the dotted lines.

There are soon twelve neatly cut-out stars on the table.

Mother comes and joins the girls. She has made tea, which she pours in silence, and she has a biscuit for everyone.

Alie fetches her red coat, her cardigan and two blouses. She lays them in a line on the sofa and places a star on each piece of clothing.

'Does it go on the left or the right?'

'Left, I think,' says Gretha.

Alie moves the stars to the left sleeves and fastens them with pins.

'Do you want me to do your coat, Mum?' asks Gretha.

Mother watches from a distance and says nothing.

Alie takes a needle and thread and sews the star to her coat as neatly as possible. Then she puts on the coat and looks in the mirror. Gretha has already done her own coat. Her star is nice and straight, because she is a seamstress, but Alie's is a little crooked. Gretha tries to straighten it, but it is too late.

'It'll have to do,' says Gretha.

Mother drinks her tea and completely ignores the stars.

'Hey, look. I can wear two like this.' Gretha holds up cut-out stars as earrings. When Alie snorts with laughter, Mother can't help but smile a little too.

'They can see I'm Jewish even without that star,' says Gretha. 'I'm proud of who I am. We should all be proud.' She gives the stars to Mother.

Mother wraps the stars back up in the brown paper. 'I'd rather be proud of you without the star.'

MAY

It is a chilly Sunday morning, and the streets are quiet. Alie, Rosa and a few other children are walking to school. They are very aware of the big yellow stars sewn to their coats.

There are not many people out and about, but every single passer-by looks at the children with their stars. They walk on quickly, trying not to make eye contact with anyone. They cross Eerste Sweelinckstraat and head towards the park, where the trees are in bloom.

Alie and Rosa wait by the fence. Annie de Leeuw walks up. The bright-yellow star is clearly visible on her coat. She waves at them.

'What did you sew your stars on?' asks Annie, when she sees the stars.

'I sewed this one onto my coat myself. It's a bit crooked,' says Alie.

'I put one on my cardigan. Then I can wear it over my other clothes,' says Rosa. 'My mother didn't feel like sewing them onto every piece of clothing.'

'I think it's pretty. It's like a brooch or a rosette,' says Annie.

A gentleman comes walking along. He stares at the girls in amazement. The girls feel self-conscious and are about to leave,

AS LONG AS I HOPE TO LIVE

122

but the man taps the brim of his hat as a sign of respect before walking on. Rosa is impressed and watches him as he walks away.

The bell of the Oranjekerk rings.

'Come on, Rosa. We have to get to school,' says Alie, holding out her arm for her friend to take.

Roosje Sarfatij

30 September 1930
27 August 1943

Lieve Ali

Wanneer je eens na lange
tijd dit Album aanschouwt
en als je dan dit versje
eens zit bekijken
Staat dan denk aan mij
Die dit hier heeft geschreven
Op dit blad versje heeft
Geschreven en die je wenst
langer zo wenst een lang
gelukkig Leven

Je klasge-
nootje
Roosje
darbity

Dear Ali,

One day, after a long time,
when you open this album
And read this poem
That is written here
Then think of me,
The one who wrote
A poem here on this paper
And wishes you nothing
More fiercely than a long
happy life.

Your classmate,
Roosje Sarfatij

Liesje Aletrino

9 June 1931
2 July 1943

9 Juni is mijn
geboorte dag dit
je nooit vergeten mag.

Lieve ...

Als ik een dichters geest bezat
Dan had ik op dit albumblad
Een mooi gedicht geschreven
Maar nu ik deze gave mis
Wens ik je al wat wenselijk is
Een echt gelukkig leven!

Je klasgenootje
...

9 June is my birthday,
which you may never forget

•

Dear Ali,

If I had a poet's soul
Then on this album page
I would have written a beautiful poem
But as I lack that gift
I wish you all the very best
A truly happy life!

Your classmate,
Liesje Aletrino

Minna Vas Nunes

20 April 1932
11 June 1943

Just	look
every	corner
to look	for

closely	in
because	you have
the date.	

•

Dear Alie.

A short greeting, but good.
My poem is small:
I hope you will be happy.

Your friend.
Minna Vas Nunes.

Tirtsa Steinberg

28–7–1932

Lieve Alie

Wij gingen naar school

En maakten altijd pret en jool

Als je mij later niet meer ziet

Lieve Alie vergeet mij niet.

Tirtsa Steenberg.

Dear Alie,

We went to school
And always had fun and laughs
If you don't see me later.
Dear Alie, forget me not.

Tirtsa Steinberg.

TIRTSA'S STORY
1943–1945

SEPTEMBER 1943

The room is dark. Tirtsa is standing at the table and watching her mother, Erna, strike a match. Her father, Solomon, is on the other side of the table. Her mother lights the candles one by one. The candlelight shines on her, and Tirtsa looks at her mother's rounded belly. Around another four months and the baby will be here. Erna blows out the match. She brings the light towards herself three times and covers her eyes.

'Barukh atah Adonai Eloheinu melekh ha'olam asher kid'shanu b'mitz-votav v'tzivanu l'hadlik ner shel Shabbat,' she says in a soft, humble voice.

She lays her hands on Tirtsa's head.

'Y'simekh Elohim k'Sarah, Rivka, Rachel, v'Leah.'

And she kisses her head and cheeks. She pulls Tirtsa close.

'Shabbat Shalom.'

The table is beautifully laid with a crisp, white tablecloth, and there are starched napkins on the plates. Tirtsa can smell the bread under the cloth. The house feels empty. Her foster sisters, Gitta and Sara, have been taken somewhere else, but she does not know where. Her aunt, grandma and cousins are gone too. They were picked up and sent to Westerbork. They didn't live in the same house as Tirtsa, but they all spent a lot of time together. Tirtsa's cousin Karen was in the same class as her at school. Did they have a school at Westerbork too?

'Why is Shabbat such a special day?' asks Mr Coppenhagen, Tirtsa's teacher.

No one raises their hand.

'Hasn't anyone done their homework? You all know how you celebrate Shabbat at home though, don't you? Tirtsa?'

Tirtsa looks up. She thinks about it.

'It's the end of the week, and you're allowed to rest. It's always nice and cosy at home with the whole family.'

'End of the week,' he writes on the board. 'What else?'

'We say Kiddush.'

The teacher writes on the board.

'We bless the bread.'

'We always sing "Lecha Dodi".'

Mr Coppenhagen writes a list of terms on the board.

'So, explain how we make Kiddush.'

Tirtsa looks at her father. There is red juice in the silver cup in front of him. He says quietly, 'Va'yehi erev, va'yehi boker.' And then more loudly. 'Yom ha'shishi.'

Before everyone was taken away, the house was always full for Shabbat. Tirtsa's mother, aunt and grandmother cooked all day before Shabbat began. They wrapped the food in cloths to keep it warm. She, her foster sisters and her cousins tidied the house. They made sure all the pens and pencils were out of sight, and they made it cosy in the house. The table was beautifully laid. When her father and the other men came back from shul, it could begin. Sometimes everyone was at their house, and other times they spent Shabbat at her aunt and grandmother's on Albrecht Dürerstraat.

'Barukh atah Adonai, mikadesh ha'Shabbat.'

'Amen,' say Tirtsa and her mother.

Her father takes a drink. He passes the cup to her mother and she drinks too. When it is Tirtsa's turn, she takes a big gulp.

'Netilat yadayim,' says the teacher, pointing his stick at the board. 'Who can explain how that works?'

Tirtsa raises her hand.

'You take the cup in your right hand and fill it with water. Then you take the cup in your left hand and pour the water over your right hand.' She demonstrates without a cup. 'Then you take the cup in your right hand and pour the water over your other hand.'

'Very good, Tirtsa.'

•

Tirtsa's father dries his hands. 'Barukh atah Adonai Eloheinu melekh ha'olam asher kid'shanu b'mitzvotav v'tzivanu al netilat yadayim.'

He sits down at the table and removes the cloth from the bread. Taking the two small loaves of challah bread, he places them next to each other and makes a small cut in one of the loaves with a big knife. Then he picks up the two loaves and holds them together. Tirtsa likes to watch her father bless the bread.

'Barukh atah Adonai Eloheinu melekh ha'olam hamotzi lehem min ha'arets.' He puts down the loaves and makes a bigger cut in the same place. Then he takes the slice of bread and dips it into a bowl of salt. He takes a bite of the bread. He cuts another slice and dips it in the salt and passes it to her mother. The next slice is for Tirtsa.

•

Mr Coppenhagen writes something else on the board: ZACHOR, SHAMOR.

'Does anyone know what those words mean?'

No one responds.

'Come on, class,' he says. 'This is important.'

A boy puts his hand up.

'Zachor is about the special things you do to remember that it's Shabbat.'

'Such as?' asks the teacher.

'Lighting candles, wearing nice clothes, singing. Eating good food.'

'Having fun doing nothing,' says a girl. The children laugh.

'And what about *Shamor*? Someone else?'

'That's about not doing the things that you normally do, like going to school, working, writing, kindling fire,' says another boy.

The teacher looks at all the terms he has written on the board.

'I can see a lot of things on the board that we either do or don't do on Shabbat, but can anyone tell me why?'

'Shabbat is the day of rest after creation,' says a girl.

'So we don't do anything that involves creating,' the teacher explains. 'But there's another reason.'

Tirtsa puts up her hand.

'We also commemorate the exodus from Egypt – when we became free.'

'Very good,' says Mr Coppenhagen. 'Remember that after work and all the ordinary everyday business, Shabbat is there to make you think of higher things. In dark days, Shabbat is a source of light.'

The bell rings.

'We'll continue with this next lesson and we'll also talk about the end of Shabbat, Havdalah.'

SEPTEMBER 1943

Tirtsa is trying to concentrate on her book.

'Studying is the most important thing there is,' Mr Roeg had said, shortly before the school was closed down for good. 'Make sure you keep studying, even though there's no school.'

The fifth-year students now had Mr Roeg. They had lessons at school as much as they could, but when there was no heating, they had to study at home. In the spring, the teacher told them that the classes were going to be merged and that they were transferring to the Jekerschool. But even that is closed now. There had been so few children those last few weeks. There will be no school year 1943–1944.

Tirtsa watches as her parents gather their belongings. The family is about to be taken away. Tirtsa's backpack is ready. She puts down her book and goes into her mother's bedroom. There she is, wearing a baggy dress. Her wig is lying on the bed, next to some knitted baby clothes.

Tirtsa looks at the little clothes. Her mother has spent all her time knitting lately.

The doorbell rings. Her mother folds the baby clothes neatly and puts them in the bag.

Two men come in. They talk to her father, and he hands them the keys. Then he comes to join them.

'We have to go now,' he says, picking up her mother's bag.

Tirtsa goes into the hallway and grabs her backpack and coat. Her mother comes out of the bedroom, now wearing her sheitel. Silently, they follow the men down the stairs. Their neighbourhood, the Transvaalbuurt, is almost empty now, and there is no one out on the streets. Windows are open, with curtains fluttering out of some of them. They walk through the drizzle to the vehicle that will take them away.

They arrive at a large building and go inside to the registration desk. Her father fetches a chair for her mother. Tirtsa stays with her mother. She can see that her mother is tired, and she takes her hand.

'Would you ask for a glass of water for me?'

Tirtsa goes to her father.

'Mum wants a glass of water,' she says.

The woman at the desk hears her.

'Your mother can drink water out there,' she says, pointing at the corridor.

'My wife's pregnant. I think this is all a bit too tiring for her,' says Tirtsa's father.

'I'll go,' says Tirtsa.

'Pregnant? But she's getting on a bit, isn't she?' says the woman in surprise, when she looks at her details.

Tirtsa's father nods.

'She's forty-one. This baby is a gift.'

Tirtsa fetches water and gives it to her mother, who sighs and rubs her belly.

Her father comes over to them.

'They'd just like to examine you,' he says. 'We might be able to stay.'

Tirtsa hopes they can go home.

It is almost Rosh Hashanah, the new year 5704 begins on 30 September and 1 October. She wants to celebrate that at home. She always likes to see the shofar being blown at the shul.

When her mother comes back from the examination, she does not look happy. She is leaning on her father.

'Do we still have to go?' asks Tirtsa.

'Your mum can stay in Amsterdam,' he says.

'Well, that's good news, isn't it?' says Tirtsa.

Her mother holds her tightly.

'I'm going to the Joodsche Invalide. It's a hospital now.' She lets go of Tirtsa. 'They're coming to pick me up.'

'And what about us? Are Dad and I allowed to go home?'

'No, we're going to Westerbork. We have to wait there until your mum can come and join us.'

'But how long will that be?' Tirtsa can't believe her ears.

'Until the baby arrives.'

Tirtsa gently hugs her mother's belly.

'Can we come and visit you?' she asks.

'I don't know. Dad will have to ask when you get there.' Her mother gives her one last cuddle and then she goes with the woman from the registration desk.

•

Tirtsa looks at the little hand sticking out above the blanket. She takes hold of it.

It was a very long time before her mother finally arrived at Westerbork.

Tirtsa went to school and did her lessons. They even celebrated holidays. And then, one day, her mother was there. With the baby. Tirtsa was over the moon.

'This is your little sister, Ruth,' her mother said.

Everyone who went by called out 'Mazel tov!' Everyone thinks her sister is really cute.

Her mother is tired and goes for a nap while Tirtsa watches her sister. She is almost three months old now. Tirtsa feels restless because it is Monday. She distracts herself by playing with her sister. Maybe they will be allowed to stay. Or maybe they will have to leave on Tuesday.

'Wake up.'

Tirtsa's mother gently shakes her. It is very early in the morning and only just getting light. All around them, women are packing up. Some of them are crying. The baby starts crying too. Tirtsa takes it from her mother.

'We're leaving,' her mother says. 'I'll pack our things.'

Then she sits down on the bed and says her prayers. She kisses the baby and Tirtsa.

As they set off, her father joins them and takes the bag from her mother. He accompanies them to the train. These are cattle wagons, so there are no seats. Her father tries to find a good place for her mother and little sister, but all the places are the same. At least they can sit down.

The journey lasts an eternity. Tirtsa has no idea where they are going. Her father has a visa for a country in South America, and they want to go somewhere they can all stay together.

Tirtsa is woken by the sound of men shouting in German, and then they are pushed off the train. There are German soldiers all around, with big dogs. They scream at them to keep walking. Worried, Tirtsa looks at her mother and sister. Her father tries to shield them with his arm, but then he is taken away. Tirtsa stays close to her mother.

They have to go to the women's camp. Her father is going to the men's camp, They are not allowed to say goodbye.

They walk through various sections of the camp. A penetrating stench hangs over everything. When they get to the women's camp, they are directed to a barracks.

'Tirtsa?' She hears a familiar voice. She looks up. It is her cousin Karen, but her face is thinner now. The two girls hug.

Her aunt, cousin Rachel and grandmother soon come to the building too. They have been here for a while. She hugs her grandmother Fanny and aunt Sarah. Tirtsa feels comforted by the fact that everyone is here. She has missed them so much.

'Come on. You can sleep by me,' says Karen, and she takes Tirtsa to her bunk bed. Her mother follows with the baby. She sits down on a bed and looks around.

'Where can I feed the baby?' she asks.

'It'll have to be here,' says Grandma Fanny. 'There's nowhere private.'

Looking embarrassed, her mother lifts the baby to her breast.

'So what are we supposed to do?' Tirtsa asks Karen.

'Nothing,' she replies. 'Except turn up for roll call. And make sure your bed looks completely smooth every day. Or you'll be punished.'

'Is there a school here?'

'No, there's nothing,' says Karen. 'And hardly any food.'

Tirtsa cuddles up close to Karen.

•

Tirtsa and her mother hurry along with the doctor. They are going to the men's camp. The Jewish doctor has come to fetch them.

'He's not going to make it. He asked for you,' he says.

Tirtsa takes her mother's bony hand. They run as fast as they can.

When they get to the men's camp, they head straight for the sickbay. Tirtsa barely recognises her father. He is skin and bone, his eyes are hollow, his skin grey. Her mother sits down beside him. Tirtsa hears her mother talking quietly to him. She goes over to sit with them too. His eyes are closed. She puts her hand on his. Then her mother takes her away.

When they get back to the barracks, Tirtsa bursts into tears. Her mother holds her in her arms. Her grandma comes and sits with them.

'Daddy doesn't want you to be too sad. He knows God has chosen him to come to him,' her mother says.

Tirtsa's little sister comes crawling up. She has just had her first birthday. She is still really small for her age. Tirtsa picks her up and gives her a big hug.

'You have no idea what's going on, do you?' she says.

She looks at her mother, who is talking to her grandmother about how they might be able to sit shiva. Everything is different here, and hardly anything is impossible. They try to follow the rules as much as they can.

Tirtsa dries her tears and plays with her sister for a while.

In the night, they are woken by loud bangs. Bombs are falling around the camp. More and more of them. Tirtsa is sure it won't be long now.

•

They move through the camp in long lines. Tirtsa looks around and sees the pits filled with the bodies of those who died of typhus. They walk past them. There is a terrible stench throughout the camp. Grandma, Aunt Sara and her cousins are leaving too. There are rumours that they will be exchanged for German prisoners of war and that they are going to Switzerland. They all have to say goodbye really quickly.

'The liberators are almost at the camp,' people are saying. They hear that the Austauschjuden have to leave the overcrowded camp.

Tirtsa, her mother and sister are going to Theresienstadt. Her mother is so thin that Tirtsa can see her bones. She is wearing a headscarf and dirty clothes. Her sister is wrapped up tight in a blanket. They are all itching. There are fleas everywhere.

They are taken in trucks to the platform where the trains are waiting. Those who are not too weak have to walk.

They have to go back into the cattle wagons. There are only sick people in there. Everyone has diarrhoea, and there are people with wounds. They are all crawling with fleas and lice.

TIRTSA STEINBERG

149

It is a long time before the train leaves. Tirtsa is starving. They have already finished the small piece of bread they were allowed to take. Her mother is still breastfeeding her little sister.

Tirtsa hovers between sleeping and waking, and she is startled when the train finally starts to move.

The train goes forward very slowly. She can see through the bars that it is dark outside. She tries to sleep, but the sobbing and wailing keep her awake.

Every now and then she manages to doze off. When her mother wakes her, she sees that the train has stopped. The doors are opened. She breathes in some fresh air. The dead are removed from the train and buried beside the railway line.

She is still terribly hungry. People are picking nettles and eating them.

The doors close and the train moves on. She can hear the bombing all around them. Then the train suddenly stops. The doors open again. Someone says that the railway line has been bombed, and the train stands still for a very long time. Then it moves off in the opposite direction, and they are on their way again.

The journey takes more than ten days. There is an outbreak of typhus, and the dead are buried beside the tracks at every stop.

Then, after the train has stood still for a long time, they begin to think that the guards have gone. Those who are capable of moving get off the train. They hear voices and see men on horseback coming toward the train. It's the Russians!

Tirtsa, her mother and sister are taken to a nearby village, Tröbitz. Most of its inhabitants have already fled, and the Russians evict any Germans who are still around. The people from the train are allowed to take over the village, and the sick are moved to an emergency hospital.

Tirtsa, her mother and her sister, Ruth, are free.

Mimi de Leeuw

21–7–1930

ver   mij

niet   1.7.42

Lieve Alie

Neem een kop vol opgeruimdheid
En een lepel goede moed
Daags 2 lepels zelfbeheersing
Waar je 'n weinig kalmte in doet
Twintig druppels geest van vreugde
En een poeder levenszoet
Is een raad als goud zo goed
Vindt je dan in dit receptje
Uwen wens nog nog niet vervuld
Neem dan voor het allerlaatste
Nog een pleister van geduld.

Je vriendinnetje
Mimi de Keur

for
get
me
not

•

1.7.42
Dear Alie

Take a cup of humour
And a spoonful of good cheer
Daily 2 spoonfuls of self-control
With a little calmness mixed in
Twenty drops of joyful spirit
And sweet-life powder
This advice is as good as gold
And if you find that this recipe
Has not made your wish come true
Then, last of all, you should take
A poultice of patience.

Your friend
Mimi de Leeuw

MIMI'S STORY
1942–1943

SEPTEMBER

Mimi feels just like she did on the day her father was buried. She is standing at the window. The occasional car drives past on Zuider Amstellaan. That day, there were as many as fifty cars outside the house, behind the one her father was in.

She was not allowed to go. Women and children don't go to funerals. Her mother and Vicky sat on low stools. There was one for her too. But she remained standing, looking down at the place where her father lay. She felt cold and lonely. Never playing cards with Dad again. Never laughing at his jokes. Never again that warm feeling that Dad would solve everything.

He was a very popular man. Everyone said so. Hundreds of people attended the funeral procession. Some Jewish orphan boys walked ahead of the car. She stood there until the entire procession had passed the square with the skyscraper – and even longer, until she could picture the procession reaching Diemen and the Jewish cemetery. Only then did she sit down on the low stool.

And now Vicky is leaving too.

She looks at the back room, where Vicky and their mother are having a serious conversation. She cannot hear exactly what they are saying, but she knows Vicky is leaving with Andries. They married in May and had been engaged for a long time before that. Dries worked at the family business, Gebroeders de Leeuw en Co. As soon as he stepped through the doorway, Vicky fell for him. He was all she could talk about. Mimi has to admit that he is really nice, and he loves Vicky a lot.

Dries works at their old branch in Van Woustraat. Now that a

MIMI DE LEEUW

155

Verwalter has taken over the business, he is no longer allowed to work in the shop, but he can work in the warehouse.

Until recently, Annie, Mimi's other sister, worked at the branch in Kinkerstraat. But she is no longer allowed to use the tram or a bike, and it would be too far too walk, given her poor health.

Mimi does her gymnastics in the living room, including the occasional handstand against the wall. She is distracting her mother.

'Go and do something useful,' she says.

Mimi lifts her leg and lays it on the window sill, then smoothly bends over it.

'I *am* doing something useful. I'm stretching.'

There is a knock at the door.

'Will you get that, Mimi?' says her mother, who is doing something to Vicky's coat with a pair of nail scissors.

As Mimi goes to open up, she does a cartwheel halfway, landing right at the door.

'Mimi, could I maybe borrow a bit of flour?' Mrs Kauffmann asks in her German accent. She is their neighbour from upstairs, and she and her family sometimes come down to eat with them. They are refugees from Germany, who have been living in the Netherlands since the late 1930s. Mimi invites her in.

Mother looks surprised to see her suddenly standing there and quickly puts a newspaper over Vicky's coat.

'Oh, Hilde, now's not a good time,' she says.

Mrs Kauffmann apologises and says she will come back later.

'She only wanted to borrow some flour,' says Mimi, trying to see what her mother was hiding.

'Then take it upstairs to her, before she comes back,' says Mother, and Mimi fetches the flour from the kitchen.

When Mimi returns, her mother is still deep in conversation with Vicky. Annie is sitting with them now too, and all three of them look sad.

'Where are you going?' asks Mimi.

'This is why it would've been better to talk about this at your place,' Mother says to Vicky.

'Mimi's not going to tell anyone. She's old enough now,' says Annie.

'What am I not going to tell to who?' asks Mimi.

Mother stands up and takes Mimi to Vicky's old room.

'Make yourself useful and unpack that suitcase. Put everything away neatly.'

Vicky has been bringing things round all week. Mimi opens the suitcase and carefully unpacks the neatly folded clothes and lays them in the wooden linen cupboard. She drops a couple of things and tries to fold them back up as neatly as before, but she can't compete with the skills of a woman who has years of experience in a fashion store.

Then she goes to her own room. There are clothes, books and craft materials all over the place. Her bed is still unmade. She drops onto the bed, raises her legs up the wall en pointe and stretches her feet, one at a time. She tilts her head back over the edge of the bed. Upside down, her room looks even messier.

'Mimi, will you come and lay the table?' her mother shouts through from the living room.

Mimi puts her hands on the floor, does a bridge and nimbly returns to standing position via a handstand. She rounds it off by stretching her arms up into the air.

In the kitchen, she sees a stack of plates and a pan of potatoes. Mimi takes a fork, pricks a potato out of the pan, and walks through into the living room.

'Mimi, the pan, the plates.'

'I'll do it,' says Annie, giving Mimi a kiss. 'Mimi's far too busy.'

Mimi sits down at the table, blowing on her hot potato. When Annie brings the plates through, Mimi takes them from the stack and deposits them on the table. Annie puts them in the right places.

'Is Dries coming too?' asks Mimi.

Vicky nods, but she is deep in thought. Mimi sits down beside her.

'Will you tell me where you're going?'

'It's better if you don't know. Then you won't let it slip.'

'But won't the neighbours notice if you suddenly disappear?'

'Everyone will think we've been called in. Which is sort of true.'

Mimi looks around the room: Mother, Annie, Vicky and Mimi. Just like it was after Father died.

Her father had been really worried. Annie was in the CIZ, the Jewish hospital, having an operation for an intestinal stricture. He could not go to see her. They all had to shelter in the bathroom because of the bombings – Mimi in the bath, with sandbags. She always used to laugh about that: what good would that do you if a bomb fell on your house?

Her father did not find it funny though. With every bomb that hit, he became more worried: what if they hit the hospital? Her mother and Vicky tried to calm him down. If a bomb did hit, at least Annie was surrounded by doctors and nurses. But Father's panic got the better of him. He decided he was going to walk to the CIZ and that Dries would help him. He was putting on his coat when a bomb fell somewhere nearby. The windows shook, and her father's breathing became more and more shallow. He did not feel at all well, so he needed to go and lie down for a moment. Then he had sharp stabbing pains in his chest: it was a heart attack.

Mimi still feels anxious when she thinks back to the panic that broke out. Her mother and Vicky were both crying and screaming. What should they do? Call for a doctor! But that was impossible, because of the bombing. Vicky broke the curfew to go to Dries, who lived nearby. They would go together to fetch a doctor. Vicky was not away for long, but to her mother it felt like an eternity. Weeping, she sat beside her husband, who was fading quickly. She told Mimi to make cold compresses to dab his forehead. By the time Vicky and Dries returned, he had passed away.

The doorbell rings. It's Dries. He is carrying a parcel, which he puts down on Father's chair before coming to join them at the table.

'Do you have everything?' asks Mother.

Dries looks at Mimi.

'I know you're going away,' says Mimi. 'And I promise I won't say anything. No one at school knows who you are anyway.'

'We can't risk giving away any details,' says Dries. 'We all have to be on our guard.'

Annie mashes her potatoes. Then she bursts into tears.

'I'm going to miss you so much.'

Their mother starts crying too, and now Mimi can't hold in her tears any longer.

'As soon as we get to where we're going, we'll let you know, alright?' Vicky says, with tears in her eyes.

'I have something for you,' says Dries, standing up and handing the parcel to Mother.

Their mother unwraps it. It is a photograph of Dries and Vicky on their way to the town hall to get married.

'It's lovely. That was such a beautiful day,' says Mother. She looks around for the best spot to put the photograph and then places it on the sideboard next to a portrait of Father.

'We need to get going,' says Vicky.

Annie and Mimi fetch their coats from the hall. Mimi looks at the star on Vicky's coat and pulls at the edge.

'Hey, this is a bit loose.'

Vicky snatches the coat from her.

'That'll make it easier.'

'What do you mean?' asks Mimi.

Annie clearly understands and tucks the loose edge back in. 'Make sure that you remove all the threads, eh?'

'Mimi, come here, sweetheart,' says Vicky, hugging her tightly. 'Take care of Mum and Annie. Try not to miss us too much and make sure you have a bit of fun too,' she says, showering her with kisses.

'I've got school tomorrow, so I won't be having too much fun.'

'School's nice though, with all your friends. And never forget that I love you very, very much, eh, Miesje?' Vicky always teases her by using her real name.

It takes them a long time to say goodbye. Everyone wants to hug everyone else.

'We'll just leave, as if we're going to see each other soon,' says Vicky.

She opens the door and makes sure no one's coming out of the lift. Vicky and Dries step quietly into the hallway. No one says anything for a moment.

'Bye, then! See you tomorrow!' Mimi says, too loudly. Annie gives her a nudge. Mimi stares at her indignantly. 'What? We're supposed to act as normal as possible, aren't we?' she whispers.

Mimi runs back inside and stands at the window. She can wave from here without being seen, even though she knows Vicky will not wave back.

Now there are just the three of them. If they had been able to get to England, they would all have been together still. And Father would be alive too. Mimi is sure of that. Just after the capitulation, her father had said: 'Pack your things. We're going to England!' Vicky did not want to go, because of Dries, but she had to. She cried all the way to the harbour at IJmuiden. But when they got there, it was being bombed. They had to take shelter. They could not go to England, so they went back home. Vicky was the only one who was relieved.

•

Mimi does a handstand, walks on her hands to the wall and rests there for a moment.

'What are you doing, standing there upside down? Shouldn't you be going to school?' her mother asks.

Mimi drops out of her handstand and straightens her pinafore, which has risen up.

'I don't feel well. Can I stay at home today?' She does her best to look poorly.

'That's what happens when you keep turning upside down. You're going to school, because I have to take Annie to the doctor,' her mother says. 'Or do you want him to take a look at you too?'

That gives Mimi a fright. She hates the doctor. She quickly grabs her sandwiches and puts on her blazer.

'Can I go to Grandma Fijtje's house after school?' she asks.

'No, you'll be home too late if school doesn't finish until quarter past four.'

'It's Wednesday,' says Mimi. 'I've only got classes until one.'

'Alright, then. Go and see her. Grandma will like that. But home by four. Agreed?' She gives Mimi a kiss and pushes her through the door.

Mimi walks past the houses on Zuider Amstellaan, turns the corner onto Maasstraat and walks to Amstelkade. On the bridge, she takes out a sandwich and breaks off some pieces of bread to throw into the water. Ducks and other birds come flocking. Then she runs on, along Tweede van der Helststraat, all the way to the Oranjekerk: it is five to nine now. One last sprint along Van Ostadestraat and she makes it on time, at one minute to nine. Up the stairs, off with the coat and into the classroom. She sits down.

Mimi is in Miss Fortuijn's class now. The classes are being joined together, as there are fewer and fewer children.

When Mimi gets to the classroom, Miss Fortuijn is already standing by the blackboard.

During the maths lesson, Mimi is constantly doing something else: drawing, whispering to Mary, writing notes that she folds up really small to flick at Ies or another classmate. The notes have little hearts on them and words of love. When someone looks at her, she feigns innocence or points at Mary.

In Dutch, Mimi draws straight lines with her ruler. She loves writing. She uses her dip pen and ink to copy the sentences from the board as neatly as she can. She gets good marks for this subject.

The bell goes. The girls have physical education next. Mimi leads the way to the gym. Their PE classes are in the Christian school they share the building with. The girls change into their sports vests and shorts. Mimi is the first one ready, and she heads into the gym. Mr van Kreveld is putting the vaulting buck and springboard in position.

'Hello, Mimi,' he says. 'Will you lower the rings?'

'What are we going to do today?' she asks, winding the handle to bring the rings down.

'A little bit of everything: vaulting, rings, the low balance beam, bridge, practising handstands and cartwheels, but none of that should be too much of a challenge for you.'

Mimi does a few cartwheels on the coconut matting to warm up. The girls are slowly drifting in. Some of them are clearly not in the mood, and they huddle on the benches to chat.

'Stand up, ladies, and form a line,' shouts Mr van Kreveld.

The girls slowly rise to their feet and stand as close to one another as they can.

'Give your neighbours some space. You don't want someone's arm hitting your head. Or a finger in your eye,' says Mr van Kreveld, and he makes them all stand at arm's length from one another.

'March on the spot! And one, two, three, four!' He claps the rhythm. 'Arms front, arms side, arms up, and one and two . . .'

Before long, most of them have red faces from all the exercise.

'A circuit of the gym. Come on! One, two . . .' Mr van Kreveld blows the whistle.

'Oh no, not running!' one girl groans. She plods along, the girl behind her pushing her forward. The rest soon overtake her.

Mimi is at the front and running fastest, taking bigger and bigger steps. She loves running. She is flying along.

'Good, Mimi. Watch Mimi if you want to see how it should be done: nice, long steps.' Mr van Kreveld blows his whistle again.

'Knees up. And . . . left, right, one, two . . .'

The girls sigh and complain. Some of them cheat by just skipping a bit. One girl takes a break, leaning against the vaulting buck.

'Well, this is going to win us the Olympic Games, isn't it?' says Mr van Kreveld.

'Jews can't do sports in public, so we wouldn't be allowed to take part anyway,' says a girl. 'Unless we go to the Maccabiah Games in Palestine.'

'Can I have a drink of water?' someone asks.

'Me too, me too . . .' Soon the class is half empty.

Mr van Kreveld shakes his head. At least he has a sense of

humour. He blows his whistle and everyone lines up neatly again. He puts them into groups of three.

'Go and stand in your groups beside a piece of apparatus and listen to the instructions.'

Some of the girls start arguing about who gets to do which exercise first. Mr van Kreveld blows hard on his whistle, and that silences them.

'The group at the low beam is going to do a balancing exercise. Mimi, could you demonstrate?'

Mimi steps up onto the low beam. She walks from one end to the other. Then she lifts her right foot, points her toes and gracefully pivots. She places her right foot in front of the left and walks back.

'Now the others can have a go,' the teacher says.

The girls give it a go but, one after another, they fall off the beam.

'It's easy for you, Mimi. You've been doing gymnastics all your life,' one girl says.

'Come on. I'll help you,' says Mimi. 'Give me your hand.'

The girl does as Mimi says.

'Now pay attention to the part of the beam you want to put your foot on. And ignore everything else,' Mimi says. 'Look at it first – and then place your foot.'

The girl concentrates – and it works. Mimi is still holding her hand. Concentrating hard, the girl walks to the end of the beam.

'See! You can do it,' Mimi says proudly. The girl has a taste for it now. She lets go of Mimi's hand and tries to pivot. But she crashes onto the mat. The other girls laugh.

'Why did you let go?' she grumbles.

Mimi smiles and helps her to her feet.

'Next.'

After the beam, Mimi helps out at the mat. A couple of the girls are very good at cartwheels, but the rest are bumbling around.

'First you have to be able to do handstands a bit. You need to get your legs up in the air.' She demonstrates a handstand and stays up for a few seconds. The girls are impressed.

Mimi helps them one at a time by holding their legs in the air.

Nearly everyone manages to do it.

'Now let's go and practise on the wall,' says Mimi, and they drag the mat over there. 'There are two ways to do it. You can take a run-up and throw your legs up into the air and against the wall in one go. Or you can stand facing the wall, bend forward so that your back is against the wall and then walk towards the wall on your toes as far as you can.' Mimi shows them. 'Then you can slowly put your legs up the wall, first one and then the other.'

Mimi helps the girls to do a handstand against the wall. Soon they are lined up in a row. The whole class has come to look. But they can't do it for long before collapsing onto the floor.

Mr van Krefeld takes Mimi aside.

'You have a talent for this,' he says.

'I've been doing rhythmic gymnastics all my life,' says Mimi.

'I mean the way you explain things and help the other girls. You'd make a good teacher. Do you know what you want to do later?' he asks.

'No.' Mimi has never thought about it.

'You could become a PE teacher. Or a swimming instructor.'

Mimi looks at him. That sounds like fun.

'It's not possible now, of course, but once the war's over, you should think about it.'

He blows his whistle, and the lesson is over.

'Are you coming out to play, Mimi?' asks one of the girls from the handstand group.

'No, not today. I'm going to my grandma's house,' says Mimi, quickly getting changed.

Grandma Fijtje lives in the Plantage neighbourhood, close to Artis, the zoo. Still warm from the PE class, Mimi walks briskly, via the River Amstel to Nieuwe Kerkstraat, then on to Plantage Kerklaan, and she is nearly at her grandma's. Grandma Fijtje lives in an old people's home on Plantage Middenlaan, which is owned by Mimi's Aunt Rosa and her husband.

She rings the bell a few times. It takes a while but then the door opens. Grandma's brother is standing at the top of the stairs.

'Who's there?' he shouts. He is a bit deaf.

'Mimi,' she shouts back.

'Who?'

'Mimi!' She is almost yelling.

'Oh, Wimmie. Come on up.'

Mimi can't help smiling when she goes upstairs and her great uncle sees that she is not Wimmie.

'Hello, Uncle. I've come to visit Grandma Fijtje. You remember me, don't you?'

He smiles, but Mimi can tell that he does not really recognise her.

'Fijtje? Say hello from me.'

Mimi knocks on the door and goes in. Grandma is knitting by the window, which looks out over Plantage Middenlaan, at the side of the zoo. When she has the window open, you can hear the animals. Mimi always tries to guess which animal she can hear.

'Hello, sjeintje,' says Grandma Fijtje, when Mimi gives her a hug.

Mimi picks up a piece of knitting too.

'Is it alright if I knit this?' she asks.

'It's seed stitch. Can you do that?' asks Grandma Fijtje.

Mimi tries, but does not get it quite right.

'Here, let me show you. It's one row alternating the knit and purl stitches like this, and then the next row you start with purl and then knit, and so on.'

Mimi soon gets the hang of it and knits a few rows.

Grandma Fijtje has some tea in a pot and she pours a cup for Mimi.

'Would you like me to knit you a scarf?' she asks Mimi. 'It's starting to get chilly out.'

'That'd be nice. Yes, please,' says Mimi. Grandma Fijtje is right. The weather is getting colder. She opens the window and hears the monkeys screeching across the road. Then some German soldiers walk past. As she looks at them, it is as if the screeching is coming from their mouths instead.

'There's a lot of activity going on at the theatre again.' Mimi puts her head out of the window and can just make out the front of the Hollandsche Schouwburg.

'They mostly come at night, on trams or on foot,' says Grandma Fijtje. 'You can hear soldiers' boots and other footsteps. Sound travels at night.'

'But what's going on there at night? Are they watching plays?' Mimi asks in surprise.

'You know people are being detained, don't you? Taken from their homes?'

Mimi nods. There have already been a lot of raids in the neighbourhood. Luckily she has not experienced it herself so far.

'They lock the people up in the Schouwburg.'

'And then what?'

'Then trams come to fetch them at night.'

'I thought Jews weren't allowed on the tram anymore,' says Mimi.

'They'll be taking them to the station. And then maybe to a camp. I don't know.'

Mimi shuts the window. She does not want to think about that.

'Come on. Drink your tea,' says Grandma Fijtje. She can see that Mimi is agitated. 'Would you like a biscuit?'

Mimi quietly continues her knitting.

Grandma Fijtje comes back with the biscuit tin. Mimi chooses a biscuit. Grandma Fijtje takes one too. She takes a bite of her biscuit and starts making strange noises. Mimi looks up and realises that her grandma is sucking the biscuit, which looks odd. When her grandmother smiles at her, she sees what the problem is: she has taken out her dentures, and her whole mouth has sunken in.

'It's not easy eating without teeth,' she says with a laugh, and now Mimi sees the inside of her mouth and lots of pink gums.

She bursts out laughing when Grandma Fijtje puts her false teeth back in and gives them a good chatter.

'Mimi, wake up,' her mother whispers urgently.

Mimi hears her, but she can't open her eyes. Her mother shakes her softly. Now she opens her eyes, but it is a struggle.

'What's wrong? Is it already morning?'

The room is in darkness. A dim light from the hall shines through the doorway. She is startled to see a man standing there, and she sits up with a jolt.

'Who's that? Do we have to go?'

'No, don't be scared. It's just me,' he says.

Mimi takes another look. Then she sees that it is her cousin Bram. Before she can say anything, her mother pulls her gently out of bed, blanket and all.

'Come on. You're sleeping in my bed tonight.'

Mimi shuffles through to her mother's room. In the hallway, her cousin gives her a kiss.

'Sleep tight, sjeintje. And thanks for letting me borrow your bed.'

Mimi mumbles something and falls straight back to sleep in her mother's bed.

A little later, she is woken by the sound of someone moving around, and she sits up in bed. Her mother is still asleep. She goes to the window and opens the blackout curtain a little: it is still dark. The noise is coming from the kitchen.

Bram is in there, eating some bread.

'Good morning. Do you want some too?' he asks, holding out a buttered slice.

'No, I only just woke up,' she says, helping herself to a cup of the tea he has made.

'As soon as the curfew is over, I'll be off.'

'Were you late for curfew yesterday?'

'No, they were going door to door, late last night. So I made a run for it.'

'Do you mean the Germans?'

'There were some Germans, but there were Dutch men with them too,' he says with a frown. 'I was lucky this time.'

Mimi gives him a concerned look.

'But don't you worry about me, Mimi. Got any fun plans for today?'

'I have to go to school.'

'Great. Buckle down to it!' He looks at his watch. 'I need to get going. Thank your mother for me. I'll pop round later this week – at a normal time.'

He gives Mimi a kiss and quietly leaves.

•

When Mimi comes home, she finds her mother and Annie in tears.

'Who can we ask?' says Annie.

Seeing Mimi, she jumps to her feet and gives her a hug.

'Vicky and Dries . . . ,' she begins, but she can't get the words out.

'They've been caught,' says her mother. 'At the border in Roosendaal. They were on their way to Switzerland.' Mimi is horrified.

'Someone has to go to the Schouwburg and ask how they're doing,' says Mother. She automatically walks to the telephone, but of course it is not connected. She slams down the receiver.

'That's the point – so we can't contact anyone in an emergency. So we all rot.'

'I can go,' says Annie.

'Your stomach ache's so bad, you can't walk ten metres,' says Mother.

'I could go, couldn't I?' says Mimi. 'I know where it is, just by Grandma Fijtje's.'

'You're not going anywhere. It's far too dangerous for a child. The place is crawling with German soldiers,' Mother says firmly. 'If they see you there with that star, they'll take you in. We need to ask one of your cousins.'

'Well, Mimi could do that, couldn't she?' says Annie.

Mother looks at the clock.

'Go and see if Bram is home and ask if he can get any more information,' says Mother. 'And come straight back.'

Mimi goes to the door, puts on her scarf and runs down the street.

No one answers the door at Bram's. She rings again. Still nothing. For a moment, she does not know what to do. She looks around, asks someone what time it is and has a think about it. Yes, she can still do it.

She looks at the star on her coat. How did Mother and Vicky do it again? She stands in a doorway and tries to loosen a thread with her teeth. Before long, she can pull off the star, and she also removes the last few loose threads. Then she stashes it in her coat pocket and looks at herself in a shop window: she does not look very Jewish with her light hair. Her coat is a bit bare without its star, but she also feels liberated. She starts running.

When she gets to Van Woustraat, she stops. In the distance, she sees the tram approaching. Does she dare? She goes to the tram stop and waits. When the tram arrives, she gets on. She sits down. No one pays any attention to her. She is just a girl taking the tram. Since Jews have no longer been allowed to travel by tram, she has had to walk everywhere. When they reach Ceintuurbaan, she gets off. She walks to Frederiksplein and catches the tram to Sarphatistraat. She walks the last part of the way along Plantage Kerklaan, her heart beating faster. What exactly is she going to do? She obviously can't just walk in there.

She takes a few deep breaths and walks to the corner of the street. It looks empty. She crosses the road. A few people walk by, and she tries to be as unobtrusive as possible. At the end of the street, she turns around and walks back. She sees a man coming out of the Schouwburg and hurries over to him.

'Excuse me, sir,' she calls.

The man looks at her. Mimi sees that he is wearing a star. She is surprised. Are Jews allowed to go in and out of the building? The man stops.

'Is everyone just allowed to leave the Schouwburg?' she asks.

The man looks around and walks to the corner. Mimi follows him.

'Why do you want to know?'

'I know someone who's in there. I'd like to find out how she is,' says Mimi.

'Everyone was sent on yesterday,' says the man, walking away.

Mimi goes after him again.

'So there's no one left inside?'

'Only staff. I'd go home if I were you, girl. This is no place for children.' The man clearly does not want to talk to her.

Mimi stops following him and walks instead to Grandma Fijtje's house, but hesitates to ring the bell. How can she tell her poor grandma about this? She runs home instead.

Mimi is walking back from school. It is cold. There is still some snow on the streets, and a thin layer of ice on the water. Mimi does not mind that the ice has melted. She is not allowed to skate now anyway.

She walks along Maasstraat. The shops are open, but she is only permitted to enter them between three and five. She is not allowed to go to the greengrocer's at all. When she is almost at Zuider Amstellaan, she sees her neighbour, Mrs Nebig, striding towards her.

'Mimi, you have to come with me. They're at your place.' The neighbour takes her arm, and Mimi hurries to keep up.

'Who?'

'Police and Grüne Polizei. They're taking everyone away.'

Mimi stops, horrified.

'It's Mum's birthday. There are visitors coming.'

'Believe it or not, everyone left just before they got here. Including your mother and Annie,' the neighbour says, pulling Mimi along.

'But I don't want to go home,' Mimi protests.

'No, you're coming with me. They won't bother us.'

Mimi allows the neighbour to lead her. Mrs Nebig is married to a Jewish man, but she is not Jewish herself. She lives with her family next door to Mimi, on the third floor.

'But then they'll see me, won't they?' Mimi says anxiously.

The street is full of police vans, with people being loaded into them. One is parked outside their front door. Soldiers and men in black are going in and out of the building. Mimi's house and the neighbours' house share an entrance. On the left is 207, and on the right is 209, where Mimi lives. In the hall, she looks at her front door, which is closed. Mrs Nebig goes straight to the lift and presses the button.

Sounds of crying and banging are coming from upstairs. She hears people speaking German: Mrs Kauffmann. They hear heavy boots pounding in the hall upstairs on the right. Mimi gasps, but the neighbour warns her to be quiet. The lift does not come. Mrs Nebig presses the button impatiently a few more times. Then she takes Mimi by the hand and pulls her up the stairs. They run to the third floor. She opens the door and pushes Mimi into the bedroom.

'Lie down,' she says, pointing at the bed.

Mr Nebig comes into the room and they quickly lift the fold-away bed with Mimi inside it. She feels claustrophobic in the folded-up bed, and tries to make some room to breathe in front of her face.

There is banging on the door. Mimi holds her breath as she hears Mrs Nebig opening up. She can't hear exactly what is said, but a moment later the door closes again.

'Just a little longer, Mimi. They're about to leave. Can you hold on?' the neighbour whispers.

Mimi answers with a stifled 'yes'.

It seems to take forever. Where are Mother and Annie? She hopes they got away safely.

Finally the bed is folded back down.

Mrs Nebig takes her into the kitchen and gives her a glass of water and a couple of sandwiches.

'You have something to eat, and I'll just go and see what happened at Mrs Kauffmann's.'

Mimi can hardly eat. She stands up and goes to the window.

'Don't do that, Mimi,' says Mr Nebig. 'They might still be waiting.'

Mimi sits at the table.

'They've all been taken, Hilde and the children,' says Mrs Nebig, horror-stricken, when she returns. 'The door has been sealed.'

'Is my mother back yet?' asks Mimi.

'I didn't hear anything. If they have any sense, they'll stay away for a while.'

The hours pass very slowly. Mimi reads a book and listens at the door every now and then to see if she can make out any sounds.

When it is almost dark, there is a knock at the door.

Mr and Mrs Nebig are on their guard. Mrs Nebig goes to the door, but waits before opening.

'Mrs Nebig, open up. It's me, Dieuwertje,' comes a loud whisper.

They open the door and Dieuwertje rushes in, closing the door behind her. Dieuwertje cleans for them and is a friend of Annie's.

'Mimi!' Dieuwertje is overjoyed to see her. 'We've been everywhere, but your mother was right. Here you are!'

She gives Mimi a big hug.

'Where are Mum and Annie?' asks Mimi anxiously.

'They're at my place, but I'll go and fetch them. You stay here.'

Half an hour later, Mother and Annie come upstairs. Mimi throws her arms around them.

'Well, this is a birthday I'll never forget,' says Mother.

'Could I just lie down on the sofa?' asks Annie. She looks very pale. She had another operation a week ago.

'Shall we go and look downstairs?' Dieuwertje asks Mrs Nebig.

Mimi goes and sits next to Annie and gives her a hug.

Mother listens at the door until Dieuwertje and Mrs Nebig are back.

'Well?'

'The door is sealed. You can't go in,' says Dieuwertje.

'Why do they do that?' asks Mimi.

'So that they'll know if anyone breaks in,' says Mr Nebig. 'Only the Krauts are allowed to steal from Jews.'

'No doubt Puls will be here tomorrow,' says Mother.

'Are they going to empty our house then?' Mimi asks nervously. 'All my things are at home.'

'I really want to go home,' says Annie.

'And then what? Stick the seal back on the door? They'll be able to tell, won't they?' says Mother.

'I'm longing for my bed,' says Annie, whose cheeks are flushed.

Mimi feels Annie's forehead. She is a little warm.

'Or we could remove the seal entirely,' says Mrs Nebig.

They all look up.

'Just get rid of it, as if nothing has happened.'

'But if they come tomorrow, then they might still take us away,' says Mother.

'Do you have somewhere else you could go?' asks Mr Nebig.

'The three of us?' says Mother. 'Annie still needs to recover from her operation. I don't think we'll be able to find anything suitable.'

Mother stands up. 'We'll do it. We'll take the wretched thing off and try not to draw any attention to ourselves.'

She picks up her bag. Then she gives Mrs Nebig a hug.

'Thanks for looking after Mimi, Griet,' she says. 'If there's ever anything I can do for you . . .'

Cautiously, they open the front door and walk down the stairs. The hallway downstairs is empty.

At their front door, Mother quickly removes the seal and opens the door. They are home.

'Let's get some sleep,' says Mother. 'Mimi, you can sleep in my bed tonight.'

Annie gets into bed with them too. Mimi lies in the middle.

'How come you weren't at home?' she asks.

'We have your sister to thank for that,' says Mother.

'Did you know they were coming then?' asks Mimi in surprise.

'No, but I had such a strange feeling all day. There was something in the air. I don't know if I was feeling anxious because of my stomach, but when Dieuwertje came, I thought: Let's go out,' says Annie. 'Just out for a walk somewhere.'

'As we were coming back, the police vans drove into the street,' says Mother. 'I had the fright of my life.'

'I'm so glad they didn't take you away. What would I have done?' says Mimi.

'If it happens again, go straight to Griet. She'll help you. And stay there,' says Mother.

Mimi cuddles up close to her mother. Suddenly she remembers the neighbours.

'I heard lots of soldiers upstairs and people shouting. They were all taken away. And Vicky and Dries . . .' She starts crying, and then Annie joins in. Their mother kisses them and tries to comfort them both.

'Go to sleep. For tonight, we're still sleeping in our own cosy beds.'

Mimi wakes to the sound of her mother banging around in the kitchen.

She sits up in bed. Annie is still asleep. Mimi gets out of bed and goes into the living room. Her mother has already laid the table and comes out of the kitchen with a pot of tea and some porridge.

'Did you manage to get a bit of sleep?' asks her mother, giving her a kiss.

Annie comes sleepily into the living room too. Mother puts the porridge in front of her.

'I can't wait until I can eat normally again,' she says, stirring the spoon around her bowl a little.

They eat and when Mimi looks outside, she sees a truck pulling up outside the building.

'They're here.' Mimi jumps to her feet and knocks the tea over. Her mother shuts the curtains and checks that the front door is locked. They go and sit in the bedroom. They sit in perfect silence. Someone rings the doorbell downstairs. Mimi holds her breath. The doorbell goes again. Then they hear someone on the stairs, and the front door opens.

'Can I help you, gentlemen?' says Mrs Nebig. She is talking extra loud, so that they can hear her.

'We're here for the property of the Jews at 209,' a man says.

'209?' she says in a surprised voice. 'They haven't been taken away, have they? You must be mistaken.'

Mimi can't hear what they are saying and wants to go into the hallway, but her mother pulls her back by her pyjamas.

They hear muttering at the door.

'There's no seal on it,' says the man.

Mimi hears him rattling the doorknob.

'I told you, they haven't been taken away. They're not in now though. I saw them leave the house this morning.'

'We have to take the things anyway. It's on the list.' The man is determined. 'Have you got the key?' he asks the other man.

'209? No, it's not there.'

'Then we'll just have to break it down. Please move away from the door, lady.'

'Not this one,' says Mrs Nebig. 'No key, no seal.'

A little later, they hear the front door slam and what sounds like the truck driving away. There is a knock on the door.

'If you're in there, open up,' whispers Mrs Nebig.

Mother hurries to the door and lets her in.

'Have they gone?' asks Mother.

'They just drove off down the street.'

They burst into nervous laughter.

'You're a one, Griet,' says Mother.

Mrs Nebig crosses her arms and stands in front of Mother.

'I stood in front of them like this, blocking their way. But I was shaking inside.'

Mimi and Annie appear from the bedroom.

'Now let's hope they don't come back,' says Mother with a sigh.

•

Mimi walks into the living room, where Dieuwertje and her mother are dusting.

'How was school?' asks her mother.

Mimi takes off her coat and throws it onto the sofa. Dieuwertje picks it up and hangs it in the hallway.

'It was quiet,' says Mimi. 'One of the teachers wasn't there – she got taken away. So another girl and I helped out with the little ones. That was fun.'

'Those poor little children. They have no idea what's going on,' her mother says, giving Mimi a kiss.

Mimi goes to the window and peers down the street. She does not see anything unusual, only people walking along, bare trees, the grass down the middle of the street, the tram tracks. No trucks or police vans.

'Do you think it'll be our turn again soon?' she asks.

'I have no idea,' her mother replies.

Annie comes out of her bedroom, still in her pyjamas. She gives Mimi a kiss.

'Does your stomach hurt?' asks Mimi.

'A bit, but it's getting better.'

Dieuwertje lays a pile of clothing on the dining table, which she has rescued from Mimi's room. Mimi helps her to fold them.

'Have you heard anything about Vicky?' asks Dieuwertje.

'Just that they're in Westerbork. They were caught at the border because someone in their group didn't have the right papers. So they were all arrested,' says Mother.

There are tears in her eyes. Dieuwertje goes and sits beside her and takes her hand.

'Why don't you come with me? I know a place where all three of you can go.'

Her mother looks at her in surprise. 'You mean go into hiding?'

Dieuwertje nods.

'But what if there's a problem with Annie and we have to go to the hospital?' Then Mother points at Mimi. 'Besides, she'd have told all her school friends about it before the day was out.'

Mimi gasps. 'I'd never do that!' she says indignantly.

'Sweetheart, I know you'd never do it on purpose, but you might let something slip. I think we need to come up with another solution,' says Mother.

20 JUNE 1943

Something wakes Mimi up. She can hear a voice that is not coming from inside the building. It sounds strange. She rubs her eyes and opens them. Then she hears it again: a voice announcing something in a monotone. It can't be the radio. They don't have one anymore.

Annie hurries into her room.

'Open the window. Listen.'

She opens the window at the back of the house. It is still not quite light.

The voice is telling all the Jews in the area to prepare to leave.

Mimi runs nervously to the living room and looks out of the window there: soldiers are everywhere. They are banging on every door. Mimi closes the curtains again.

Her mother comes sleepily out of her bedroom.

'What's going on?'

'They've come for us,' says Annie in a weak voice.

'They can't,' says Mother. 'We have a stamp.'

'You have a *Sperre*? How did you get it? When?'

Mother shows it to her. 'We all have one – doesn't matter how or when. All that matters is that we're not going.'

They can hear the voice still summoning everyone outside.

'But they're telling everyone to prepare to leave,' says Annie. 'Let's get our things ready.'

'No, we don't have to go.'

'But then if we do have to leave, we won't have any luggage,' says Annie, going to her room. 'Mimi, pack your things. Just in case.'

Will they really have to leave now? Mimi can hardly believe it. She goes to her room and stands there, not knowing what to do.

'What should I take?' she shouts.

'All the warm clothes you can find,' Annie calls back.

Mimi looks in her wardrobe. She grabs a pile of clothes and throws them onto her bed. She does not want to leave. She lies in her bed, under the covers.

'I'm not going,' she shouts.

Her mother comes into her bedroom.

'Annie's right. We'd better be prepared,' she says, pulling the covers off Mimi. 'But we're not going out to them. We'll wait for them to come and fetch us.'

Mimi stays there, lying on the bed. Her mother takes some clothing off the pile and sets it aside on her bed. Annie comes in and puts Mimi's things into a backpack.

'Do you want to take a book?' she asks.

'Go on then,' says Mimi.

'Which one?'

'I don't know. Anything,' says Mimi.

'Just tell me which book you want to take.' Annie sounds irritated.

'You're the one who's insisting I should take a book. So you can choose one.'

Mimi angrily tugs the bedcover back over herself and starts to cry.

Annie pulls down the cover.

'I'm sorry. I'll choose a nice book for you.'

She gives Mimi a kiss, takes a book off the shelves and adds it to the pile. Then she pulls Mimi up.

'Come on, let's have breakfast first.'

No one is hungry. Their mother butters extra slices of bread for sandwiches and removes the crusts from Annie's. She divides them between three bags.

They sit in silence when the doorbell rings downstairs.

It rings again. They hear the front door of the building open. Footsteps in the hallway, boots.

Then a knocking on the door. They hold their breath.

'*Aufmachen*,' says a gruff voice. Open up.

The banging continues.

Their mother stands up and takes some documents from her bag.

'You're not going to open the door, are you?' Annie says in dismay.

'They'll keep banging away if I don't,' says Mother.

Mimi can't hear exactly what her mother is saying. The conversation is short and a little later Mother comes back into the room, looking pale.

'We have to go to the assembly point anyway,' she says, in a daze. 'We'll just have to sort it out there.'

Mimi has tears in her eyes. Her mother and Annie gather up their belongings and put the backpacks in the hall.

'Get dressed, Mimi. We're going,' says Mother.

Mimi puts on her sandals and her summer dress with a cardigan over the top.

There is a knock on the door. It's Mrs Nebig.

'Is there really nothing more that can be done?' she asks with teary eyes.

'Maybe we'll be able to sort something out when we get there,' says Mother.

'Those stamps should be enough though,' says Mrs Nebig. 'Why else would they give them to people?'

'Griet, would you take that box? And Annie's key? Then you can come in and take a few things to look after for us,' says Mother. Then they say goodbye and leave the house.

Mimi looks back for a long time, trying to absorb everything.

They walk to Daniël Willinkplein, at the end of the street. There are already lots of people on the grass in front of the skyscraper, and more keep arriving. Everyone is carrying a backpack or some other kind of luggage.

'What now?' asks Mimi.

'I'm going to look for someone who can help us,' says Mother. 'You stay here with Annie.'

They put down their luggage and sit on the grass. The weather is lovely. Perfect for a day at the beach. Mimi basks in the sun.

'Wish I'd brought a folding chair,' says Annie. 'My dress is going to turn green.'

'Then go and fetch one. It's not far,' says Mimi.

'I'll go in a bit, when Mum gets back,' says Annie, who thinks it sounds like a good idea.

Half an hour later, their mother returns. Annie has forgotten about the chair.

'Well? What did they say?'

'They're going to see what they can they do. We have to stay here for now,' says their mother. The hours go by. The square is packed, and more and more people come to join them.

Mimi spends time with some little children on the grass, playing tag and doing cartwheels. They eat and drink what they have brought with them.

'We could just as easily have left later,' says Mimi in a bored voice. 'Then we'd still be at home.'

'At least the weather's good,' Annie replies.

At the end of the afternoon, Mother goes to make inquiries again. She walks over to a group of Germans.

Mimi is scared. Her mother looks so small next to those German soldiers. She can tell from her mother's expression that the conversation was not very hopeful.

'We'll keep trying,' says her mother.

It is almost evening by the time the trams arrive. There is an announcement that everyone must prepare to board. Mother becomes very anxious and gives it one last try. She kicks up a fuss with one of the soldiers, refusing to get on the tram until she has spoken to someone. She shows her papers again. The soldier goes to talk to his superior. Mimi cannot hear what is being said, but she sees the soldier returning the papers. Her mother comes back.

Mimi looks at the trams. They really do have to leave now.

'Get your things. We're going home,' says Mother, gathering up her belongings. Mimi is confused.

'Hurry – before they change their minds.'

Without looking back, they return to Zuider Amstellaan as fast as they can walk without running.

Once they are inside, they collapse onto the sofa, feeling so relieved.

'How did you manage that?' asks Mimi.

'Bram,' says Mother.

'But how?' Mimi still does not understand.

'Diamonds,' says Annie.

'He bought a *Sperre* for everyone in the family,' says Mother. 'And it worked. Well, at least we aren't going to be sent away.'

She stands up, walks around the room and looks at the furniture.

'What are you doing?' asks Annie.

'We were allowed to stay,' says Mother. 'But we still have to leave the house.'

'But you said we didn't have to go!' Mimi can't make any sense of it.

'We have to move house. To the Transvaalbuurt. To the ghetto.'

Rosa Snijders

9 MAY 1931

Lieve Mi

Als je later bent gezeten
Die weet je ... wel
Zal je Rosa dan niet zijn vergeten
Die eens met jou heeft ... gezeten

Je vriendinnetje
Rosa Snijders

Dear Ali,

One day later when you are sitting
Who knows how far from here
Will you not forget Rosa
Who once went to school with you?

Your friend
Rosa Snijders

10–6–'42

JUNE

Mr Roeg reads out the names of the children in the class. Rosa is sitting behind Alie and Jenny.

The headmaster, Mr Stibbe, comes into the classroom, carrying a book. He looks at the names with Mr Roeg. Mr Stibbe takes the list from Mr Roeg and adds it to the lists from the other classes.

'Where do you live again, Ro?' asks Alie.

'Nieuwe Keizersgracht, at my grandma and grandpa's.'

'Posh,' says Jenny. 'It must be a big house.'

'There are eleven of us living there,' says Rosa.

'Do you like living in Amsterdam?'

'No,' she says quietly. 'I'd rather have stayed in Enkhuizen.'

ROSA'S STORY

1942–1943

Rosa looks at the men in their long raincoats. It is not cold, but they are wearing hats. One of the men is holding a clipboard with lots of sheets of paper.

'Is your mother at home?' The man gives her a friendly smile, but Rosa has an unpleasant feeling. She runs down the hallway and calls her mother.

'Mum, there are two men at the door!' Her mother, who is cooking, wipes her hands on her apron and walks to the door.

'We're here to do the inventory,' says the man, with the same friendly smile.

Rosa can see that her mother is on her guard, but she lets the men in anyway.

'Ro, go to your bedroom and do your homework.'

Rosa leaves the room, but stops and peers through the crack in the door.

She sees her mother putting aside a few bits and pieces, but one of the men stops her.

'Leave everything where it is,' he says forcefully. The men look with great interest at the antique blue plates hanging on the wall. The man with the clipboard busily makes notes. Then they open all the drawers and cupboard doors. They note everything down. Rosa has a shock when one of the men suddenly opens the door.

'Where's the kitchen?' he says. Rosa points the way. She follows him and watches as he opens all the drawers and cupboards in there too. Her mother hurries in and takes the pan of food off the heat.

The man points at the counters on either side of the kitchen. 'Kosher?'

Her mother nods. The man opens the cupboards and makes a note of what is inside. He licks his thumb and index finger and turns the page.

'Do you have a pantry?' he asks, looking around. Her mother hesitates. 'You're going to Amsterdam,' he says. Her mother nods again.

'You can't take anything with you, and certainly not food,' he says, lifting the lid of the pan with the fingers he just licked.

Her mother replaces the lid. She points at the door. 'Down the stairs, on the left. That's where you'll find the pantry,' she says. The man heads off that way.

'What are they going to do with our things, Mum?'

'Not now, Ro,' says her mother, quickly following the man.

The man looks calmly at his list again.

'I think we're more or less finished here.'

Rosa's mother closes all the drawers and cupboard doors.

'So you're leaving in two weeks?' asks the man, still looking at his list.

'That's right,' says her mother.

'No need to lock the door. Leave the keys behind in an envelope on the table, including the spare ones.' The man puts his pen behind his ear and calls his colleague.

Rosa and her mother follow the men to the front door. Rosa

notices that the coat pockets of the man who went into the pantry are bulging with tins of food. She taps her mother's arm and points at the man's pockets, but her mother pushes her hand away. As the men are leaving, one of them turns around for a moment.

'Oh, and don't forget to cancel your gas and electricity,' he says, with a broad grin. 'Wouldn't want you to waste the money.'

Mother slams the door when the men have left.

'He'd filled his pockets!' Rosa exclaims. But her mother is already putting on her coat and not listening to Rosa.

'I'm going to fetch your father. Stay here and don't open the door to anyone.'

Rosa looks around. Staying at home alone feels a bit frightening now. The men could come back at any minute. She goes to her room and closes the door.

In her bedroom, her suitcase for Amsterdam is already packed. It is full, but she still puts another jumper on top of it. And another dress. And another book. She keeps going until there is a big pile on top of the case.

When the front door slams, Rosa jumps. She walks to the landing and to her relief she hears her parents talking.

'Dad, two men came to the house,' she says, giving her father a hug. 'And one of them stuffed loads of our tins of food into his pockets.' But her father is not listening.

'Do you have a copy of the list?' he asks her mother.

'No, they didn't give me one,' says her mother, opening a drawer. 'They made a list of all the silver cutlery. And the antique blue plates.'

Rosa's father looks angry. 'Then we've lost those.'

They sit at the table in silence.

Mother goes to the kitchen. She puts the pan of food back on the heat. Rosa picks up a spoon.

'No, not that one. That's for meat.' Rosa's mother takes the spoon from her and points at the other counter. 'Take one from that drawer instead.'

Rosa does as her mother says. Her mother looks into the kitchen drawers. First one counter and then the other. She has a big smile on her face. She gives Rosa a hug.

Rosa has no idea what is going on, but she follows her mother back into the living room, where Father is still thinking.

'Or maybe we haven't lost them . . . ,' says her mother. Rosa and her father watch in surprise as her mother takes all the silver cutlery and the dishes out of the cupboards and drawers.

'We'll leave copies. Stainless steel.' Rosa does not really understand what Mother means, but a smile appears on Father's face now too.

'And the breakfast plates are blue as well,' says her mother.

Rosa watches as her father carefully removes the beautiful antique plates from the wall and hangs up the ordinary breakfast plates instead. The three of them look at the result.

'Spot the difference,' says Father with a satisfied smile.

TWO WEEKS LATER

Rosa watches as her father lifts the suitcases onto a handcart. It is a dry, fresh day. The sun is shining weakly. She buttons up her coat. In the distance, she sees her aunt and uncle approaching with her two cousins. Her cousins have the same names as Rosa and her brother, Marcus, who is generally known as Max. The whole family is going to Amsterdam.

Her mother dashes in and out of the house, checking that she has not forgotten anything. Rosa pops back inside. She has already said goodbye to her bedroom. Who knows when she will see it again? She goes into her room, one last time. It is so neat and tidy. She has stripped the bed, put the rest of her clothes in the wardrobe and given the floor a bit of a sweep.

She closes the curtains. Now she is ready to leave. Her mother is waiting for her in the hallway.

'Come on, let's go,' she says quietly. Her mother leaves the key on the table. One last look into the hallway and then they close the door behind them. Father and Mother shake hands with the neighbours. Some friends and acquaintances come to say goodbye.

'We'll see you again soon,' her father says firmly.

They walk down the street to the corner, where her father's shop is. She still calls it her father's shop, even though he has had to sell it. They pause in front of the building. There are people coming from every direction now. Rosa is surprised to see that all the children from her old class have come to wave them off.

'Here, for the journey.' One of her friends hands her a bag of sweets. 'We all saved them up for you.' Rosa takes the sweets and gives all the girls a hug.

'We have to get going.' Her mother takes her hand.

More and more people come to see, lining up on the roadside. Rosa, her family and all the other Jews in Enkhuizen make their way through the crowd of people to the station. Men pat her father on the shoulder. Women gather around her mother, hugging her. Rosa can see her mother is struggling not to cry. Her own eyes are full of tears too, but she is not crying.

Women and children come up to her and kiss her.

'Good luck!' they shout. As they walk on, some people look curiously at what is going on. Lots of people are crying. Nearly everyone walks all the way with them to the station, where a train is waiting. There are other passengers already on the train, who have been taken from other villages. They are all Jewish families. The train is accompanied by Dutch police officers and a few German soldiers. The locals who walked with them stand and wait on the platform.

Rosa boards the train and gets a seat by the window. She waves to her friends for so long that her arm starts to feel numb. When the signal sounds for the train to leave, there are still lots of people standing there. The train starts moving. Rosa waves harder. The people on the platform wave back and blow kisses. Handkerchiefs come out, and people are crying. Her parents have tears in their eyes too, as they wave back. Rosa can't hold in her tears any longer. This really is her farewell to her home.

Rosa holds her nose – it stinks in Amsterdam. It smells of the big city. They walk with their suitcases along Sint Antoniesbreestraat towards Jodenbreestraat and Nieuwe Keizersgracht. Rosa holds her mother's hand tightly. The streets are so busy. People are swarming all around. Street vendors are hawking their wares.

Rosa looks around in amazement: so many people, so many shops. It is nothing like Enkhuizen at all. Walking on, they come to a big square. She is looking straight at the Portuguese Synagogue. To the right of it is the Grote Sjoel. Being here gives her a warm feeling. There are important people here. Nothing can happen to them in this place. Rosa looks back at the market on Waterlooplein. They cross the bridge and walk onto Weesperstraat, the main road through the Jewish neighbourhood. It is even busier here, if that could be possible. There is more traffic: people with handcarts, bicycles, the occasional motorbike and even a car.

The second canal on the right is where her grandma and grandpa live, at number 22, on the second floor. Rosa runs ahead with her cousins. She rings the doorbell and looks up. Her grandma and grandpa are waving from the window.

'Grandpa, Grandma, we're here!' The front door opens and her big brother, Max, is standing there. Rosa is so happy to see him. They give each other a hug. Grandpa and Grandma are waiting upstairs with Aunt Rosalie. She is a widow. When they are all together in the living room, Rosa counts how many people are there: Grandpa, Grandma, Aunt Rosalie, Aunt Celina and Uncle Daniel, Mum, Dad, Max, and her two cousins. With her, that makes eleven in total.

'Where are we all going to sleep?' she asks.

'Come on, I'll show you,' says Aunt Rosalie.

She takes the children with her to the attic, where there are beds lined up for them. The parents have their own rooms.

•

Rosa looks out the window at the house across the canal. She has been in Amsterdam a few weeks now. She is still not quite used to it and likes to retreat to the top floor. It has the best view in the house: to the left she can see all the way across the River

Amstel and if she leans out the window and looks right, she can see along the canal and down to Weesperstraat. It is quiet out. But then a car turns onto their street, and she is alarmed to see it stop at their door. She quickly pulls her head back in and closes the window.

'Mum, there's a car in front of the house,' she calls, running to her parents' room.

'Go and warn Grandpa and Grandma,' her mother says.

Rosa goes to her grandparents' room.

'There's a car outside the front door,' she says.

Her grandpa and grandma do not hesitate for a moment, but climb into bed and pull the covers over themselves.

The doorbell rings. Her mother waits for her to come back. Now there is loud banging on the door downstairs.

'Ro, go and sit with Grandma,' says her mother, pulling the rope to open the door downstairs.

'Who's there?' she calls down. There is no reply.

Rosa hears feet quickly coming up the stairs. She peeps through a crack in the door. There are two men in long coats out there. They are both wearing hats, so she cannot see their faces clearly. They are speaking Dutch.

'We are looking for Marcus Snijders, born in 1929. He is supposed to be living here on his own,' says the man.

Rosa shivers: Max! She can see her mother is nervous, but she quickly pulls herself together.

'That's my son,' she says.

The men look at each other in surprise.

'That's not possible. He is registered as living alone,' the man says gruffly.

'But he's my son. He came here on his own last year, but the whole family lives here now,' her mother says.

'We have to take him with us. Where is he?'

Rosa's mother remains extremely calm and polite.

'He's at school now. He has classes until late today.'

'Then we'll come back later,' says the man, turning to leave.

'But you can't take him. My husband and I work for the Joodsche

Raad. We have a stamp,' she says, walking to the living room to fetch her papers. She frowns when she sees Rosa standing at the door.

'I told you to go and sit with Grandma,' says her mother, taking the papers from her handbag. The men want to come into the living room, but Rosa's mother manoeuvres them back into the hallway. Rosa listens at the door again.

'We have an exemption. So do the children,' says Mother, showing him their identity papers and the stamps.

'Bis *auf weiteres* . . . ,' reads the man. 'Exempted until further notice.'

The man shows it to the other man, who shrugs.

'We have to see the boy first,' says the man.

'Why don't I phone the office? Then someone can tell you exactly what kind of stamp we have and that my son has also been exempted,' says Mother, sounding a little more desperate now. 'Please. Our neighbour isn't Jewish. She might let me use her telephone.'

He gives permission, and the two men accompany her to the neighbour's house.

Rosa leans out of the window to watch what is happening. She sees her mother and the men coming out of the house and ringing the neighbour's doorbell. The neighbour puts her head out of the window and shouts something. Then her mother goes into the building with the men. She sees another neighbour coming outside, and she hides quickly when he looks up. That neighbour is a member of the NSB, the Dutch National Socialist Movement, and she is terrified of him. She feels like he is watching her, so she is always on her guard.

Very carefully, she sticks her head back out of the window. The NSB man is walking over to the car and looking around. Then her mother comes out. She says something, but Rosa can't hear what she says. Then the men go back to their car, and the NSB neighbour goes to have a chat with them. They point at her mother and at the house. Rosa shuts the window. Her mother comes running up the stairs. She closes the door and locks it.

'Does Max have to go with them?' Rosa asks anxiously.

Her mother hugs her tightly. 'Fortunately not,' she says. 'Not this time.'

'Will he have to go next time?'

'I don't know, sweetheart. But we're going to do everything we can to make sure that doesn't happen.'

It is the end of the afternoon. Rosa has just come home from school. She is eating a sandwich and looking out of the window. Suddenly a truck comes tearing along from the Amstel. It stops at the end of the canal, blocking the road. Then, at the other end of the canal, by Weesperstraat, another truck appears.

Rosa drops her sandwich and runs to the kitchen.

'Mum, they're blocking off the street.'

Her mother follows her and they both look out of the window: there is nowhere to go. Everyone who lives along the canal is trapped. Soldiers jump out of the vehicles and start taking people away. A woman who lives a few doors down is pulled from her house. She is holding a toddler's hand and carrying a baby in the crook of her other arm.

'What do they want with that poor woman and those two little ones? Isn't it enough that they've already taken her husband?' says Mother. 'Come on, get away from that window.'

Rosa stays put.

When they try to load the woman into the truck, she panics. She starts screaming and runs away, but there is nowhere she can go.

Rosa gasps. 'No! She's jumping into the water. We have to do something.'

Her mother opens the window. They see another neighbour, who does not hesitate for a moment and pulls the woman out of the canal. The neighbour tries to take her back to her house, but some soldiers grab the soaking woman and throw her into the truck.

Rosa's heart starts racing when someone bangs on the door. Her mother goes to Grandpa and Grandma's room. The banging becomes louder and there is a shout: '*Aufmachen!*' Open up!

Her mother opens the front door. The soldiers walk into the hallway.

'*Herr und Frau Akker*,' says the German.

Rosa knows that they are here for her grandparents.

'*Nein, sie sind gesperrt*,' says her mother. They have exemptions. 'Heart problems,' she says in Dutch. She shows them the doctor's papers and points at Grandpa and Grandma's room. The German takes the documents and strides into the room. A little later, he comes back out, hands Mother the papers and leaves.

Rosa is shaking from head to toe. She curls up in a chair in the living room. She can still see the woman who jumped into the canal. She takes off her glasses and closes her eyes. Outside, she hears the trucks driving away. When her mother comes to sit by her, she snuggles up close to her.

Rosa is walking home from school with her cousins along the River Amstel. A few other children are walking with them. It is a fresh day, and the leaves are a reddish orange.

'You're off the line,' a girl says to Rosa's cousin. They are trying to see who can walk along the line for longest. They pause and then carefully get going again.

They walk to the Magere Brug, the 'skinny bridge' across the River Amstel.

Rosa is concentrating hard on the line she is walking along, but the girl in front of her stops suddenly and Rosa bumps into her.

'Now *you're* off the line!' she says, when she sees the girl put her foot down beside the line of the paving stones. But the girl does not respond.

When she looks up, Rosa sees big green trucks driving into the neighbourhood. The children stand there, frozen. There is a

German patrol on the other side of the bridge. No one is allowed across.

'Come on, quickly!' Rosa's cousin pulls her back to the other side. They run along the riverside and see trucks across the water driving onto their street.

'But what about Mum and Grandpa and Grandma?' says Rosa.

'They have stamps.'

They walk over to a boy who is in her cousin Marcus's class and lives on the other side of town, and they ask if they can go back to his place.

Just before curfew, they walk home.

'It will be safe now, won't it?' asks Rosa.

'We'll check if it's safe first. And if it isn't, we'll turn around and go straight back,' says her cousin Marcus.

When they come to the Magere Brug, the road is open. People are walking and cycling across it as if nothing happened. Rosa wants to get home as quickly as possible, so she runs the last part of the way. The street looks quiet. She races up the stairs – and finds her mother in tears.

'Your father, Aunt Celina and Uncle Daniel have been taken,' she says.

Her cousins are upstairs now too, both crying.

Her mother tries to comfort them.

'They actually came for Grandpa and Grandma,' she says. 'But then they took the others. They let me stay behind to look after your grandparents.'

'Where did they take them?' her cousin asks.

'Probably to the Schouwburg.'

'Let's hope those stamps work.'

Rosa is woken by the sound of voices from the living room. She looks for the light switch in the dark and puts on her glasses. Sleepily, she gets up. Her father, aunt and uncle are all sitting in the living room. She runs up to her father and jumps into his arms.

'Where were you?'

'Dad was saying that a policeman helped them at the Schouwburg,' says Max.

'I thought, I'll just ask him. I saw the trams coming and I knew it wasn't good. I had to keep my wits about me,' her father says. 'He said he wasn't sure it would work, but he took me to a broom cupboard and told me to wait there. But your aunt and uncle had to come too. So I was allowed to fetch them. I have no idea how long we were in there, but when he finally let us out, the whole building was empty. He unlocked the back door for us. It led out into the courtyard and we escaped through the gardens and an alleyway.'

'It was a close thing,' says her aunt.

'He must have been a really nice German,' says Rosa.

'He was a Dutch police officer,' says her father. 'But you're right. He was a nice man, very nice indeed.'

'The only problem is that we've all been registered,' says her uncle. 'If they check the list, they'll know we escaped.'

No one says anything for a while.

'Come on. Time for bed,' says her mother, breaking the silence. 'You have to be up in time for school tomorrow.'

Rosa is awake early and is surprised to see that her father is up too. He has not turned on the lights yet and is looking out of the window. When he sees Rosa, he gives her a hug. She has a sip of his tea.

'Can you see something outside?' she asks in a concerned voice.

'No, everything's quiet.'

'Are you worried about them coming back?'

'Yes, we were lucky this time. Next time we'll need to be better prepared.'

Rosa's heart sinks. Next time. So it's going to happen again.

'Come on, let's lay the breakfast table.'

After breakfast, Father gets up from the table.

'We had a long talk yesterday about what to do if anyone comes and asks about us,' says her father. 'And I want to show you something.' They follow him upstairs to the attic.

He opens the cupboard with the water tank inside. It is a large, rectangular tank, lined with lead.

'The rainwater from the gutter comes straight into here,' her father explains, opening the tank.

'Five of us can just about fit in there. Four adults and Max,' he says, climbing inside. Then he tells the others to get in too.

'We won't fit in there. It's too small,' grumbles Max.

'What if we face in opposite directions?' says Uncle Daniel. They try it.

They squeeze into the tank, sitting very closely together.

'Pull your knees up,' says Rosa's father, bending his head forward. That way, five of them can fit into the tank.

'Nice and cosy, eh?' her father jokes.

Very quickly, they climb back out and go downstairs.

'What about us?' asks Rosa.

Her parents and aunt and uncle look very serious.

'If they come back,' says her mother, 'we'll quickly climb into the tank and Grandma and Grandpa can go to bed. Tell them your parents have already been taken away. And give them the date when your dad and aunt and uncle were taken in.'

'The day they were taken to the Schouwburg?' asks Rosa.

'Exactly. They leave children alone.'

Rosa thinks it's a good idea.

'Get dressed now. You need to go to school,' says her mother.

In the middle of the night, Rosa is woken by the pounding of feet on the stairs and banging on the door. She is suddenly wide awake. Her mother opens the bedroom door, and her father, uncle and aunt follow.

'Max, come on,' her father whispers urgently.

Max gets up sleepily, and his father pulls him by the hand towards the tank. Her mother makes Max's bed neatly, as if no one has been sleeping there.

'Are they coming for us?' asks Rosa.

'They're downstairs at Mr Davids's place,' her mother says in a whisper. 'But you never know.'

She gives Rosa a big hug.

'You stay here. They'll leave you children alone. Grandpa and Grandma are in bed and have their papers with them. You know what to say, don't you?'

The children nod.

When they hear someone downstairs shouting in German for the door to be opened, they freeze. The banging on the front door of the building gets louder and louder. There is cursing. Then they hear boots on the staircase: they are coming up. There is loud banging on the door.

'Open up!'

The children check to see if the door to the tank cupboard is closed and then carefully open the front door. Two men come rushing in. One is Grüne Polizei, in their green uniform, the other is dressed entirely in black. Rosa shrinks away. The man in black looks around the room.

'Where are your parents?' he screams.

Rosa fumbles for words before clamming up.

'Our parents have already been taken away,' says her cousin Marcus, and he tells them the date when his parents and Rosa's father were taken.

'So you're all on your own?' asks the man in astonishment, his tone softening.

'Our grandpa and grandma are downstairs. They're ill. We're helping them,' says Marcus.

The man looks at the police officer, who turns around and heads downstairs.

'Why don't you get dressed? And then we'll make sure you can go to your parents. You'll see them again soon,' says the man in black.

Rosa hesitates. She knows their parents can hear everything. She waits for them to come out of the tank, but they stay where they are. The children get dressed.

'What are you going to wear?' she asks her cousin Rosa.

'Let's wear as much as possible. You never know if it's going to be warm or cold.'

They put on warm jumpers, their winter coats and extra socks.

Dressed in layers of clothes, they walk past their grandparents' floor. The colour drains from their faces when they see the children being taken away, but they continue to play the part of invalids.

'Come here, and give Grandpa and Grandma a cuddle,' says Grandma, and she gives them each a kiss.

'No need to say goodbye. We'll be back for you later,' says the man in black.

'But we have papers. We're sick,' says Grandpa.

'Then we'll take you to a hospital first,' the man in black replies coldly.

Grandpa and Grandma give each other anxious looks, but there is nothing they can do.

When they walk past Mr Davids's floor, they see that the door has been kicked in and Mr Davids is being dragged away.

They are put into a truck with a lot of other people.

The truck takes them to Adama van Scheltemaplein, where they stop at a school. Inside the building, they have to go to a desk, where three women register everyone. It takes a long time. All their details are noted: name, address, details on identity cards.

Finally it is their turn.

'Children have to register together with their parents,' says the woman who registers them.

'We're on our own,' Rosa's cousin Marcus replies.

The woman looks puzzled.

'Where are your parents?' she asks.

'We don't know why we were brought here, but here are our identity cards and copies of our parents' documents,' he says.

Rosa shows hers as well.

'My parents work for the Joodsche Raad too,' she says.

The woman looks around to see if anyone is paying attention to them.

'Come with me,' she says, leading them to a side room, which is full of old and sick people. 'I'm going to find out what's going on, because this doesn't seem right.'

The children sit down on the floor. An old woman is crying, and her husband is trying to comfort her. Will her grandpa and grandma be brought here soon? They sit there quietly, and Rosa tries to think about something else.

An hour later, the woman returns. She takes the children out into the corridor.

'They're taking someone to the NIZ, the Jewish hospital, and that's near your house,' she whispers.

'I know where it is,' says Rosa. 'It's five minutes from our place.'

'You're going too. Get into the ambulance and hide in the back. Alright?'

The woman lets them out through the back and opens the door of the ambulance. They jump in, and she shuts the door behind them.

Before long, a sick person is brought into the ambulance on a stretcher. The driver and the nurse do not seem at all taken aback to see the children there.

They drive through the night towards home.

When the door opens again, the children are surprised to see they are outside their house. Quickly, they climb out of the ambulance and ring the front doorbell.

It is some time before the door pops open. They run up and see Rosa's mother on the staircase. She lets out a cry of joy and calls the others.

They hear footsteps and the rest of the family come downstairs. They are overjoyed.

'I nearly had a heart attack for real when I saw the ambulance,' their grandpa says. 'I thought they were coming for us. They said they were going to.'

The family sit at the table, drinking tea. It is almost morning. Rosa is exhausted and tearful.

'Do I have to go to school tomorrow?' she sobs.

Her mother comforts her.

'No, you're staying at home tomorrow, and then you children are leaving town for a few days, to recover.'

Rosa calms down a little. She is glad she won't have to go to school tomorrow.

•

It is a chilly day. The wind whips Rosa's face as she walks to school. Then it starts raining. She walks close to the houses on Weesperzijde. The tram is crossing the bridge from Ceintuurbaan. If only she could get on it. She is so tired. She walks along Ceintuurbaan to the Sarphatipark and crosses the road. At the end of the street, she rounds the corner and is at school.

She hangs her soaking coat on the rack, where only a few other coats are hanging. The classroom is quiet. Not only are the children silent, there are not many of them left now. Mr Roeg is pleased to see her.

'Rosa, you're back.'

Rosa shakes her teacher's hand.

'Take your seat and we'll get started.'

'Shouldn't we wait for the others?' she asks.

'This is it. A few stayed at home. And the rest . . .' He goes to the board and starts writing. Rosa looks around the classroom: Alie, Erna and a couple of other girls. A few boys – and that is it.

The others must all have been taken away. Did they go to the same building as her? Or to the Schouwburg like her father?

Mr Roeg is explaining something, but Rosa is not listening. She is looking outside. She wants to go home.

•

The family are sitting around the table. The parents are having a serious discussion.

'We have to leave for the children's sake,' says Rosa's father. 'We can't go on like this.'

'I agree with Leo,' says Uncle Daniel.

Rosa can see the tension on her grandfather's face.

'We know plenty of people in Enkhuizen who want to help us,' says Rosa's mother.

Rosa really wants to go back to Enkhuizen, the sooner the better.

'Dad, you can come with us. The two of you can stay together,' her uncle says, trying to persuade her grandpa.

'What if I can't get kosher food? What then? And I certainly won't be able to go to shul,' her grandfather says.

'We're seventy-eight and seventy-two. What if we get sick? How will we get to a doctor or hospital?' her grandma asks.

'And what if I die? What about the funeral?' Grandpa shakes his head. He does not like the sound of it at all. 'We're better off staying here. You go with the children.'

'If we go and you're here alone, then they're sure to take you,' says Rosa's mother.

No one speaks for a moment.

'Then we'll stay too,' says Uncle Daniel.

Rosa wakes up and heads downstairs. It is quiet in the living room. Her father, mother, uncle and aunt are sitting in silence around the table, which has not yet been laid. When her mother sees her, she quickly wipes away a tear.

Rosa feels her stomach flip.

'Grandpa and Grandma were taken away in the night,' her mother says quietly.

Rosa can't believe it: every other time there was a raid or someone was taken away, she heard it. But this time she slept right through it. She starts crying. 'I didn't even get to say goodbye.'

Her mother pulls her close. 'Maybe that's for the best. There was nothing you could have done anyway. None of us could have.'

Rosa is inconsolable.

TWO WEEKS LATER

Rosa is helping her mother to make parcels. She packs an item of clothing belonging to her father, mother, Max and herself into each of the packages. Then she closes the box and writes an address in Enkhuizen on it.

Her mother comes into the room with a black dress and a box. 'Grandma wanted her nice black dress and Grandpa asked for his box with the tweezers and . . . What else did he want?' she asks.

Rosa looks at Grandma's letter. 'His reading glasses,' she says.

'Oh, yes,' her mother replies, walking out of the room again.

'We're doing fine. Don't worry about us,' Rosa reads. It is a short letter.

Her mother brings some tins of food and puts those in the parcel too.

'Do you really think they're doing fine?' asks Rosa.

'I hope so, sweetheart. But if Grandma's asking for her nice dress, then she must have some reason for wearing it. So that's good news.'

Rosa feels better.

'As long as Grandpa and Grandpa are in Westerbork, we can still help them,' says her mother.

'But where are they going after that?'

'I don't know, but we have to be ready to leave as soon as they're moved on.'

She fills another box with more clothes. When they have finished, there are six parcels.

'Will you take one? Then I'll take the one for Grandpa and Grandma.'

'What about the others?' asks Rosa.

'We'll do one the day after tomorrow and then the next one two days after that, until we've sent everything.'

'Ro, wake up.'

Rosa slowly opens her eyes and sees her mother sitting on her bed.

'It's time. We're going.'

Rosa jumps cheerfully out of bed. Then she realises what that means. Her grandpa and grandma must have been sent away from Westerbork.

She gets dressed and goes into the living room.

Everyone else is already there: her father, mother, Max, her uncle and aunt and her two cousins.

'We're going first,' says her father. 'They're leaving later.'

'Ro and Max, you're going together on the tram to Centraal Station. We'll meet you in the hall there and we'll go on the train together to Enkhuizen.'

'I've parcelled up some sandwiches. Put them in your bag,' says her mother.

The food packets are on the table with their identity cards.

'First let's have breakfast together one more time,' her aunt says, giving Rosa and Max a kiss.

Rosa realises she might never see her cousins again. They are going to a different address.

They have breakfast together, but everyone is too anxious to eat properly.

'Go and finish getting dressed, and then we'll be off,' says her father.

Rosa goes to the bedroom and puts on the rest of the clothes she still has. She looks in the mirror. There is no star on her clothing.

One last look around the room – she is not going to miss this house. She is going to miss her family though. They take their time to say goodbye to her aunt, uncle and cousins. Then they leave the house, her parents going first.

Rosa and Max walk along the other side of the canal. Rosa is clutching a notebook to her chest, in case they see anyone they know. Max is carrying something over the spot where his star should be too. They walk to Weesperstraat and catch the tram.

Without the star, they simply get on, and no one pays any attention to them.

Acting as normally as they can, they head straight for the hall at Centraal Station, where they see their parents waiting for them. They look at the departure boards and walk to the platform and the train.

They board the train. The guard blows the whistle. Slowly the train leaves the station, heading for Enkhuizen.

Everyone has their ticket and an identity card. Rosa opens hers: it is her photograph, but without the J for Jew.

From now on, Rosa Snijders will be Jopie Terlien.

Annie de Leeuw

3 May 1932
22 July 1942

Beste Alie
10 mei 1942

Een aardig meisje vroeg mij
Of ik zo goed wou zijn
Een versje in haar album
              te schrijven
Ik was het nog zo klein
Ik heb aan haar verzoek
             voldaan
En ziet mijn naam hier
             onderstaan

Je vriendinnetje
Annie de Leeuw

10 May 1942

Dear Alie

A nice girl asked me
If I would be so kind
As to write a poem in her album
Even if it was just a small one
I agreed to her request
And there's my name below

Your friend
Annie de Leeuw.

JUNE

The classroom is still quiet. Alie goes to sit at her desk. The teacher comes in, followed by a few children.

'They were throwing everything out onto the street, sir,' says one boy.

'I saw it with my own eyes, sir,' says another.

'We'll talk about it later. Go and sit down at your desks first,' Mr Roeg says. When everyone is sitting, Alie notices that Jenny and Annie are not there.

'There's something I need to tell you,' Mr Roeg says sadly. 'I've heard that Annie de Leeuw was taken away last night.' Mr Roeg is silent for a moment.

'Annie?' Alie feels a pain in her stomach.

Then the door of the classroom flies open, and Jenny bursts in.

'Sir, sir. They're emptying Annie's house!' Jenny is standing in the doorway, pointing outside. She still has her coat on.

Alie is so relieved to see her friend.

Mr Roeg walks over to Jenny and tries to calm her down.

'I don't think there's anything we can do, Jenny,' he says quietly.

'Why can't you do anything? You're the teacher!' Jenny says tearfully.

Alie gets up and helps Jenny to her desk.

'Read a book or something,' says the teacher. 'I'll be back in a minute. I'm just going to see the headmaster.'

As soon as Mr Roeg has left the classroom, Herman and David come over to Alie and Jenny.

'Right after they were taken away, some thieves turned up. It woke my dad up. They were throwing all kinds of things onto the street,' says David in a whisper.

'By the time we walked past this morning, most of the stuff had already been swiped,' says Herman.

'Did you take anything? Something that belonged to Annie?' asks Alie.

'Why would I do that?' David exclaims indignantly.

'For when she comes back, of course!' says Alie.

'No, I didn't think of that.' The boys slink back to their seats.

'Let's go round later and see if anything's still there,' says Jenny, putting her arm around Alie.

When the bell goes for lunchtime, Jenny and Alie run straight to Tweede Jan van der Heijdenstraat. When they get there, they see a big removal van with the name PULS on it parked in front of Annie's house. The men are almost finished. They are taking the rope off the pulley at the top of the house. The back of the van is still open, and Alie and Jenny look inside. They see the dining table, the sofa, the chairs. Annie's little brother's highchair. All the De Leeuw family's furniture is in the back of the removal van.

'But they won't have anything left when they come back!' Alie looks away. Her stomach really hurts. She puts her arm around Jenny.

'Let's go,' says Alie. They are about to leave when they see Herman and David coming.

'What are they going to do with that furniture?' Herman wonders out loud.

'My dad says it's going to Germany. To Krauts who have lost everything in the British bombings,' says David.

'Serves them right,' says Jenny fiercely.

'Where's Annie going?' asks Alie.

'Probably somewhere in Germany,' says David.

'But what's she going to do there?' Alie does not understand at all.

'If her father has to work there, I suppose she'll be going to school.' Herman clearly does not know either.

Beni, a boy in their class, comes over with a few other boys to take a look. They look scruffy, and they are all eating sweets.

'Want one, Alie?' asks Beni.

Alie looks into the big bag of sweets that Beni holds out to her. Jenny and the other boys eagerly reach into the bag.

Beni laughs. 'Help yourselves. I've got loads more at home,' he says.

'Where did you get it all from?' asks Alie.

'Nicked it,' says Beni.

Alie gives him a worried look, and Beni notices her expression. He takes a handful of coins out of his pocket.

'Bought them. With this.' He gives Alie a wink, and she takes a couple of sweets.

The boys crowd around the front of Annie's house.

Alie peers into the removal van and sees that there are blankets over all the furniture now. Then a man pushes the children out of the way and slams the tailgate shut. The loud bang makes Alie flinch. She flattens herself against the front of the house. As she looks up, she sees that Annie's window has been smashed.

The removal van drives off. The people in the street have seen enough and drift away.

Jenny and the boys come over to stand with Alie. They look up too.

'Is the house completely empty now?' asks Jenny.

Beni gives the drainpipe a quick tug and then starts nimbly shinning up it.

'What are you doing?' the other children exclaim. 'Come down!'

Alie looks around nervously. The police could come along at any minute, or the Germans. She looks up anxiously at Beni, who has reached the balcony.

'What can you see?' asks Jenny.

Beni looks in through the broken window.

'It's a complete tip!' he shouts. 'They've turned everything upside down. There's glass and broken stuff all over the place.'

'Come down,' Alie shouts, panicking.

Beni climbs back down, just as smoothly as before.

'They'd better go and live somewhere else when they come back,' says Beni.

He picks up a few stones off the ground. So do the other boys. Beni passes some to Alie and Jenny.

'What am I supposed to do with these?' asks Alie.

Beni looks up. The others follow his gaze. Herman and David each choose a big stone.

'For Annie, the prettiest girl in the class,' says Beni.

ANNIE DE LEEUW

215

Alie shivers when she realises what he is going to do.

'Now!' shouts Beni.

Alie throws as hard as she can. All the stones fly towards the broken window.

They sprint away, towards the park. As they are running, they hear the broken window making an almighty noise as it crashes to the ground. They look back.

'That was for you, Annie.'

Alie runs for home. She runs and runs.

•

The doorbell rings. Alie looks at the clock: it is half past nine in the evening. A shock goes through her.

'Have they come for us?'

Roosje barks.

'Quick! Lights off!' Mother turns off the light above the sofa. Alie flicks another switch.

'Keep that dog quiet!' hisses Mother, carefully pulling aside the blackout curtain. She does not see anything out there.

'Shh, Roosje.' Alie holds the dog tightly to keep her calm.

Someone is knocking on the front door of the building, rapidly, urgently. Loud enough for them to hear it through the upstairs door.

'Mum, Alie, open up!'

'Greet!' Mother hurries to the door and pulls the rope.

Gretha comes racing up the stairs. She is wearing a headscarf and has no star on her coat.

Roosje pulls away from Alie and runs to Gretha. She jumps up happily, but Gretha ignores her.

'Have you gone mad? Do you know how dangerous it is to go around without a star? I thought you were staying at a friend's place!' Mother is beside herself with worry.

'Berry was picked up this afternoon, when he was out shopping. They swept through the market and took everyone away.' Gretha sinks onto Father's chair, crying.

Alie and Mother are horrified.

'I spent all afternoon wandering the streets after I found out he'd been taken.'

Alie sits down next to Gretha and holds her tightly.

'I waited until it got dark, took off my star and then came here.'

'Will they come here, do you think?' Alie is frightened.

'I don't think they specifically came for us. Berry was just unlucky that he was in the wrong place. I'm going to the Joodsche Raad tomorrow, to ask where he was taken. He doesn't have anything with him. Maybe I can take a few things.' Gretha removes her coat, shoes and headscarf.

'Have you eaten anything?' Mother asks.

'No, I completely forgot. I forgot everything. My bag, my keys . . .'

Mother pours a cup of tea for them and puts out some crackers for Gretha, who eats them right up.

'I'm shattered. I just want to sleep,' she says when she has finished eating.

'Can I sleep with you?' Alie asks a little later.

Gretha makes room for her. Alie climbs into the narrow bed. She cuddles up to her sister and smells her hair. Gretha smells nice, like face powder.

'Just like we used to,' says Gretha. 'You always did this when you were little.'

'You're so beautiful,' says Alie.

Gretha laughs. 'Beautiful? Me? Ah, I suppose I'll do.'

'Berry thinks you're beautiful, doesn't he?' asks Alie.

'He thinks I'm the most beautiful woman in the world. He's not too bad himself,' Gretha says sadly. 'Remind me to put a photograph of me with his things.'

Alie gives Gretha a kiss.

'I'm really, really sorry they took Berry,' says Alie. 'Do you think he'll have to go to a labour camp, like Dad?'

'I don't know. I don't know anything.' Gretha turns over. 'I just hope he's in Amsterdam, so that I can still see him. Maybe they'll be able to tell me more when I go to the Joodsche Raad tomorrow.'

'Can I go with you?' asks Alie.

'We'll see. I'm going to sleep now.'

Before long, Gretha is asleep. Alie carefully gets out of bed and goes to Mother's bedroom. She snuggles up close to her.

'I don't want you to work at the market anymore,' says Alie.

'I don't really work there. I just help out Aunt Sara now and then,' says Mother.

'But I still want you to stop,' Alie says anxiously.

'Then what will we have to live on?' asks Mother.

'Dad sends money, doesn't he?'

Mother does not reply.

'He does though, doesn't he?' asks Alie.

'As soon as we get some money from your father, I'll stop working at the market,' says Mother.

Gretha reaches for her key when she is nearly home.

Roosje runs up to her. Alie is walking a little further behind. Gretha stoops to stroke Roosje. When she stands up, she sees two men in hats and long leather coats.

They are heading straight for Alie, who has not noticed them.

'Do you live here?' one of the men asks her, pointing up.

Alie freezes and does not reply. Gretha walks up to them. She has casually draped her scarf over her star, so that it is hard to see.

'Can I help you, gentlemen?' she says in her most charming voice.

The men look at her suspiciously.

'We are looking for Margaretha Waterman. The wife of Pinehas Waterman.'

Alie's breath catches in her throat.

'Hmm, Margaretha?' Gretha pretends to be thinking.

'Her maiden name was Lopes Dias,' says the man gruffly.

'Oh, you mean Greet? I just saw her leaving.' She points in the direction of Van Woustraat. 'Isn't that right, Truus? We saw her a few minutes ago. She was carrying a big bag,' Gretha bluffs.

Alie does not move. She holds on to Roosje, who tries to wriggle free and starts barking.

'Was she alone?' asks the other man, clearly irritated by the noise Roosje is making.

'I didn't notice,' says Gretha.

Roosje keeps barking. She wants to play.

'Can't you shut that stupid dog up?' the man snarls at Alie.

Alie tries to get Roosje to be quiet.

'I'll take it home to its owners. It belongs to the Bakkers, down that way.' Gretha grips Alie's wrist and quickly pulls her and Roosje along the street.

The men watch Gretha and Alie go, but then stride off towards Van Woustraat.

Gretha does not stop. They walk all the way to Ferdinand Bolstraat.

'Greet, stop!' Alie can't keep going and she stops and leans on a wall to catch her breath.

'What am I supposed to do now?' Gretha's eyes fill with tears. So do Alie's. They sit on the kerb and Roosje drops down to lie on the ground beside them.

'They're sure to come back. I'll have to sleep somewhere else.'

'But where?'

'Somewhere. I don't know.'

'You can't just go. What about Mother and me?'

'Mother's too old and you're too young. They'll leave the two of you alone.'

'That's not what I mean,' Alie protests. 'What are we supposed to do without you? Dad's already gone, and so has Berry now. I don't want you to leave too.'

'Do you think it's what I want? I don't know what to do either, but I'm going to have to come up with something. And soon. Go home, and I'll see you later.'

Alie hesitates, but then heads home with Roosje. She looks back at Gretha, who is turning the corner onto Ferdinand Bolstraat.

At the end of the afternoon, Gretha comes home. She goes to her room and gathers some belongings together. Mother and Alie help her.

'But where are you going?' Mother sounds really concerned.

'Don't worry about it. It's better if you don't know,' Gretha says, trying to reassure Mother. She puts her things into a large handbag and a shopping bag. The white canvas backpack is lying empty in a corner. It will look as if she has just been shopping.

'I'll send you a message tomorrow to let you know I've arrived safely.'

'Do you really have to go?' Alie clings on to Gretha.

Gretha gives her mother and Alie a hug. The three of them stand there until Roosje starts trying to squeeze her nose between their feet.

'Daft dog,' Gretha says with a smile, stroking Roosje. 'I have to go. They're waiting for me.'

Who?' asks Mother. Gretha gives her a stern look, and Mother stops asking questions.

'Aaltje, could you go and see if there's anyone out on the street?' Gretha puts on her headscarf.

Alie carefully pulls aside the net curtain and peers along the street. It is not dark yet. Nothing out of the ordinary, only a few children and people who are coming home from work. It is busy enough for Gretha to be able to join them without being noticed.

'The coast's clear.' Alie helps Gretha with her bags and opens the door for her. Roosje wants to go out too.

'Stay, Roos.' Alie pushes her back inside.

They give each other a quick kiss, and then Gretha leaves.

Alie runs to the window and looks through the net curtains. She sees Gretha walking close to the houses across the road, towards Van Woustraat. She is staring at the ground. When she is almost out of sight, she looks back one last time, but she does not wave. Alie does.

Mother, standing behind her, gives a deep sigh.

'Did she really not tell you anything at all about where she's going?'

'No. And I don't want to know,' says Alie. 'Then I can't give it away by accident. Those men were really scary.'

'Greet is going to make it.' Mother pulls Alie away from the window and closes the curtains. 'If luck's on her side, she'll make it. May God protect her.'

Alie is walking along, close to the houses. The street is quiet.

When she is almost at her house, Albertine jumps out of a doorway.

'Where was your sister going with all those bags yesterday?'

Alie's breath catches in her throat.

'What do you mean?' she says, pulling herself together.

'I saw her sneaking off.'

'Gretha was still asleep in bed this morning when I left,' she says, as casually as she can.

'You're lying!' says Albertine and she stands threateningly in front of Alie. She points at her window. 'I saw her with my own eyes.'

Alie says nothing and tries not to look at her.

'I've got my eye on you, Alie.' She gives Alie a shove and walks away.

Alie's whole body is shaking. She stands there until she cannot see Albertine any longer, and then she runs upstairs, storms into her room and slams the door.

'What's wrong? Has something happened?' Mother asks.

Alie does not reply.

'Alie? Open the door.'

Alie climbs into bed and pulls the covers over her head.

'Go away.'

'Why are you acting so strangely?' Mother rattles the door.

Alie says nothing.

'Don't you want something to eat?'

Alie wakes up with a start. She must have dozed off. Then she remembers Albertine. She quickly gets up and shuts the curtains.

'I've made a nice cup of tea. Do you want to come and drink it? And we can play a game.'

Alie cannot stand her mother's cheerful tone. 'Stop it. There are other things going on in the world than tea and games,' she yells. 'Or hadn't you noticed?'

It is quiet on the other side of the door. Then she hears her mother shuffling off to the kitchen.

Alie looks through a gap in the curtains at Albertine's window opposite. The curtains there are closed.

She sticks up the blackout paper. Then she closes the curtains too.

Roosje scratches at the door, and Alie hears the sound of her mother knocking on it gently.

'What's wrong? Has something happened? I saw you talking to Albertine,' Mother asks. Alie does not reply.

'Alie? Open the door.'

Alie climbs in bed and pulls the covers over her head. 'Go away.'

'Why won't you tell me what's the matter?' Mother rattles the door.

'I have a stomach ache. Leave me alone!'

She hears her mother sigh and walk away.

Alie is sitting on the sofa in her pyjamas when the doorbell rings.

She freezes. 'Mum! The door.' Roosje barks.

Mother comes into the living room and walks nervously to the window.

'Roosje, quiet!'

'Who is it?'

'It's a woman,' says Mother, sounding surprised.

'Do you know her?' asks Alie, jumping up from the sofa.

'Maybe Greet sent her.' Mother hurries to the door. Alie follows her.

'Who's there?' Mother calls cautiously down the stairs.

'Hello, Mrs Lopes Dias. I'm Mrs Friedman from the Joodsche Raad's social-pedagogical department.'

'I see,' Mother says suspiciously. 'What do you want?'

'Could I come up for a moment? I'm here to see Alida,' the woman shouts.

Mother looks at Alie.

'Have they come to fetch me?' She shakes her head. Mother mustn't let the woman come in.

Mother hesitates.

'Just tell me why you're here.'

'Please. I'm standing out here in the street. There's no need to be alarmed. I'm just here for a chat, on behalf of the school.'

'Alright, come on up,' says Mother.

Alie quickly fetches the hot-water bottle from beside her bed and drops back down onto the sofa.

'I'm sorry for startling you both,' says the woman when she comes in. 'You must be Alida.'

'I'm Alie,' she says feebly, as she shakes Mrs Friedman's hand.

'Oh, I can see you're really poorly,' she says, when she sees the hot-water bottle on Alie's tummy.

Alie looks guiltily at her mother.

'She's had a bad stomach for weeks,' says Mother. 'She was coming home from school with stomach ache every day. So I'm keeping her at home for a while. You never know. It could be contagious.'

'But it's been two weeks now,' says Mrs Friedman sternly, looking through her notes. 'The school is concerned.'

'Is Mr Roeg worried about me?' Alie asks in surprise.

'Mr Roeg and Mr Stibbe. And so am I,' she says.

'Shall I make some tea?' asks Mother, taking Mrs Friedman's coat.

'Could you tell me a little more about your symptoms, Alie?' asks Mrs Friedman, sitting down in Father's chair.

'I keep getting stomach ache,' says Alie.

'And have you always had that?' asks Mrs Friedman, making notes.

'Not always,' says Alie, feeling a little shy. 'Are you a nurse?'

'Something like that.' The woman goes on writing. Then she gives Alie a searching look. 'Has this been going on since the war began, Alie?'

Alie nods.

Mrs Friedman nods too and puts down her pen and paper. 'I see.'

Mother comes in with the tea and is surprised to see Mrs Friedman packing up her things and getting to her feet. 'Are you finished already?'

'I think Alie can go back to school tomorrow. She is simply suffering from nervous tension. There's nothing wrong with her. I sympathise, but you must understand that she has to attend school. You can't keep her at home for every little trifle. After all, she's already had to retake a year.'

Mother explodes. 'Now you listen carefully, Mrs Social-Peda . . . bla bla bla. I am not going to let someone waltz into my own home and tell me what I can and cannot do. The Krauts out there do enough of that already! If Alie has stomach ache, then she's staying at home with a hot-water bottle. And that is that.'

Alie fiddles nervously with her pyjamas.

For a moment, Mrs Friedman looks completely at a loss, and then she bursts into tears.

'Do you think I enjoy telling off parents who are already having such a hard time? Every discussion is a battle. I'm trying to do what's best for the child. In some cases it's better to stick to a regular routine. To go to school every day so they can forget their worries for a little while. And those damned Krauts have taken our bikes and we can't get a cycling permit, so I have to walk everywhere. All over town. From the old Jewish neighbourhood all the way to Plan Zuid.' She takes a handkerchief out of her bag.

Alie and Mother look at each other in surprise after this torrent of words.

'Please, have a cup of tea.' Mother quickly pours her a cup. Mrs Friedman takes it without looking at Mother or Alie.

'I can see you're a decent family. But if you knew some of the cases I have to deal with. Beni, for instance – he's in your class, isn't he, Alie?'

'Is Beni in trouble?' asks Alie. She knows he has been stealing. Otherwise he could never have so many sweets. But she does not say anything.

'He's fallen in with a gang of juvenile delinquents. The gang's getting bigger and bigger. They spend all their time roaming the streets, mainly in the old neighbourhood. Their parents have too many other things to worry about. Especially in families with lots of children and their fathers are in labour camps.' Mrs Friedman shakes her head and blows her nose. 'I'm so glad Alie's being looked after properly. I'm sure you're not having an easy time of it either. Is your father in a labour camp?' she asks, taking a sip of her tea.

'Molengoot,' says Mother.

'You must be missing your dad, Alie,' she says sympathetically.

'I miss him so much,' says Alie.

'Take all the time you need, dear,' says Mrs Friedman. 'I'll sort it out with the school.'

Alie feels guilty.

'I'll go back to school tomorrow.'

Alie knocks quietly on the door.

'Come in,' the headmaster, Mr Stibbe, calls through the door. Feeling shy, she goes into his office.

'Mr Roeg told me to come and see you.'

'Sit down, please, Alie. I'll be with you in a moment.' He points at a chair by the wall.

Mr Stibbe is writing on the last pages of a big notebook, making lists of names. He is writing very quickly and doing all kinds of calculations.

She tries to see exactly what he is doing, but Mr Stibbe suddenly closes the book and stands up.

'Right then, Alie,' he says, shaking her hand. 'I'm glad to see you're back. I heard from Mr Roeg that you've been working hard this year and so you can move up into the next class.'

'Did he really say that?' Alie asks in disbelief. 'But I've been ill so much.'

'You have good marks, even though you were ill. Which is very clever of you.' Mr Stibbe picks up his chair and comes over to sit beside her.

'Well, I'd already learned most of it last year, of course,' says Alie, downplaying her success.

'Yes, you should be in my class by now,' says Mr Stibbe. 'Are you still enjoying school? Of course, you know most of the children already, don't you?'

'Yes, sir. I like the children in my class. The ones who are still here.'

Mr Stibbe nods sympathetically.

'I was thinking, maybe we could all have a bit of fun before the school holidays.' Mr Stibbe picks up a pen and some paper. 'What do you like doing, Alie?'

'What do you mean?'

'Well, what do you think we could organise? Something for the whole school.'

'A trip maybe? But we aren't allowed to travel, are we?'

'Unfortunately not. I thought we could do something in the assembly hall though,' says Mr Stibbe.

'You mean like a play?' asks Alie.

'A play! That's a good idea. Who could we ask to do it? A cabaret artiste?' says Mr Stibbe, thinking out loud.

'You want to invite real performers?' Alie asks in surprise.

'Yes. Did you think Mr Roeg and I were going to become a double act?' he says, laughing.

Alie smiles. 'No, sir.'

'Or how about songs?' Mr Stibbe makes a note. 'What kind of songs do you like?'

'I always used to listen to Jacob Hamel on the radio. But that was before the war.'

'An excellent idea,' says Mr Stibbe and he writes down the name Jacob Hamel in capital letters. 'We'll sort it out.'

He stands up and walks to the door. 'Shall we tell the other teachers right now?'

Alie has never been inside the staff room before.

'You know everyone in here, don't you?'

Alie looks around the room. Mr Roeg is reading a newspaper. Miss van Pels is marking some work. Mr van Moppis is smoking a cigar.

'Mr Roeg, Miss van Pels, Mrs Polak, Miss de Paauw. And Mr van Moppis and Mr Coppenhagen over there. So we're just missing Mr de Vries and Miss Fortuijn. Oh, and Mr van Kreveld, the PE teacher.'

Alie does not know all of them, but she says hello politely.

'Alie has a good idea for how we could bring in a little entertainment for the children.'

The teachers all look up from what they are doing. Alie feels shy again.

'Jacob Hamel,' says Mr Stibbe. 'My children like him too.'

There are murmurs of approval.

'But how are we going to pay for that, Elias? Jacob Hamel is a well-known artiste.'

'That's exactly why I want him. Everyone's heard of him,' says Mr Stibbe.

'You should put in a request through the Joodsche Raad,' says Mr Coppenhagen. 'He does performances for their extracurricular activities programme too.'

'What do you think, Alie? Do you want to help me to organise it?' asks Mr Stibbe.

'What will I have to do?' she asks.

'I was thinking of a colourful poster.' Mr Stibbe looks at the door. 'To go on some of the school doors.'

Alie hesitates. 'I'm not very good at drawing.'

'It doesn't have to be a work of art. You have nice handwriting, don't you?' asks Mr Stibbe. He does not even wait for Alie to reply. 'I'm sure you'll do a good job.'

'You can ask some of your friends to help,' says Mr Roeg.

'But it has to be a surprise for everyone else,' says Mr Stibbe, winking at Alie. 'Ask Miss van Pels to help you with the materials.'

Miss van Pels takes Alie to the crafts room.

'All the materials you'll need are in here. Help yourself,' says Miss van Pels.

Alie chooses a few nice coloured pencils and some paint for the posters and goes in search of her friends.

JULY

The poster Alie made is on the door of the assembly hall. Some of the younger girls are admiring it.

'Alie from Class 4 year made that poster,' says one of the girls. 'She knows Jacob Hamel really well. And I know Alie really well, so that's how I know,' the girl brags.

'Who's Alie?' asks a smaller girl.

As Alie walks into the corridor, the girl who knows her 'really well' comes racing up.

'Alie, is it really true? Is Jacob Hamel really coming to sing with us?'

'Yes, and I'd hurry up if I were you. It's about to start,' she says.

'Did you organise all of this?' the children ask. 'Do you really know him that well?'

'Don't you believe me?' asks the first girl. 'I told you she knows him really well, didn't I? Otherwise she wouldn't be allowed to make his posters, would she?'

Alie smiles.

The girl pulls the smaller girl away before Alie can reply.

'Very nicely done, Alie,' says Mr Stibbe, who has come to stand beside her and is looking at the poster. Alie feels proud. 'Thank you, sir. I made them with Jenny and with Rosa Levie. Rosa's good at drawing.'

There is an excited atmosphere in the school hall. The children are lined up on benches in front of the stage, which has been set up specially for the occasion, complete with a piano.

Alie looks over to where her class is sitting and sees Jenny beckoning her. She goes and sits between her and Guta.

'The posters you two made are lovely,' says Guta.

Alie notices a younger girl nearby, who looks sad among all the happy, excited children.

'Adele? Do you want to sit with us?' asks Guta.

Adele walks over and sits down between Alie and Guta.

'Have you heard of Jacob Hamel?' asks Guta. 'You haven't been in the Netherlands that long, have you?'

'Yes, but I'm not sure where I heard of him, maybe in the home where I was with my brothers when we first got here,' says Adele.

'I always used to listen to him on the radio. I loved the children's choir,' says Alie.

Then the children start cheering and Alie looks up: a man with grey combed-back hair has come onto the stage. It's Jacob Hamel. He is wearing a smart suit and has a conductor's baton in his hand.

As the children applaud, he gives a deep bow.

'Hello, boys and girls,' he says. 'I feel very honoured to perform here today. But it's lonely up here on the stage. Who would like to come and stand by the piano?'

Dozens of children raise their hands.

Alie and Jenny look at each other: they are definitely not going up onto the stage.

He chooses a number of children, and they climb up there to join him.

A lady sits down at the piano and plays a few chords.

Mr Hamel waves his conductor's baton to set the beat.

'Who knows this one?' he asks.

Lots of children put up their hands. Everyone knows the song.

'It's "The Bird's Song", isn't it?' asks Adele, enthusiastically nudging Alie.

'If you all know it, then no introduction is needed,' says Mr Hamel. 'Sing along, boys and girls!'

All of the children join in. Alie does not really dare to sing out loud. 'It's as if he wants to say, "I'm singing this song for you . . .,"' she mouths.

Jenny and Guta are not as timid and sing their hearts out.

The children belt out one song after another. The little ones listen open-mouthed.

'Now, everyone, stand up!' shouts Jacob Hamel. Alie hesitates, but Jenny pulls her to her feet.

'Who can finish this sentence?' he asks. '*Klepper de* . . .'

'*Klepper de klep, klep, klep!*' the hall sings with one voice.

Alie laughs and when the song continues, she sings along, just as loud as everyone else.

Guta Maliniak

23 April 1932
1 July 1944

Zolang die meeuwen
Niet zwemen gaan
Weet je dat onze vriendschap
Blijft bestaan.

Beste Atie
Vriendschap is staat zo vast
Als muren maar zy
Kan nog langer duren
Muren vallen met den tijd
Maar vriendschap duurt
In Eeuwigheid.

Je klasgenootje
Gut. Maliniak

Ik to do best
doe ik school
goed te
best

As long as the seagulls
Don't start to buzz
You know our friendship
Will go on.

•

Dear Alie.

Friendship stands as firm
As walls but it
Can last even longer.
Walls fall over time
But friendship lasts
For Eternity.

Your classmate Guti Maliniak

•

Ti to to test
at school do your best.

Adele Zimmer

19 May 1931

10-7-42

Beste Alie

Roosjes groeien in de hoven
Roosjes krachten dan stat robijn
Lieve Alie laat je hartje
Net zo als die roosjes zijn

Je schoolvriendinnetje
Adele Zimmer

Jij zijn logi
De datum
staat
erop.

10–7–42
Dear Alie

Roses grow in gardens.
Roses softer than satin
Dear Alie, let your heart be
Just like those roses.

Your schoolfriend
Adele Zimmer

.

ip bip bop
the date is at the top.

JULY

It is silent in the classroom. The children are doing a maths test.

Alie glances out of the window now and then. The weather is beautiful outside.

'Do you want to go roller skating with me and Roosje later?' she whispers to Jenny. Jenny nods.

Alie looks at the clock. It is almost home time. She has done all the sums, and she turns her paper over.

The classroom door slowly opens and Mr Stibbe beckons Mr Roeg. Alie sees them having a serious conversation in the corridor. Mr Roeg comes back into the classroom and looks at the clock. He sits down at his desk and waits. Alie looks curiously at her teacher.

'Time to finish your last sum, everyone,' says Mr Roeg.

He walks around the classroom, collecting the papers of the children who have finished. A few of them are still writing. When he gets to Alie's desk, she hands in her test.

The bell should have gone by now. Some of the children stand up, and everyone starts talking.

'Boys and girls, I need you to stay here a little longer,' Mr Roeg says gravely. 'I've just heard that a number of streets in the city have been blocked off, and that it's not safe to go home. So far, all I know for certain is that the old neighbourhood has been closed off.'

The children are shocked: a raid!

'Until we find out more, everyone has to stay at school,' he says.

A wave of disappointment runs through the classroom.

'But I live just around the corner, sir. And it's such a nice day!' one boy cries.

Alie's disappointed too, but she can see that Rosa is really worried. Her face has gone pale.

'You can go and play in the playground. The teachers will hand out some food and drink.'

The children leave the classroom. Alie, Jenny and Lientje go over to Rosa and put their arms around her.

Lientje is anxious too.

'The Transvaalbuurt isn't part of the old neighbourhood, is it?'

'No, that's in Oost,' says Alie. 'Don't worry.'

The girls walk downstairs and into the crowded playground. There is hardly any room to play, so they sit down in a corner. The teachers of the junior classes hand out drinks.

'When can we go home, Miss van Pels?' asks Rosa.

'I don't know. It's better if you stay here for now,' the teacher says.

'But what if my father and mother get taken away without me?' says Rosa.

'People who work for the Joodsche Raad usually have a *Sperre*. Your parents are probably just at work as usual, or at home.' Rosa looks a little reassured.

The teacher goes on handing out drinks. Some of the younger children are crying. Miss van Pels looks after them.

'Why don't we play a game?' asks Jenny. 'How about "Do you see what I see?"'

'I see, I see . . . something that's green and hangs down,' says Lientje quickly.

'A leaf on a branch,' says Alie.

'Wrong.'

'A branch,' says Jenny.

'Wrong.' Lientje looks at Rosa. 'Ro?'

But Rosa is deep in thought.

'Do you want to take a guess?'

'I just want to go home.'

'So do I,' says Alie.

'Me too,' says Jenny.

They sit in silence for a bit.

'Shall I tell you the answer?' says Lientje, looking impatiently at the other girls.

'The hand on the clock of the Oranjekerk,' Alie calls out at the last minute.

'Wrong,' says Lientje, peering at the clock in the distance. 'Is it really green?'

'No idea. What's the answer?' Alie is not in the mood for playing the game anymore either.

'A bogie hanging out of one of those little kids' noses,' says Lientje with a big grin.

The girls laugh – even Rosa.

'Can we play too?' asks Guta, coming over with Adele to stand with them.

'We don't know what to do,' says Jenny in a bored voice.

'I've got an idea,' says Alie, running back inside. She heads upstairs to her classroom to fetch her album.

'I've already written in it,' says Jenny.

'Me too,' says Lientje.

'Then you can go and find something else to do,' says Alie, handing the album to Guta.

'Do you want to go next, Adele?' asks Alie. Adele nods.

Alie goes and sits in the shade and watches Guta and Adele writing in the album.

JULY

'What are you doing?' asks Rosa, walking up with her skipping rope.

'They're writing in my friendship album. Would you like to as well?' Rosa nods and looks to see what Guta is writing.

Then Mr Stibbe comes out into the playground. He has a discussion with the teachers.

'Class 4A, to me!' Mr Roeg puts his hand in the air. The children gather around him.

'We're going back into the classroom. Follow me,' says Mr Roeg and he heads inside.

'But we want to go home!' a boy shouts.

The children trudge upstairs after him. They all sit down at their usual desks.

'All the children who live on this side of the Amstel can go home. Children who live across the Amstel will have to go home with a friend.'

They all cheer.

'I think it would also be a good idea for the boys to walk the girls home.'

Alie looks at Jenny. 'But we're taller than all the boys in the class.' They both laugh.

'Alie, can I come home with you?' asks Lientje, who lives across the Amstel.

'Yes, of course.' Alie turns to Rosa, who looks a little forlorn. 'Ro, do you want to come home with me too?'

Rosa nods.

The girls leave school. A boy from the top year comes over to them. It is Rosa's cousin.

'Ro, are you coming? We're going over to a friend of mine's place on Herengracht.'

She hesitates.

'I think I'd better go with my cousin,' she says to Alie and the girls. 'I want to be with my family.' The girls understand, and Rosa runs off with her cousin. Alie, Lientje and Jenny quickly head home.

ADELE'S STORY

1942–1943

Adele is walking with her brothers Salli and Moritz along Van Woustraat, eating ice cream as they head for the riverside. They are speaking German – it reminds her of the old days, back home in Cologne.

Moritz is nineteen and he has changed from a boy in a woollen jumper into a young man in smart trousers and a jacket. Adele thinks he is handsome; all of her brothers are handsome. They sit down on a bench by the water. Moritz stares gloomily into the distance.

'Don't you like it at your new place?' asks Adele, moving up the bench to sit close to her brother. 'Aren't the people you live with very nice?'

'Yes, but it's different. They don't eat kosher. I miss the farm. And my friends,' he says.

'Maybe he's missing his girl,' says Salli.

'Have you got a girlfriend?' Adele exclaims.

Moritz gives a little grin and nudges Salli.

'Is she sweet?' asks Adele.

'No one's as sweet as you,' says Moritz, giving her a cuddle.

Adele is happy when both her brothers are with her. They meet up once a week. Moritz fetches Salli from the Reindorps' house on Boterdiepstraat, and they go together to Diamantstraat, where Adele is living with Mr and Mrs Konijn and their two children. Until recently, Moritz worked at a farm in Wieringermeer, but the project has been closed down. All the young people who were there had to leave. Moritz was given accommodation in Amsterdam.

Adele misses her big brother and her parents.

'Have you heard anything from them?' asks Adele.

'All I know is that they went to Belgium, but there's been no news since then,' says Moritz.

'I want to go home,' says Adele, cuddling up closer to Moritz.

243

'We've only just come out. The Konijns aren't expecting you back yet.'

'Not here. I mean home, real home. Cologne. And for us all to be together again. With Mum and Dad.'

'Agrippastrasse,' says Moritz with a sigh. 'Oh, to be in my own home, my own bed, my own town.'

'And all the Nazis,' says Salli. 'I'd rather stay here.'

Adele knows Salli is right. Their life was never the same after Kristallnacht. There was such a terrible noise on the streets that night. Frenzied people looted Jewish shops and set them on fire. The noise had woken her, so she looked out the window and saw the fanatical face of a man with an axe, chopping away at something. When she went out the following day, the woman upstairs spat at her. Adele had no idea why.

It became too dangerous for Jews in Cologne. There was so much aggression on the streets. Lots of parents sent their children to the Netherlands, and Adele's mother and father thought that was a good idea too. Then they would be able to prepare for the journey to America, where her mother's brother lives. They would apply for visas, and the children could join them later. Until then they would be safe.

In January 1939, Adele, Salli and Moritz had boarded the train to the Netherlands, where they were met by people from the Kindercomité.

They were then sent to a children's home and had to go into quarantine. Later they went to a home in Driebergen, where they were given kosher food and Shabbat was celebrated on Friday. All the children in that home were refugees. The people at the home took good care of Adele, and she learned Dutch and how to crochet and knit. Though she was not pleased that her brothers had been put in with the older children, while she was with the little ones. She missed her parents and wanted her brothers to sit with her while she went to sleep. Salli and Moritz helped her however they could – until they were all moved to different addresses.

Moritz stands up and walks to the water. He picks up a pebble and flings it at the water. The pebble skips over the surface of the water a few times. Salli does the same. Adele tries, but the stone sinks.

'Let's do something else,' she says.

'Yes, let's go to the cinema,' says Moritz, throwing another pebble.

'Or how about the swimming baths?' says Salli, tossing a stone.

'Or the zoo? Oh no, I forgot. We're not allowed to do any of that now, are we?'

'As long as I can be with you,' she says. 'Then I don't mind where we go.'

'Do you want me to show you how to skim a stone properly?' He takes Adele's hand and does it together with her. After a few attempts, she succeeds. Salli and Moritz take it in turns to help her, and she enjoys being so close to her brothers.

·

School has finished. Adele walks down the stairs. Children are running up and down and round and round.

'No running on the stairs,' says Mr Stibbe sternly. He stands on the stairs so that everyone will slow down.

Once they are outside, they start running and playing again.

'Adele, do you want to play hopscotch?' asks Guta.

Adele is about to answer when she sees Moritz. He is waiting nearby. She runs over to him.

'Moritz, what are you doing here?' she asks.

'Come on. I'll take you home.'

They walk to Van Woustraat, holding hands.

'I've been called up,' says Moritz.

'What for?'

'I have to go to a labour camp.'

'Are you going back to that farm?'

Moritz hesitates.

'You know, to Wieringe . . . what was it called again?' asks Adele.

'Wieringermeer,' Moritz says with a smile.

They cross the road and head onto Lutmastraat.

'No, I'm going somewhere else,' he says.

Adele stops.

'But you will come back when Mum and Dad are here, won't you? We're going to America.'

'I know,' says Moritz gloomily. 'I don't think I'll have to stay there long. As soon as we can go to America, I'll come back.'

Moritz walks on, with Adele clutching his hand.

'Is it nice at this new place?'

'I think it's like Wieringermeer. That was pretty good. Lots of young people, all working on the land together.'

'When are you coming back?'

'I don't think it'll be every weekend, but maybe once a month.'

They are almost at Diamantstraat.

'You and Salli can meet up. I'll write to the two of you. Alright?'

Adele nods. They are at the house.

'Do you want to come in?' she asks.

'Yes, and then I can say goodbye to Mr and Mrs Konijn too.'

Adele gives Moritz a hug.

'And I can do a drawing for you.'

•

Adele and Salli are sitting at the table at Salli's place, playing Ludo. Salli is winning. Adele's mind is not on the game.

'Do you think we'll hear from Moritz soon?'

Salli shakes the dice.

'He hardly ever wrote from Wieringermeer.'

'But he promised,' says Adele.

'Maybe he's busy, or he's not allowed to write,' says Salli, throwing a double six. He moves his counter.

'Why wouldn't he be allowed to write?' asks Adele.

Salli can see that he is going to win and counts a couple of moves twice.

'Because they're always finding things to ban us from doing,' he says, passing the dice to Adele.

'It's your go.'

Adele throws the dice and looks at the board and then at Salli's counter. She counts the number of moves. She knows Salli is letting her win, but she moves her counter and is the first one home.

'Hey, you've won,' says Salli.

Adele smiles.

Salli puts the counters back at the beginning.

'Come on. Let's have a rematch.'

'Fine, but this time I'm letting you win!' They both laugh.

'You know I'd do anything for you, right?'

Adele does not reply.

'At the home, do you remember?' he asks, pulling a face.

She does not know what he is talking about.

'What did you have to take every evening?' he asks.

'Oh yes. Cod-liver oil. Yuck!'

'And who took it for you?'

'Moritz,' she says quickly.

'And whose idea was that?'

Adele can't help laughing. 'Yours, but do I remember you taking it for me sometimes too,' she says, giving him a kiss.

∙

Adele wakes up to the sound of voices in the living room. She listens as they become louder and louder.

'What are you talking about? She's eleven years old,' says her foster father.

Adele gets up and walks quietly to the bedroom door. Her foster brother and sister are fast asleep. She opens the door a crack.

'Adele Zimmer must come with us,' says a Dutch-speaking man, who is dressed in black and red.

Adele has goose bumps. They're here for her?

'No, you can't take her. She's all on her own,' her foster mother pleads. 'You don't take children who are on their own, do you? It's two in the morning. She's asleep in bed.'

The man looks at the list again.

ADELE ZIMMER

247

'Go and fetch her,' he orders.

Adele quickly jumps back into bed and pretends to be sleeping when her foster mother comes to wake her.

'Adele, sweetheart, you have to wake up.'

Adele opens her eyes and looks into the pale face of her foster mother.

'Are they here?' she asks.

Her foster mother nods.

'Come on, you have to get dressed. I couldn't talk them out of it.'

Together they pack some things in a backpack.

She steps into the living room, still a bit sleepy.

'Look how small she is,' says her foster father. 'Why does she have to go with you? Please, can't you just leave her here?'

'Adele Zimmer is on the list and has to come with us.' The man raises his voice.

Adele flinches.

'We'll do everything we can to get you out. Don't be scared,' says her foster mother, kissing her and giving her a hug. Her foster father kisses her too.

'Be brave, Adele.'

One man walks ahead of her, while the other pushes her towards the stairs. He slams the door behind him.

It is dark outside. She walks between the two men. They put her in a car and they drive to another street. Then they stop in front of a house and tell her to get out. There are German soldiers and Grüne Polizei at the door.

Adele looks around and sees that they are on a street with a canal. What are they going to do? They're not going to throw her into the water, are they? She stands perfectly still by the car. When one of the men pulls her by the arm, she struggles. The man simply pulls harder – she is no match for him.

To her relief, they head into the house. She has to wait in the hallway. The men walk through a door, and Adele sees a family inside, with three children. The mother is crying and screaming and trying to protect her children.

'These children can't go. They're sick. Feel their foreheads. They have temperatures,' begs the father.

The German ignores him, and the man brings in another family with two children and pushes Adele into the room too. He orders her to sit down on a chair, and she watches the man going through the people's belongings. She looks to see if the people have noticed, but they are too busy trying to talk the German around.

The man looks at a few trinkets and opens a tin. There are biscuits inside. He takes out a couple and crams them into his mouth. When he sees that Adele is watching, he takes another one.

'Biscuit?' he asks, holding one out. She shakes her head.

The mother does not stop crying.

'Now shut your mouth and get dressed. Everyone!' shouts the German. Adele winces.

The father goes to the bedroom and returns with backpacks and rolled-up blankets. The mother sobs as she helps the children to get dressed. The other family sits there listlessly.

When everyone is ready, the procession heads downstairs. Escorted by the soldiers, they have to march quickly. They are taken to an air-raid shelter.

In the darkness, Adele cannot see where they are. It looks like the square behind the school. But before she knows what is happening, she is pushed roughly into the shelter. There are other people in there already.

The door slams.

People start screaming. Women and children are crying.

With all the pushing and shoving, Adele is forced into a corner. She looks at the strangers who are trying to get to the door. She wants to be with her brothers.

'Come on,' a woman's voice says quietly. Adele opens her eyes and sees that the door is open. It is just getting light outside.

They are pushed into a truck.

After a while, the truck stops outside a big building. In the early morning light, Adele recognises the neighbourhood. They are near the zoo, Artis, at the Schouwburg.

As soon as they enter the building, they have to form a queue. Everyone is registered. Even though it is so early in the morning, there is a lot of activity. People are walking around, shouting, arguing, crying and even laughing. Everyone is waiting. It is hot and stuffy. When her turn comes, she says her name. The woman behind the desk writes it down.

'Where are your parents?' she asks. 'They have to register too.'

'My parents are in Belgium,' Adele says quietly.

'Where? You'll need to speak up, child,' says the woman, leaning over the desk.

'I'm here on my own. My foster parents are at home.'

The woman looks surprised and walks around the desk to Adele.

'How old are you?'

'Eleven.'

'But then you shouldn't be here at all,' says the woman. Adele is relieved. Surely she'll be allowed to go back home now.

'Come with me. You're going across the street.' She picks up Adele's backpack and walks with her to a line of children who are waiting with their parents.

A little later, two nurses come in and read out the names of the children. Some of the children are crying. Adele goes with some other children to the other side of the street.

The crèche is full of children of all ages, big and small. Adele is one of the older ones. They are all given a glass of milk and a couple of sandwiches. She realises now that she is starving, and she wolfs down the food and drink.

'Looks like you needed that,' says one of the nurses. 'What's your name?'

'Adele Zimmer,' she says, still chewing.

'Did you and your parents have to wait for long?' she asks.

Adele does not understand what she means.

'Was it a long time between getting picked up and being brought to the Schouwburg?'

'I was brought in on my own,' she says. 'My parents are in Belgium and my foster parents didn't have to come.'

'You're all on your own?' asks the nurse. 'I don't think you should be in here at all.'

She goes to discuss it with the head of the crèche. Before long, she returns.

'We're going to look into it, but you won't be staying here long. Come on, let's go to the dormitory,' says the nurse. 'Give me your backpack. My name's Rosa, by the way. If you need anything, come and see me, alright?'

Adele nods and, relieved, takes hold of her hand as they go to the dormitory.

EIGHTEEN DAYS LATER

Adele is sitting at the window facing the garden. She is reading a book.

'Adele, will you help me with the food for the little ones?' asks Rosa.

Adele goes to the kitchen, where the bottles are being prepared. She measures out the powder and boils the water. Another nurse comes into the kitchen. She has a list in her hand and she shows it to Rosa, who gasps.

'Adele, come here,' she says. 'You're on the list for transportation.'

'What does that mean?' she asks.

'Come with me,' says Rosa, taking her by the hand.

They go to the sickbay.

'Do I have to go to Germany?' asks Adele. 'But my brothers are still here.'

'Get into bed and pretend to be ill. I'll fetch your pyjamas,' says Rosa. 'I'll make sure you get off the list.'

Adele sits on one of the beds. There are sick children all around her. They are sniffing and crying. She waits patiently.

When Rosa comes back, she stands up.

'Can I go home now, to my foster parents?' she asks.

'They probably haven't been able to do anything to help you. Or you wouldn't be on that list. Just stay here.'

Adele puts on her pyjamas and lies down like the other children.

She wakes with Rosa shaking her gently and looks up at her sad face.

'I'm sorry.'

Adele gets up and puts on the clothes that Rosa gives her.

'Is it morning already?' asks Adele, sleepily looking outside.

'It's still evening. You and the other children are leaving at ten. The little ones are getting a bottle. Would you like something to eat?'

Adele is not hungry.

'I'll make you something for the journey,' she says, giving Adele a kiss. Adele follows her to the kitchen, and Rosa puts a packet of food in her backpack.

The nurses are busy feeding the little ones.

When everyone has been fed, changed and dressed, the littlest ones are wrapped up in blankets and the children who can stand and walk by themselves are lined up in a row. They are ready to go across the road, to the Schouwburg, where they will be reunited with their parents for transport.

'Adele Zimmer,' comes a voice from the doorway.

'Adele?'

Adele looks up to see one of the nurses waving at her. There is no sign of Rosa, and Adele is not sure what to do.

'Step out of the line,' says the nurse.

Adele goes over to her.

'You're staying here,' she says with a smile.

Adele does not know how to feel about that. She is glad she does not have to go, but she can see all the other children leaving.

Rosa comes back from across the road and is pleased to see Adele.

'Can I go home now?' she asks.

'I don't know. I have no idea how you got off the list. Someone must have done something to help you after all. You go and snuggle down in bed, and I'll ask around.'

Adele puts her pyjamas back on and lies back down in bed. The dormitory is almost empty now.

The next time Adele is woken up, she finds herself looking into Mrs Konijn's face. Her foster parents have come to collect her.

'Let's get out of here as quickly as possible,' says Mrs Konijn.

Adele throws her arms around her foster mother's neck. She is delighted to see them.

After saying goodbye to Rosa, they leave, very quickly and without looking back. They walk along Roetersstraat to Sarphatistraat. They walk as far as the Paleis voor Volksvlijt, and then on to Van Woustraat. Adele is tired. She can't wait until she is home and can see Salli again.

At the Konijns' house, everything is as if she never went away. They have left her things as they were, as if they knew she would return.

'How did you get me out of there?' asks Adele.

'That doesn't matter now. The important thing is that you're back with us,' says Mr Konijn, stroking her hair.

Mrs Konijn goes to the kitchen. Adele sits on her own in the living room. It is quiet without the noise of children around her.

She follows Mrs Konijn into the kitchen.

'Where are the children?' she asks.

'They're still at school,' says Mrs Konijn, who is cooking.

School – she had almost forgotten about that.

'I've told Mr Stibbe you'll be back at school tomorrow.'

Adele is keen to see all her friends again. Now everything is going to be fine. She is going back to school, Moritz won't be away for too much longer, and Salli . . . she misses him.

'Can I go and see Salli?' she asks.

'Shouldn't you rest for a bit? I need you here,' says Mrs Konijn.

'I can go on my own. I know the way.'

Mrs Konijn hesitates.

'I promise I'll be careful. I want to surprise him.'

'Go on, then, but get Salli to bring you home well before curfew.'

Adele walks quickly down the street to Jozef Israëlskade, which is now called Tooropkade. She crosses the street and walks as far as Van Woustraat. Then across the bridge, and onto Rijnstraat. The closer she gets to Salli, the faster she walks, until she's almost running. Finally she reaches Boterdiepstraat.

Impatiently, she rings the doorbell at number 26. No one answers. She rings again. Then she sees the curtains twitch, and the door opens a second later. She dashes inside.

'Adele!' exclaims Mr Reindorp. 'You gave us a fright.'

'Sorry,' she says. 'I shouldn't have rung the bell like that.'

She looks into the living room.

'Where's Salli?'

'How did you get out?'

Adele goes to Salli's room, but it is empty.

'Salli's not home from school yet. He'll be home soon. Sit down, dear, and tell us how you're doing.'

Mrs Reindorp comes out of the kitchen and is delighted to see Adele.

'Adele, Salli will be so glad you're back,' she says, giving her a hug.

The Reindorps have no children of their own, and they adore Salli and Adele.

Adele keeps looking at the clock. It is half past three.

'How long does it take Salli to walk home?' she asks.

'About a quarter of an hour if he comes straight home,' says Mr Reindorp.

She waits, looking out of the window now and then.

'Adele, I'm going to the Jewish market. Would you like to come with me?' asks Mrs Reindorp.

'No, I might miss Salli,' she says.

Mrs Reindorp smiles. 'I'll bring back something nice for the two of you.'

It is quarter past four when she sees Salli coming down the street. She is so nervous that she can feel butterflies in her stomach. He is going to be so glad to see her.

She looks around the room. She wants to surprise him, so she dives behind Mr Reindorp's big chair.

'Will he be able to see me here?' she asks.

Mr Reindorp peers around. 'Huh? Where are you?'

'Here, behind the chair,' she says, popping her head out.

Mr Reindorp laughs.

When she hears the front door opening, Adele can barely hold in her giggles. She has to put her hand over her mouth.

Then there are footsteps in the hallway.

'Did you have a good day at school, Salli?' asks Mr Reindorp.

'It was alright,' he replies.

At the sound of his voice, Adele cannot control herself anymore. She jumps out.

'Boo!' she says, giggling nervously.

Salli gasps, freezes and then bursts into tears.

Adele starts crying too and then laughing. In the end, both Adele and Salli are laughing – and kissing and hugging.

'I thought you were gone,' sobs Salli.

'Well, I'm back,' she says quietly.

They sit together in the big chair, holding hands.

'Everything's going to be alright again, isn't it, Salli?'

'Everything's going to be fine now that you're back.'

•

It is cold in the classroom. Mr van Moppis is wearing a scarf. He writes a few sums on the board. Adele copies them neatly into her book. Her fingers are chilly and she pulls down the sleeves of her cardigan as far as they will go, so that she can keep writing. Doing sums in her head is tricky today.

She looks up from her book. The windows are steamed up, and it is raining outside. A girl coughs and wipes her nose on her sleeve. Lots of the children have colds.

How are the other children doing? Treesje, Esther, Frieda, Inge, Sem, Greetje? Four rows are completely empty. There are gaps in the other rows, like a game of draughts. One child gone and one child there.

•

Adele jumps when she hears the doorbell. Her eyes are red and puffy. She gets up off her bed and goes to the door. It is Mrs Bethlehem from over the road. She hurries inside. Mrs Bethlehem is big and tough and afraid of no one.

'What's wrong, child?' she asks, when she sees Adele's red eyes.

'Salli has to go,' she says. Mrs Bethlehem puts down the heavy shopping bag and tries to comfort her.

Salli and his foster parents have been told to report to be sent to a labour camp. Mr Reindorp works for the Joodsche Raad, but lots of people who work there have to leave. Their stamps are no longer valid. No *Sperre*, no more exemption from deportation.

'He's going with his foster parents and I can't say goodbye.'

Mrs Bethlehem leads her into the kitchen. She takes vegetables, fruit and a loaf of bread out of the bag and places them on the counter.

'Why can't you say goodbye? Has he already gone?'

'They have to leave tonight. But I'm not allowed to go there on my own, and my foster parents can't take me because it's too dangerous. They're afraid that they'll be taken away too.'

Mrs Bethlehem understands.

'When Jopie gets back, ask him to come round to mine. Maybe we can sort something out.'

Adele nods and waits for her foster father to get home.

He sees the groceries in the kitchen.

'Mrs Bethlehem would like you to pop round to hers,' says Adele at once.

'What for?'

'I might be able to go and see Salli after all.'

'Adele, we've already talked about this. It's too dangerous. You've already been taken away once and if we go . . . You never know what might happen.'

'Then I won't have anyone left,' she says quietly.

The doorbell rings and Mr Konijn goes to answer it.

'I saw you come home,' says Mrs Bethlehem.

'Thank you for the groceries,' he says. 'We really do appreciate it.' He shakes her hand.

'So what do you think? Should I take Adele round to Salli's?'

Mr Konijn sighs. 'It's too dangerous.'

'Think about it, Joop. Those children probably won't see each other for a long time. They've already stopped hearing from Moritz. Give her the chance to say goodbye.'

Mr Konijn hesitates. Adele looks at him, pleading.

'Will you keep a close eye on her?' he asks.

'You know me, don't you?' she says with conviction.

Adele follows Mrs Bethlehem. She wants to go faster, but they must not draw attention to themselves. It is getting close to curfew, and the streets are emptying.

When they get to Boterdiepstraat, they see Salli and his foster parents coming towards them.

Adele runs to them.

Salli picks her up.

'You came after all,' he says happily.

'Just in time.'

They do not say anything, but walk hand in hand to the tram. Just this once, they are allowed to travel on the tram. Mrs Bethlehem stands on the street corner and watches.

'We really need to go now, Salli,' says Mrs Reindorp. She gives Adele a big hug and Mr Reindorp does the same.

'I can't do it,' says Adele. 'I don't want to say goodbye.' She feels tears rolling down her cheeks. Salli wipes them away.

'I'm sure I'll see you again really soon, and until then I'll write to you.'

His foster parents nod to say that it is time to get on the tram now.

'If we weren't brother and sister, then . . . then I'd want to marry you, Salli.'

He gives her one last hug. They board the tram. Salli leans out from the open balcony at the back. Adele reaches out her arm. Salli takes it. They hold on tight.

Adele cannot let go, even as the tram slowly pulls away. She keeps on holding tight. She can feel that Salli is not letting go of her either, and her arm is stretched over the balustrade. Still she holds on. Then the tram speeds up and she has to let go.

Her arm feels chafed, and she has red marks on her skin.

Salli stands at the back of the tram, getting smaller and smaller. She watches the tram go until it disappears from sight.

•

Mr Konijn comes running up the stairs and bursts into the house.

'They're closing off all the streets. Take everything you need. I'm going to ask the upstairs neighbour to watch the road.'

He runs upstairs.

Mrs Konijn grabs two backpacks, blankets and pillows.

'When the Germans come, take off your bolero jacket with the star on. Then go to Corrie's mother next door. Ask if Corrie can come out to play and then go away somewhere. Just get out of the neighbourhood,' she instructs her, going into the kitchen to fill bottles of water. 'Her mother knows about it. We're going up to the attic.'

Mr Konijn storms into the room and grabs the things.

'You know what you have to do?' he asks.

Adele nods.

Her foster parents run upstairs to the attic.

'They're here!' the man upstairs shouts down.

He has barely spoken the words when the entire street is flooded with German soldiers and Grüne Polizei.

Adele takes off her bolero jacket, heads outside, goes to the next-door neighbours' house, up the stairs and knocks on the door.

The door opens. The woman looks at Adele.

'Can I play with Corrie?'

The neighbour slams the door.

Adele stands there. She has no other instructions.

Soldiers are running up the stairs of the building.

Adele turns around and, as she walks back down the stairs, her eyes meet those of one of the German soldiers, who carries on up the stairs.

Calmly, she walks on. Down the stairs and along the street.

On the other side of the road, a woman is leaning out of the window.

'Adele's out on the street without her star,' she shouts.

Adele hurries on without looking around. No one heard the woman. No one stops her.

She turns onto a street where there are dozens of Germans.

'Get off the streets!' policemen are shouting.

She walks close to the houses, looking at the nameplates. She pretends to be looking for someone.

Adele walks on until she reaches the end of the street. Everything has been cordoned off. She turns around and goes back past all the houses, reading the names: BREUKER, DE HAAN, POLET, GROEN, VAN LOEN.

She does this a few times.

Meanwhile people are being hauled out of their houses and herded together.

Adele walks past the houses. It is as if she is invisible.

After some time, the streets become emptier. People are taken away in police vans, and Adele realises that she has become conspicuous.

She sees a girl she knows from her street and goes up to her.

'Can I walk with you?'

They walk together through the streets, and the girl eventually takes Adele home.

'Adele, would you like to see the baby rabbits?'

Adele looks round and sees Mrs Bethlehem waving at her from her doorway. They do not have any rabbits, but Adele does not hesitate for a moment. She runs across the street and quickly goes inside.

Mr and Mrs Bethlehem give her kisses and cuddles.

'Thank goodness you're safe.'

It is almost curfew time. Adele is looking out of the window at her house. It has been quiet for a while now. The Germans have gone. The cordons have been removed.

'Come on, let's go and see if Jopie and Peppi are alright,' says Mrs Bethlehem.

Adele hesitates.

'What if they've been taken away?'

'Then at least we'll know,' says Mr Bethlehem, who is even bigger than his wife.

They cross the street and walk cautiously upstairs. There is a German seal on the door. They go up to the attic and knock quietly on the door.

No one answers. They knock again.

'It's us. We have Adele with us,' Mr Bethlehem whispers.

The door slowly opens. Mr Konijn is in the doorway. His face is grey.

'You can come out now. They've gone.'

'No, I'm not going downstairs,' says Mrs Konijn, her voice hoarse in the background.

Mr Konijn looks at them in despair.

'She's too scared to go home.'

'You can't anyway, because the door is sealed,' says Mrs Bethlehem.

'Come back tonight when it's dark. I'm going to see if we can go to my brother's,' says Mr Konijn. 'Can Adele stay with you until then?'

Adele goes back across the street with the Bethlehems.

That night she sleeps between Mr and Mrs Bethlehem.

She feels safe.

•

In the following weeks, she and her foster parents went into hiding with Mr Konijn's brother-in-law. During those weeks, Adele had no idea what was going to happen. Every step she took too close to the window was met with shouting. Everyone was afraid of being discovered.

And now she is walking out on the streets without a star.

'You have to go left, then right,' her foster mother has instructed her.

She sees her in the distance. She recognises the woman with the scarf in her hair – she came before to pick up her foster sister and, later, her foster brother.

Their eyes meet. The woman turns around, and Adele follows her.

'She won't speak to you. You mustn't say anything to her either. She knows who you are. Follow her wherever she goes.' Adele does exactly what Mr and Mrs Konijn have told her to do.

She follows the woman onto the train and keeps a close eye on her. The train leaves Amsterdam. After a long journey, they arrive at their destination. Adele is taken to a small room, where she is to spend the night.

'As soon as you get there, send a birthday card. Then we'll know you're safe.' This is the last instruction she receives from Mr and Mrs Konijn.

Adele tries to sleep, but she is too scared. The room is full of crucifixes.

The next morning, the lady comes to fetch her again. They catch a train that takes them deeper into the countryside. They get out at a little station. The woman takes her to a farm. Adele walks across the yard, looking around. There are cows and rabbits here. The sky is blue and the air is fresh. This is a place she would like to stay.

AUGUST

Alie races around the corner on her roller skates. Jenny tries to catch up with her, and Roosje follows behind, barking and panting.

Alie heads straight for the corner building and slaps her hand against the wall.

'Home!' she says triumphantly.

'Wow, you're so fast.' Jenny slumps, exhausted, against the wall. Roosje drops onto the ground too and makes a groaning sound.

Alie and Jenny burst out laughing.

Alie sees a group of children in the distance. Coby, who lives across the road from Alie, is with them.

'Come on, let's go and ask them if they want to play.'

As they get closer, they see that Albertine is there too.

'Albertine's with them,' says Alie.

'So?' says Jenny. 'I'm not scared of her.'

'Shall we make a train?' suggests Alie, when she sees that some of the girls are on roller skates too. The girls join up and soon there is a line of six girls with Alie and Jenny at the front. Albertine stops one of the girls.

'Are you coming, Truusje?' asks Coby.

'We don't play with Jews,' says Albertine, coming over to them. Truusje stares at the ground, looking confused.

'We play with Alie though, don't we? You've known her all your life,' Coby exclaims.

'But not with her,' says Albertine, pointing at Jenny.

Jenny and Alie look at each other.

'Well, that's good, because my mother says I'm not allowed to play with stupid cows,' says Jenny.

Albertine walks threateningly up to Jenny. Alie is scared, but Jenny makes her feel brave. She puts up a hand to stop Albertine.

'I wouldn't do that if I were you,' says Alie. 'Jenny's grandpa is the wrestling king of The Hague.'

Albertine hesitates. Jenny glares at her defiantly. Albertine takes a step back.

'Who wants to play?' asks Alie, taking Jenny's hand. The other girls link up again.

The procession of girls continues. Albertine and Truusje stand at the side. As they skate past them, Jenny sticks out her tongue. So do the rest.

'Let's go to the park!'

The girls skate in a straight line along Eerste Sweelinckstraat.

Alie stops at the cigar shop and looks to see if Mimi's there.

'She hasn't been at school for a while. I never see her parents anymore either,' says Alie sadly.

'Come on, let's keep going.' Jenny puts her arm around her.

When they reach the corner, they see a group of people in and around the edge of the park. They are watching some men with a machine removing the Sarphati memorial from the park.

The girls let go of one another and head over to watch too.

Alie and Jenny stay behind by the gate when the rest go into the park.

'Are you coming, Alie?' asks Coby.

'We're not allowed,' she says.

'Oh yes, I forgot,' says Coby. She takes a quick look around. 'You can do it just this once, can't you?'

Through the fence, Alie can see some policemen and a few Germans working on the monument.

'We'll watch from here.'

Coby walks over the gravel in her roller skates. Roosje looks at Alie.

'Go on, Roosje. Go with Coby.' Roosje trots off after her.

'I'd really like to go into the park again,' says Jenny.

'Sometimes I dream about it,' Alie replies.

They gaze through the fence and into the park.

'Come on, let's go. This is no fun,' Jenny says, skating off. Alie follows her.

On the corner of the street, the sign saying SARPHATIPARK is being removed from the wall. A man picks up the new sign. Alie reads the name: BOLLANDPARK.

A couple of little boys come to watch.

'What are you doing, sir?' asks one of them.

'New name. All the Jews have to go, right?' the man jokes.

Alie and Jenny look at each other in surprise.

'Come on, Aal, time we got going,' Jenny says, pulling Alie along.

'I think I'll go home,' says Alie. 'See you tomorrow?'

At home, everything looks as it was before the war began: Father's chair in the corner by the fire. The little sofa that she and Mother always sit on, and the dining table with the thick red woollen rug as a tablecloth. The curtains and nets that you can use to shut yourself away from the world. Alie curls up on the sofa. Mother comes out of the kitchen.

'Stomach ache again?'

Alie does not reply. She curls up even tighter. Mother goes over to her and puts her hand on her forehead.

'Do we have to go too?' Alie asks in a worried voice.

'Who said that?' Mother asks.

'Those men who are changing the signs. It's called the Bollandpark or something now.'

'The Sarphatipark? It's the Bollandpark now?'

'The man said that all the Jews have to go.'

'Why not the Hollandpark?'

'Do we have to leave?'

Mother sits down beside her, and Alie lays her head on her mother's lap.

'I don't know,' Mother says, stroking her head. 'Whatever happens, we'll stay together. I'll never leave you all alone.'

Roosje barks up from downstairs. Alie pulls the rope and Roosje struggles upstairs. When she reaches the top, she flops down on the floor in the hallway. Alie fetches some water for her and sits down next to her. Roosje rests her head on Alie's hand.

'Hey, Roosje. Did you have a nice poo in the B-O-L-L-A-N-D-park, girl?' asks Alie.

Erna Fleischhauer

24 September 1929
23 July 1943

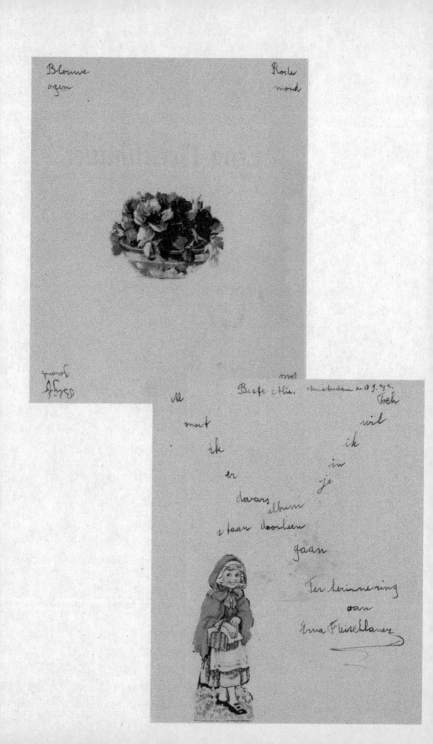

Blauwe ogen   Roode mond

Beste Alie.   Amsterdam de 19.9.'42.

Al   Toch

moet   wil

ik   ik

er   in

dwars   je

album

staan doorheen

gaan

Ter herinnering

van

Erna Fleischhauer

| Blue | Red |
| eyes | mouth |

| healthy | Alie |
| Stay | Dear |

•

Amsterdam, 18.9.42

Dear Alie.

Even if I have to go right across the page
I want to be in your album.

•

To remind you of
Erna Fleischhauer

SEPTEMBER

Alie goes into the classroom.

She sees Minna, Lientje, Agatha, Rosa and Jenny and heads over to sit beside Jenny.

'Sit down, everyone,' says Mr Roeg. 'We have two new girls in the class today. Anna Poppers and Erna Fleischhauer.' He points at the back row of desks, where two girls are looking shyly at the other children. 'That's Anna on the left, and Erna is on the right. Anna's from the Netherlands, and Erna's from Germany.'

'But I've been living here four years. I'm from Groningen,' says Erna with a slight German accent.

'Yeah, it sounds like it!' one of the boys jokes. The children laugh.

Erna looks embarrassed and does not say anything else.

At break time, Alie and Jenny walk up to Erna. Agatha approaches them.

'Erna lives in the same home as me. Do you two want to come round one evening?' she asks. 'Erna needs to decorate her room a bit. Maybe you two could help.'

Alie looks at Jenny.

'My mother says I can only play with friends in my neighbourhood,' says Jenny apologetically. The girls understand.

'Are your parents still in Groningen, Erna?' asks Alie.

Erna shakes her head.

'Anyone want to play a skipping game?' she asks, running over to a few other girls from their class.

'She doesn't know where her parents are,' whispers Agatha.

The girls look at Erna, who is happily skipping now.

The teacher calls the children back inside. In the classroom, he hands out sheets of paper and puts a set of crayons on every desk.

'We're going to fool around a bit today.' He has barely finished talking when the cheering and laughter start. 'On paper, that is.' He looks sternly at the boys in the first row. The boys look at each other in mock surprise.

The girls go and sit together.

'Everyone take a crayon and draw whatever you want most. It can be anything you like.'

'That's easy,' says Alie. 'For my father to be back at home and selling flowers again.' She draws some flowers.

'I want a really beautiful satin dress,' says Jenny.

'I want the war to be over,' says Agatha, but she does not know how to draw that.

Adele and Rosa draw good things to eat: ginger buns, cake, a big bar of chocolate.

'Ooh, me too,' cries Agatha and she draws some sweets.

Erna has drawn a meadow with big light-brown cows. And a father and mother with a baby.

'Is that where you come from?' asks Alie.

'It's Adelsdorf in Germany, where my parents live,' says Erna and she goes on drawing.

'It looks beautiful,' says Alie.

'It's Germany. How can that be beautiful?' says Jenny.

Erna looks up from her drawing, upset. 'It is the most wonderful place in the world. Or it will be when the Nazis leave,' she says angrily.

'But all the Germans can't leave Germany, can they?' Alie exclaims.

'Not all Germans are Nazis,' says Erna fiercely. 'Before the Nazis came to power, we were German too.'

'We call all the Germans Nazis,' says Alie hesitantly.

'I just call them Krauts,' says Jenny.

'What's going on here?' asks the teacher when he sees Erna's angry face.

'Erna says that not all Germans are Krauts,' says Agatha.

'Nazis, I said. Not all Germans are Nazis,' Erna growls.

'Sir, can we talk about something other than the Krauts?' asks Rosa. 'They're already everywhere. Do we have to talk about them at school too?'

'You're right. Come on, let's see what lovely things you've drawn.' The children put their coloured sheets on the desk and talk about their drawings.

The teacher looks at the clock and sees that it is almost twelve o'clock.

'Tidy up, everyone,' he shouts.

'And it's time for the children to go home to rest . . .' The teacher starts singing the song, and the class join in at the top of their voices.

'The children called . . . Polak and Poppers!' sings the teacher.

The children whose names are called are allowed to go home.

'The children called Polak and Poppers can go home to rest. The children called Polak and Poppers have done their best,' everyone sings. Anna and the boy whose surname is Polak leave the classroom.

'And the children called . . . Lopes Dias, Cohen, Fleischhauer and Van Schaik can go home to rest. The children called Lopes Dias, Cohen, Fleischhauer and Van Schaik have done their best . . .' The children laugh as they stumble over the long list of names. Alie leaves the classroom and waits for Jenny.

Agatha and Erna come out of the classroom with Jenny.

'Are you coming home with us, Alie?' asks Agatha.

'I don't think my mother will let me. But you can both come home with me,' she says.

Mother is not at home, and Alie makes some tea. She looks to see if there are any biscuits left.

Agatha finishes her biscuit in a second. Erna slowly nibbles hers.

Alie fetches her friendship album from her room.

'Will you write in my album?' Alie asks Erna.

Erna carefully takes hold of the book and opens it.

'It's beautiful,' she says, admiring the poems and the pictures.

'Do you do that in Germany too?' asks Alie.

'I can't remember,' says Erna. 'But I saw some at Mrs Asscher's house in Groningen.'

'Is that a relative of yours?' asks Alie.

'No, she's a famous writer. Clara Asscher-Pinkhoff.'

'And you lived with her?' Alie exclaims.

Erna nods, but she does not look up at Alie.

'Hey, I wrote in your book too. Is it still in there?' Agatha pulls the book from Erna's hands.

'Of course it's still in there. Give it back.' Erna takes it from her.

'Careful,' says Alie anxiously.

'Why don't you tell Alie how you got here?' says Agatha, picking up a few crumbs from her lap and putting them in her mouth.

'What do you want to know?' asks Erna.

'You don't have to tell me, not if you don't want to,' says Alie.

'My parents are trying to get a visa for America. So I won't be staying here much longer.'

'Have you spoken to them?' Agatha asks in surprise.

'No, but it can't be much longer now,' says Erna, as she writes her poem for Alie.

'Where are your parents now then?' asks Alie.

'Somewhere on their way here, to me,' says Erna casually.

'That's not what you told me.'

'Why are you sticking your nose in?' Erna snaps at Agatha. This time she does look up from what she is writing. 'I can tell people whatever I like. You don't know whether they're on their way here or not, do you?'

'No, but—,' Agatha begins.

'Well, then,' says Erna, cutting her off.

No one says anything for a moment. Then Erna starts crying quietly.

'Erna, I'm sorry. I didn't mean to upset you.' Agatha sits down beside her and tries to comfort her. Erna quickly dries her tears.

'Would you like a glass of water?' Alie asks.

'I'll fetch it for you.' Agatha jumps to her feet and leaves the room. Alie sits down with her instead.

'You really don't have to tell me anything at all if you don't want to. I never tell everyone everything.'

There is a long pause before Erna starts to speak.

'When I was nine, I came to the Netherlands with a lot of other children.'

'You've been without your mother for that long?' asks Alie. 'Were you in Groningen all that time?'

Agatha comes back in with a glass of water for Erna.

Erna gazes out of the window for a moment and then puts down the pen.

'I was in different homes. First I went to Rotterdam, where I had to go into quarantine. As if I was sick, even though I wasn't. But that was what we had to do. Then, in the summer, that was 1939, I was in a home by the seaside. In Wijk aan Zee.'

'The war hadn't started then. Why did you have to leave your mother?' Alie wonders.

'A couple of months before I left, there was a pogrom in the village where I lived.'

Agatha gives Alie a meaningful look.

'What's that?' asks Alie.

'Kristallnacht,' says Erna.

'Was it bad?' Alie asks tentatively.

Erna nods and looks sad.

ERNA'S STORY
1938–1942

NOVEMBER 1938

Erna is asleep in bed. Something crashes against her window with a loud bang. She wakes with a start. Then there is another bang and the window shatters: hundreds of pieces of glass fly all around her. Erna's heart is pounding.

'Mummy, what's happening?' she shouts in fear.

Her mother runs to her and pulls her away from the window. BANG. Another window shatters. Erna and her mother scream.

'Justin!' her mother cries.

Her father comes running upstairs. He leaps out of the way just in time as a burning rag comes flying through the window straight towards him. He quickly stamps out the fire.

Erna throws herself into her father's arms. He comforts her as he brushes the glass out of her hair.

'Why are they doing this?' asks Erna.

'We have to get out of here. Quickly!' He pulls Erna and her mother with him.

Downstairs, people are kicking in the front door. With a bang, it flies open.

Furious men are standing in the doorway. They are carrying torches and axes, and they have bands around their sleeves with the SS symbol on.

'Nazis! Dad, it's the Nazis.'

Before her father can say anything, the men storm in and drag him outside.

'*Raus, Jude!*' they are screaming and yelling.

Erna's father is thrown onto the street. Her mother tries to stop them, but they push her away. Erna sees them kicking her father.

'Daddy!'

Erna's mother protects her, hugging her head tightly to her chest. She does not want her to watch any more. More and more Nazis bring Jewish men from the village to the small square in front of Erna's house. Sobbing women and children follow them.

The men throw things out of the upstairs window of Erna's house; books, chairs, clothes, and someone stabs a pillow with a knife and hundreds of feathers come swirling down.

Erna and her mother have no idea what to do. These people are destroying everything!

One of the men throws a burning torch onto a sofa and within a few seconds everything is ablaze. Erna's mother falls onto her knees and screams. Erna drops down beside her, unable even to cry. The fire spreads until her bedclothes, her toys, her books – everything is burning. The Nazis bring the furniture of the other Jewish families to the fire, which grows higher and higher.

Erna watches some men carrying the big kitchen table out of their house. They do not put that on the fire, but carry it away. They take the candlesticks and the crockery too. Some of the village women go into the house and come back out carrying the family's belongings.

Erna stares at the fire. She hears the Jewish men being beaten, the Nazis laughing, women and children crying.

The fire crackles in the cold night.

When she wakes up in the morning, she is confused for a moment. She thinks she is lying in bed, but she is on a layer of hay in the cowshed next to her house. Then she remembers what happened. She sits up. She can't see her father and mother. And then she panics.

'Mummy? Daddy? Where are you?' She gets up and runs outside. People from the village are standing around the smouldering remains of the fire. Everything is burnt. Erna has tears in her eyes. Those who see her look away, ashamed. Some of the children are showing off and imitating the Nazis by throwing sticks into the fire.

One of Erna's neighbours comes over to her. Her eyes are full of tears too.

'Erna, I'm so sorry. There was nothing we could do.' The neighbour tries to put her arm around Erna, but Erna shrugs her off.

'You're our neighbours. But you did nothing to help!' She runs away, to her friend Martha's house. But no one answers when she bangs on the door. Erna can see someone is at home, so she bangs again.

'I know you're in there!'

Shamefacedly, Martha's mother opens the door a crack.

'Martha can't play with you anymore. I'm sorry, but you have to leave, Erna.' She looks at Erna with pity.

'But Martha's my best friend,' Erna pleads.

'There are very bad times coming. Especially for you Jews. I want Martha to stay as far away from that as possible.'

Erna says nothing and simply walks away.

'I wish you the very best, Erna. I really do.'

Erna does not look back, but starts running. She heads back home. Her mother is waiting for her at the cowshed.

'Where were you?' her mother asks anxiously, grabbing hold of her.

'Martha's not allowed to play with me anymore,' says Erna sadly.

'They've done this to Jews all over Germany. Do you understand how serious that is? Martha is the least of your problems,' says Mother.

'Where's Daddy?' Erna suddenly wonders.

'I've heard that all the Jewish men are at the police station, but they wouldn't let me in to see him. The mayor wants them to be released, but the Nazis want them to go to a labour camp. Come on, let's go and give it another try.'

'At the police station, my mother and I got bad news: the men had just been picked up and transported to Dachau.'

'What's Dachau?' asks Alie.

'It's a labour camp, for the enemies of the Nazis,' says Erna.

'Is he still there?' asks Agatha.

'A few weeks later he came back,' says Erna. 'The mayor had got them out. He had to work nearby, building a road to the station. He was allowed to come home every day though. Because our house had been looted, my mother and I were staying with an aunt. My father didn't get paid and our cows had been stolen, so we had no money for the rent.'

'Did you have cows?' Alie asks.

'My father was a cattle dealer. He bought cows for the butcher and kept some himself. Before the war, we always had the best meat. In the months after Kristallnacht, the people in the village got meaner and meaner. We were treated really badly, and not just by the Nazis. They hit my father for no reason, and they called my mother names. I didn't go out onto the streets anymore. There was nothing left to go outside for. They wanted all the Jews to leave the village.'

'And that all happened before the war began here,' Alie exclaims. 'So then you came to the Netherlands?'

'I did, but my parents didn't,' says Erna sadly.

Erna hears her parents whispering. When her mother raises her voice in anger, her father looks around to see if Erna has heard anything.

'Will you go and give your aunt a hand?' he asks, as if nothing is wrong.

Erna quickly leaves the room, pretending to go and look for her aunt, but then heads straight back to the kitchen.

'I don't want to do that,' her mother says.

'We'll see each other again later,' says her father. 'It's the only way.'

'What's the only way?' Erna says in a worried voice.

Erna's parents look very serious.

'There's a special programme for Jewish children,' her father says enthusiastically. 'You can go to England!'

'Just for children? Then no one's going to go,' says Erna. 'Who would want to go without their parents?'

Her parents look at each other sadly.

'It's not safe here for children anymore, sweetheart,' her father says. 'There are already lots of children on the list. If we want you to go with them, we'll have to be quick.'

'But . . . Dad,' Erna protests.

'You'll be free in England. You can go to school. No one will call you names,' says her father, looking happy at that thought.

'But what about you two?' asks Erna.

'As soon as you're on the train to England, we'll make sure we get a family visa for America,' her father says brightly.

'To go to my uncle?' asks Erna.

'Yes, you can wait for us in England and when we have the papers, we'll fetch you and the three of us will go and join your mum's brother.'

'But the three of us could just go now, couldn't we? Together. I can help!' Erna says.

'No, your father's right. You have to get away from here, before anything worse happens,' her mother replies.

'And we can arrange things faster if you're not here. We'll probably be in with a better chance if you're already in England too. Everything is going to be fine,' says Father.

Erna is standing on the platform with a big suitcase. It is very busy: hundreds of children with their parents and lots and lots of luggage. Erna has slung a canvas bag across her body with some food and other things for the train journey. She has a card on a chain around her neck with her details on it: her name, where she comes from, her address in England. She is struggling to hold in her tears.

'You'll try to call as soon as you get to England, won't you? Your aunt's neighbours' telephone number is on the card.' Her mother's voice sounds hoarse.

They walk over to one of the escorts.

'She's all on her own. She doesn't have any brothers or sisters or other family members who are going,' her father explains to the woman.

The kind woman shakes Erna's hand and ruffles her hair. 'I have a few other girls who are travelling alone. We'll put them together. By the time we board the ship in Holland, they'll be the best of friends. I promise.' She smiles at Erna and her parents.

Erna looks at the station clock: it is five to nine.

'The train's leaving in five minutes,' she says to her parents.

Erna's mother gasps and holds her tightly, clearly trying not to cry. Erna looks at her father, who is standing behind her mother, and sees that he has tears in his eyes too. Now Erna can't hold them back any longer. She starts weeping.

'Will you come soon?' she sobs.

Her mother lets her tears flow now too. 'Yes, sweetheart. We'll come as soon as we can. Your father's already working on the papers.'

'We'll see you very soon. Have fun at school in England. And learn the language, because you'll need it when we go to America,' says her father, and he takes her in his arms and squeezes her tight.

The whistle blows. All the children have to board the train now. Erna's father climbs onto the train with her to see where she will be sitting.

Erna sits down next to another girl. They smile at each other. Her father takes a quick look inside her bag.

'Do you have everything?' he asks nervously.

Erna looks out at her mother outside. She stands up and walks over to the door to give her mother one last big hug.

'I love you, Mummy.'

Her mother is so tearful that she cannot say a word.

Other parents all around them are saying goodbye to their children too, hugging and crying.

Her father gets down from the train, giving Erna one last cuddle.

'Go and stand by the window,' he says, and he walks up the platform to the other side of the window.

The train doors close. The guard blows his whistle. The train starts to move. There are only adults left on the platform now.

Erna and the girl beside her reach out of the window. Parents wave.

'Bye, Mummy! Bye, Daddy!' Erna waves as hard as she can.

Her father runs alongside the train.

'What is your name?' he shouts in English.

'I name ... My name ... ,' she says, correcting herself. They laugh. 'My name is Erna Fleischhauer! What is your name?' she asks her father.

'My name is Justin Fleischhauer. And your mother's name is Bertha Fleischhauer! We love you!'

Erna nods through her tears. Then the platform ends and her father can't run with the train. She goes on waving.

'Are your parents in England now?' asks Alie. Erna's story has given her a lump in her throat.

Erna sighs. 'They didn't get permission.'

Alie gasps. 'So they're still in Germany?'

Erna shrugs.

'I don't know. I haven't heard anything from them for almost a year. The last thing I know was that they were moved to Nuremberg.'

'So why didn't you go to England?' Agatha asks.

'When my parents didn't get a visa for America, they weren't allowed to go to England either. My mother wanted me to wait for them in the Netherlands, so that we would be together.' Erna's voice falters.

'You don't have to talk about it if you don't want to,' Alie says again.

But Erna keeps talking. 'They said we'd be much safer in the Netherlands than in Germany. My mother tried to come to me, but she wasn't allowed to enter the Netherlands. And then the war started here, and she couldn't leave Germany anymore. And then Daddy was sent to a labour camp.'

'But didn't you want to go to her, in Germany?' asks Alie.

'Of course, but my mother made it very clear: I was absolutely forbidden to go back to Germany. She was going to do whatever she could to come to me.'

'Maybe she still will,' says Alie.

'She'll come as soon as she can.' Erna pauses and looks worried. 'I'm afraid she won't be able to find me, though, because I've moved house so many times. I hope someone's keeping a record.'

Erna looks at the clock and gasps.

'I have to go home. Or I'll break the curfew. Are you coming, Agatha?'

Erna looks at the friendship album. 'Shall I take it with me?'

Alie hesitates.

'I'd rather keep it here, just in case . . .' Alie hardly dares to say it. 'I might lose it if there's another raid.'

Erna understands.

OCTOBER

Alie is walking carefully past the houses, trying not to be noticed. It is strangely quiet on the street. It is a warm day, but she feels cold. She buttons up her cardigan. On Ceintuurbaan she sees two big removal vans standing in front of a house, with the name PULS written on the side of them. Alie shivers and quickly crosses the street.

The street with her school on is really quiet too. When she sees Erna and Agatha, she waves and runs over to them.

'Did you hear it last night?' asks Agatha.

Alie is surprised. 'Did it happen in your neighbourhood too?'

'All night long. Must have been four trucks there,' says Erna sadly.

They walk in silence to school.

When they enter the classroom, only half of the children are there.

Alie looks around the classroom, but where is Jenny? The children are talking about only one thing: last night's raids.

Alie does not want to listen. 'Where's Jenny? She should have been here ages ago,' she says to Erna.

Mr Roeg comes into the classroom, with a very worried look on his face.

'Children, as you know, I live on Plantage Middenlaan. A lot of people were taken to the Schouwburg last night.' He looks around the classroom. 'And not everyone is here today.'

'Do you think all of them have been taken away?' asks a girl. 'Maybe they didn't sleep very well and wanted to stay at home today.'

'Yes, that'll be it,' says Alie. 'Jenny's just tired.'

'We're going to start today's lesson. So get your books out,' says Mr Roeg.

Alie takes out her book and copies down the sentences the teacher writes on the board.

The clock ticks slowly on. The seat beside her remains empty.

At break time, Alie, Erna and Lientje lean against a wall in the playground.

'Who's still here?' asks Lientje.

Alie looks around the playground. 'Rosa, Agatha, Guta, Mimi, Inge, Liesje and Minna.'

'And who's not?'

'Rosa Levie, Esther, Flora, Estelle, Herman, Maupie . . .'

Alie is silent.

'Jenny,' says Erna.

'Jenny's tired. She's staying at home today,' says Alie quickly.

The girls are relieved. 'Oh, that's good. Did you go round to her place this morning then?'

'No, I just know. Jenny loves sleeping,' Alie says abruptly.

Lientje and Erna look at each other.

'I'm certain.' Alie walks away. She goes over to Guta and some of the other girls and asks if she can skip with them.

'Adele was taken away last night,' Guta says sadly. 'They took her all on her own, without her foster parents. What about in your class?' asks Guta.

'A few, but are you sure about Adele? She might be staying at home today,' says Alie.

'I went round to call for her this morning, but she'd gone. The girl next door told me,' says Guta.

Alie does not feel like playing anymore. She goes and sits in a corner in the sunshine.

The rest of the morning feels as if it will never end. Alie's mind is on other things. Finally, the bell rings.

Alie jumps up. She runs out of the classroom and heads straight for Van Woustraat. When she gets to the corner and looks down the street, she sees a removal van. All she can see is the front of it. She stands and watches.

The street is busy. People are shopping and walking around the removal van. Hardly anyone is wearing a star.

Slowly she walks on and then she sees the big letters on the side of the van: PULS. The Puls men are taking the furniture out of Jenny's house.

She stops in front of the house and watches the men lowering the dining table out of the window. An antique wardrobe with clothes still inside. Jenny's shoes. Her father's haberdashery case. Jenny's bed.

'Jenny's bed . . .' Her eyes fill with tears.

Alie feels a hand on her shoulder. She looks around. It's Mr Roeg.

'Sir . . . ,' says Alie. 'They've taken her bed.'

Mr Roeg gives her a handkerchief.

'How did you know I was here?' asks Alie.

'I was walking past on my way home. I wanted to see if she . . .'

He searches for the right words.

'If she was having a lie-in,' Alie says, finishing his sentence.

'Exactly,' he replies. He smiles at Alie. 'Go home – and be quick about it. I'll see you at school tomorrow.'

Alie walks close to the houses, with her head down, so that she does not have to look at anyone.

Alie and Mother eat in silence. Alie stabs another bean with her fork. With every stab, her fork makes a nasty scratching sound.

'Will you stop doing that?' her mother says.

Alie puts the bean into her mouth. She does exactly the same with the next bean. That sharp noise again.

'What did I just say?' says Mother, snatching the fork from her hand.

'What are you doing?' Alie snaps back. 'I can't eat without a fork!'

'So eat with your spoon.'

Alie tries to scoop up a bean with her spoon. She deliberately makes the spoon scrape loudly over the plate and then looks defiantly at her mother.

Mother stares back at Alie. Then she grabs the spoon out of her hand and throws it onto the table.

Alie says nothing, but glares at her mother. Then she starts eating with her hands and smacking her lips.

Mother watches for a moment before taking the plate and smashing it onto the floor.

'Hey!' Just as Alie is about to start yelling, Roosje leaps out of her basket and noisily gobbles down all the food in a second.

'Roosje! Stupid dog!' Alie yells.

She grabs Roosje and opens her mouth.

'My beans!'

Roosje tries to wriggle out of her grasp, but Alie holds her tightly. They wrestle. Roosje wins and runs away.

'Why did you throw my plate onto the floor? You've gone mad!' Alie fumes.

'Yes, because of you and that infernal noise,' says Mother, calmly eating her beans.

Alie snatches her mother's plate. 'Then I'm going to eat yours.'

Mother gasps. 'Will you stop being so cheeky! I'm your mother – remember?'

'A good mother wouldn't give her daughter's food to the dog.'

'A good mother would have given you a clip around the ears long ago. Now give me that plate.' Mother pulls it from her hands.

'No! I'm hungry.' Alie grabs hold of the plate.

'I'm warning you . . . ,' says Mother.

'I'm warning you . . . ,' Alie says, mimicking her mother.

'That's enough!' Mother yanks the plate out of her hands.

The beans fly everywhere. Like a vacuum cleaner, Roosje goes after every single bean. And, again, everything vanishes in an instant. Roosje goes around licking the floor where the beans were.

Alie and Mother are speechless. Mother would like to be angry, but Alie bursts out laughing.

'Roosje! You're a rubbish bin!' She looks at her mother, who can't hold in her laughter now.

Alie imitates Roosje licking and sniffing and they both collapse into fits of giggles. Roos stares at them dopily.

'At least someone had a nice dinner,' Mother laughs.

The clock in the living room rings the hour.

'Eight.' Alie freezes. She looks anxiously at her mother.

'Go and get dressed,' says Mother calmly.

Alie goes to the bedroom and puts on extra clothes.

When she comes back, Mother has shut the blackout curtains. The fire is out.

'Shall I put my cardigan or my dress over the top?' asks Alie.

'Your thick cardigan. It might be chilly,' says Mother, fetching some extra clothes for herself.

Alie sits on the sofa. Roosje climbs up on to her lap.

'Do you want your book?' asks Mother.

Alie shakes her head.

Mother fetches a blanket and joins them on the sofa with her own book.

Alie nervously runs her fingers through Roosje's fur, but the dog does not like it and tries to escape. Alie puts her on the floor.

'Go on. Give me my book,' says Alie.

Mother passes it to her: 'n Zomerzotheid.

Alie opens it up and starts reading.

They hear a car outside. Alie moves closer to her mother.

'Are you wearing thick socks?' asks Mother.

'No need. I'm warm enough,' says Alie.

'Put them on anyway. You never know,' says Mother.

There is shouting out on the street.

Alie gasps when she hears a glass falling in the kitchen.

Roosje runs towards the sound.

'Go away, you've already had enough to eat,' she hears her mother snapping at the dog.

'Come back here, Roos. I've got a tasty biscuit for you,' says Alie.

Roosje comes running. Alie throws a bit of biscuit into her mouth.

An engine roars in the street. It comes closer and closer, until it sounds as if it has stopped outside their house.

Alie listens, holding her breath. Doors open. She hears boots stomping.

Mother comes back into the living room and turns off the light. She sits down beside Alie.

They listen. There is a commotion outside and someone screaming. Alie wants to see what is happening. She goes to the window.

'Alie, sit down. You don't need to see this,' she says firmly.

Alie does not listen and pulls away a corner of the blackout paper.

'Do as you're told.' Mother tries to drag Alie away from the curtain.

Alie stands there.

'No, I'm not going!' someone shouts outside.

Alie and Mother peep through the curtain: the woman from across the road is holding on to a door and trying to get back inside, while two German soldiers are tugging at her and cursing.

The woman slips through the door and tries with all her might to close it, but one of the Germans gives the door an almighty kick and the woman falls to the ground. They pull her up and take her to the truck. She screams and kicks. Then one of the Germans hits her hard with his rifle. They throw her into the truck.

Alie turns her head away from the window. Across the road, she can see Albertine standing half-hidden behind the curtain.

'Do you get it now?' says her mother. 'You don't need to know everything.'

More commands in German ring out. Footsteps.

Alie is almost panting. Mother holds her breath as the footsteps come closer.

Then they hear the doors of the truck shut and the engine start up again. It drives away.

Alie sighs and Mother dares to breathe again. She switches on the light over the sofa.

'That poor woman,' says Mother.

Alie is lying on the sofa with Roosje. They are both asleep. Mother covers Alie with the blanket and takes the book off her stomach. Alie wakes with a start.

'Do we have to leave?'

'It's half past twelve. They're not coming back,' says Mother quietly.

Alie feels relieved.

'Come on, let's go to bed.' She helps Alie up off the sofa. 'Try to sleep a bit. You've got school tomorrow,' she says, gently stroking Alie's forehead. When Alie gets into bed, she falls straight back to sleep.

Alie looks up from her sums. She can't concentrate. The seat beside her is still empty. She looks at the trees outside. It is raining softly and she can hear birds singing.

She looks around: the classroom is only half full. Hardly anyone is working.

Mr Roeg has also noticed.

'Alright, boys and girls. I think it's time for a story. Who would like to read to the class?'

No puts their hand up.

'Will you read to us, sir, from *Winnetou*?' a boy asks.

'I was actually thinking of a nice story from the Torah, but Indians are fun too.'

The teacher picks up the book, and the children come and sit in a circle around him. Alie listens to Mr Roeg's voice.

At break time, the boys run outside to play cowboys and Indians. Alie and a few other girls stand in the doorway, because it is still raining a bit.

Then Alie spots Adele in the playground. She goes over to her. 'Hey, I thought they'd taken you away.'

'Yes, everyone had to go to the Schouwburg,' says Adele. 'I was sent to the crèche across the road, to where all the children were.'

'Did you see Jenny there?' asks Alie. 'Jenny Cohen?'

Adele thinks about it for a moment. 'No, I don't remember seeing Jenny. There were lots of people at the Schouwburg, but they all got taken away at night on trams.'

'Where were they taken?' Alie asks.

'I don't know,' says Adele.

'But how did you get out of there?' asks Alie.

'I don't really know. My foster parents came for me. They managed to arrange something.'

'Were you there all on your own?' Alie can't believe it.

Adele nods.

Alie puts an arm around her. 'I'm glad you're back.'

The teacher calls the children back inside. Again, Alie can't keep her mind on the lesson.

When the lesson is over, she goes up to the teacher and hands in her work.

'Didn't you understand the exercise, Alie?' asks Mr Roeg when he sees the unfinished sums.

'If Adele came back from the Schouwburg, might Jenny come back too?' Alie asks, without answering her teacher.

He thinks about her question for a moment.

'It is possible, isn't it, sir?' asks Alie.

'I don't know. I think it depends on people's own particular circumstances whether they get released or not,' says Mr Roeg.

'But there is a chance, isn't there, sir? Do you know any people who were released?' Alie is not giving up.

'I know some people with a *Sperre*, but . . .'

'So she might come back. Because her mother knows people at the Joodsche Raad,' Alie says, interrupting him.

'Let's hope so, Alie,' he says with a sigh.

Mother is waiting for Alie in front of the school. She is carrying a large shopping bag.

'Come on. We need to hurry, because we're only allowed into the clothes shop between three and five.'

Alie gives her mother a kiss and they walk together to Van Woustraat.

'I've got some extra textile points. Enough for some warm underwear for your father.'

At the corner of Van Woustraat, Alie stops for a moment. She looks left, at Jenny's house. To her astonishment, she sees that the window is open and a rug is hanging over the edge of the balcony. She runs to the house.

'Alie, what are you doing?' Mother sees her running towards Jenny's house and goes after her.

Alie rings the doorbell impatiently.

'Jenny!' she shouts, looking up.

'Who's there?' A blonde woman appears on the balcony.

Alie is stunned. 'Is . . . Jenny in?'

'I don't know anyone called Jenny,' says the woman, turning to go inside.

'But she lives here,' says Alie indignantly. 'Jenny Cohen.'

The woman looks alarmed when she hears the name. She takes a good look at Alie. At the star on her coat. When Mother comes and stands next to Alie, the woman looks around.

'Not anymore,' the woman barks, going back inside.

Alie bangs on the door. 'Jenny does live here!' she says, ringing the bell again.

'Come on, Alie. Jenny isn't here,' says Mother, pulling her away. Suddenly the door opens. Alie walks up to the woman, who has something in her hands.

'I've got nothing against you Jews, but you can't come here again.

People might start talking,' she says, handing Alie a stack of books. 'These were left behind in the bedroom. I think they belonged to your friend.'

Alie stares at the catalogue from De Bonneterie, which is on top of the pile.

'Her father gave her that,' says Alie, her eyes filling with tears.

'Keep it. For when you see her again,' says Mother. They are about to leave, but then Mother turns around.

'So you're just living here temporarily, are you?' asks Mother.

'Why do you want to know?' the woman asks suspiciously.

'Because the Cohen family are coming back,' says Mother.

The woman looks shocked. 'When?'

'I don't know,' says Mother calmly. 'But they're coming back. I just wanted you to know.'

'Then they can take it up with the authorities. We have to live somewhere too,' snaps the woman, and she slams the door.

Mother puts the books in her shopping bag.

'Do you really think they'll come back?' asks Alie.

'I don't know, sweetheart. But that little madam won't be sleeping quite as soundly now,' says Mother, taking Alie's arm.

Alie looks back at Jenny's balcony. The rug has been taken in and the balcony door is closed.

It is busy at the Joodsche Raad. People are standing in line, and everyone is talking at the same time. Alie and her mother have been waiting for two hours now.

'Finally!' sighs Mother, when a man calls them forward.

'This is going to Westerbork,' says Mother, handing over the package, which is tied up tightly with string.

The man looks up from his form. 'Then you're in the wrong place. Parcels go through the Central Post Department.'

Mother looks at the man in surprise. 'So what now?'

The man gives a deep sigh. 'You'll have to take it there.'

'Where is it?'

The man hands Mother a piece of paper with some details on.

She glances at it and pushes it back across the counter. 'If I go there now, I'll break the curfew.'

'Then go tomorrow,' the man says in a weary voice.

This does not go down well with Mother. 'I most certainly will not go there tomorrow,' she says in a loud voice. 'I've waited two hours, after walking all the way from Zuid, and now you're telling me to try again tomorrow?'

Everyone is looking at her.

'Mother, not so loud,' says Alie.

Mother looks around and sees everyone staring, but she does not care. She starts speaking even louder. 'And if you worked a bit harder, everyone here wouldn't have to wait so long.'

The man does not react. He is clearly used to people speaking to him in that way.

Mother picks up the parcel from the counter. Alie does not dare to look up as they walk past the queue of people.

As Mother and Alie head to the exit, a young man comes over to them.

'Give it to me. I'll make sure your parcel gets to the right place,' he says with a smile.

Mother smiles back at him and hands him the parcel.

'We'll just need to fill in this form. What's his barracks number?'

'Barracks number?' asks Mother. 'I don't know.'

'Date of arrival?' asks the man.

'He left Molengoot on 3 October. So how long would it take to get there?'

Alie looks at the man.

He gives Alie a friendly wink. She blushes and looks away.

The man takes the form and slips it under the string around the package. 'Your husband will get it. We'll make sure of that.'

Mother is so happy that she gives the man a hug. 'Thank you so much.'

'Don't hold it against the man at the counter. He found out this morning that his parents have been moved on from Westerbork, and he doesn't know where to,' he says.

Alie and Mother are stunned.

'Why didn't he say anything?' Mother asks, looking shamefaced.

'Maybe you should go and apologise,' says Alie.

'There's no need. He can take it. That kind of thing happens here all the time,' says the man, holding out his hand for Mother to shake.

'Shake the nice young man's hand, Alie,' says Mother, as Alie turns to leave.

When he smiles, her face turns as red as a beetroot again.

'All the best, ma'am, miss,' says the man and he walks away.

Alie watches him go. Mother notices. 'Well, he's easy on the eye,' she says with a smile, giving Alie a nudge.

'I don't know what you're talking about,' mutters Alie, and she hurries along the corridor to the exit.

Alie gets home from school. When she opens the door, she hears voices from the living room.

'Greet!' Alie races through. 'You're back!' She practically leaps on Gretha and gives her a hug.

Mother and Gretha are sitting at the table, with some paperwork in front of them. Mother looks meaningfully at Gretha, and Gretha tries not to smile. Alie can tell that something is up.

'You two are acting so strangely!' She studies Mother and Gretha. 'Is something wrong?'

'No, nothing. Did you have fun at school?' asks Gretha.

Alie shrugs. 'It's not the same without Jenny.'

Roosje is hopping about next to Alie. She wants some attention too. Alie gives her a quick cuddle.

Mother pours the tea.

Then Alie notices a letter. She picks it up and sees that it is from Father.

'Is this from Westerbork?' she asks.

She pulls the letter out of the envelope, but Gretha stops her.

'Why don't I read it out?' asks Gretha, looking at Mother.

'You're acting strange again. I can read it myself.'

But Gretha snatches the letter from her and scans it.

'Alright. He starts by saying that it's busy at Westerbork. And that they're being treated well. Better than at Molengoot. He says thank you for the parcel. He was the first in his group to get one.'

'All because of that nice boy, eh, Aal?' says Mother, teasing her.

Alie feels her cheeks getting warm.

Gretha looks up from the letter and sees that Alie's blushing. 'Oh, was he a *sjnokkeltje*?'

'He was just some old man,' Alie says with a scowl, and she goes to her room.

Mother and Gretha laugh.

'Don't you want to hear what Father wrote?' asks Gretha.

'I can hear it from in here. Then at least I won't have to look at the two of you,' Alie says.

'He sends everyone hugs and kisses,' says Gretha. 'Oh, and he asks if you'll give the nice man who sent the parcel a big kiss and a hug too.' Gretha cackles.

'You're pathetic. We finally have news from Father, and you go and spoil it with your stupid jokes.' Alie closes the sliding doors.

Gretha opens the doors again and sits down beside Alie on the bed.

'I'm glad you have a bit of a distraction during this miserable war. Having a little crush is nice, isn't it?'

'I do not have a crush!' Alie says. 'Just stop it!' Alie pushes Gretha off the bed.

'Sorry, Aaltje. I shouldn't tease you,' says Gretha, who can see that Alie really has had enough.

Mother comes into the bedroom too. 'It's not that bad, is it? You're allowed to have a bit of fun.'

Alie stands up.

'Oh, really? And what about Father? We're here having fun while he has to work his fingers to the bone?' she says, her voice cracking.

Mother and Gretha look at each other, aghast.

'Of course we're allowed to have fun. And your father would be glad to see it. Do you think he wants us to sit here sobbing all day?' says Mother, putting her arm around Alie.

'He'd be happy if you could think about something else for five minutes,' says Gretha. 'You know what he's like.'

'Daddy Honey Cake,' whispers Alie.

Mother and Gretha laugh.

'Why do you two always call him that anyway?' asks Alie.

'Because he's soft and sweet, just like honey cake,' Mother and Gretha say as one.

'The gentlest man I know,' says Mother affectionately.

'When is he actually coming home on leave?' asks Alie.

'Father won't be coming home for now. He's staying in,' says Gretha.

'I miss him so much,' says Alie softly.

'Me too,' says Gretha, putting her arms around Alie.

'I miss you too,' says Alie and she holds Gretha tight.

Alie looks at the trees in the back gardens. A weak sun is shining through the leaves, which are already starting to fall.

Gretha lies down beside her.

'You and Mother have received a letter that says you can go and join Father,' says Gretha. 'Family reunification, they call it.'

'We can go to Father?' Alie can hardly believe it. 'And then we'll stay together?'

'Your father doesn't want us to come,' Mother calls through from the living room.

'What?' Alie can't believe her ears. 'Why not?'

'He wrote that you shouldn't come, that they'll keep you apart anyway,' says Gretha.

'But then why did they send the letter?'

'We can give it a try, can't we?' says Mother.

'Mum, he wrote: "Do not come." Why are you being so bloody-minded?' Gretha says angrily.

'I haven't seen your father for six months,' Mother replies. 'Maybe there's a chance we'll be able to see each other now and then. That's enough for me.'

'I want to see Father too. I don't mind going to Westerbork. Jenny might be there as well,' says Alie.

'And what if he gets sent to another labour camp?' asks Gretha.

'Whole families are going to Westerbork,' says Alie. Gretha has no answer to that.

'Yes, what do they actually want with all those women with children?'

'Or we could try to find out if we really are fully Jewish,' says Gretha.

Alie snorts. 'Us? Not Jewish? Oy vey!'

Mother laughs at Alie.

'Laugh all you like. We might be descended from the Spanish or Portuguese royal family,' says Gretha.

Alie laughs even louder now. 'And maybe Princess Beatrix is my second cousin twice removed.'

Roosje trots up to Alie, happily wagging her tail.

'And what about you, Roos? Who are you descended from?' Alie takes hold of Roosje's ears and holds them up. 'From Little Red Riding Hood's wolf? What big ears you have, Grandma!'

Now Gretha joins in with the laughter.

'You see how ridiculous it is?' says Mother.

'Father wants us to look into it,' says Gretha.

'Is that really possible?' Alie is surprised. 'That we're not Jewish?'

'We need to do some research,' says Gretha. 'If Father wants us to be on that list, we have to give it a try, don't we?'

'What list is that?' Alie asks.

'It's called the Calmeyer list. If he says you're not really Jewish, then you're not.'

'And then they won't come to take us away?'

'Not if you're Aryan or Mediterranean, no. Then you can take off your star and live normally,' says Gretha, looking at Mother.

'Live normally,' Alie dreams. 'Out on the street, to the cinema. Back into the park . . . let's find out,' says Alie enthusiastically. She looks pleadingly at Mother. 'For Father. Then he can come home soon.'

'It's not that easy. You have to go to the registry office and send letters,' Mother protests.

'Then I'll do it without you,' says Gretha to Mother.

'I'll help,' says Alie. 'What do you want me to do?'

Alie and Gretha sort through the paperwork on the table in the living room, and Alie picks up a pen and a sheet of paper.

Mother busies herself, picking things up and putting them down again. Gretha walks over and puts her arms around her.

'If we're not Jews anymore, then what will be left of us?' Mother wonders sadly.

'It's only on paper, not inside us,' says Gretha.

1943

1943

Leendert Lopes Dias

11 April 1896
9 December 1942

JANUARY

'How is that possible? He'd only just got to Westerbork. He had to work. Like all the other men. He was supposed to have leave. I just received his pay for August.' Mother puts the letter down. 'No, this has to be a mistake.'

Gretha takes the letter from the table and reads it again properly.

'Isn't it his cousin? He's called Leendert too,' says Mother.

Alie can't stop crying.

'Stop that sobbing. Because he's not dead. Do you hear me? He is not dead!' Mother's voice catches.

Alie leans in close to Gretha, who is reading the letter.

'Govert Flinckstraat, Mum. That cousin lives in east Amsterdam,' says Gretha quietly. Her face is pale.

'I don't care. It's not right. It's simply not right.'

Mother puts her coat on. Gretha follows her.

'Where are you going?' she asks anxiously.

'To the Joodsche Raad. Maybe they'll know how he ended up in Germany. Your father is forty-six! You wouldn't send him to Germany, would you?'

'They won't be able to do anything for you there.'

'Someone has to do something or say something. This can't just happen, can it? That people go away and never come back?' Mother cries out in despair.

'It's the Krauts, Mother. It's what they've decided to do, and they get away with everything,' says Gretha, trying to calm Mother, who is wracked with sobs.

'They want all Jewish men dead. That's the aim,' says Mother. 'First all the boys in Mauthausen and now old men too. They just don't care. Everyone has to work themselves to death.'

'Go and lie down, Mum. I'll make you some tea.' Gretha helps Mother out of her coat.

Mother sits down on the sofa beside Alie.

Roosje is lying on Father's chair. She rests her head on the arm and looks sadly at Alie and Mother.

'Why didn't we go to Westerbork? Then at least we'd have seen him. Now we have nothing at all. No goodbye. Nothing,' says Mother, in a defeated voice. She stands up and goes to the bedroom.

Oh, but didn't Father write something? Alie suddenly remembers. She goes to her bedroom and picks up her album. She leafs through to find the poem:

Dear Alie,

Roses wilt.
Flowers wither.
But our love,
will last forever.

Your Father

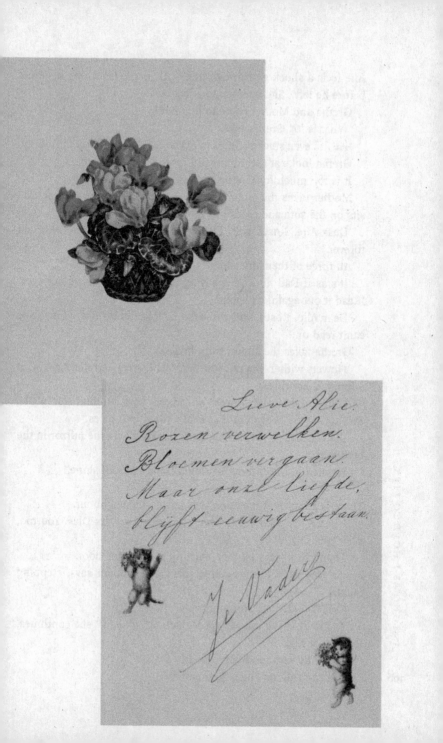

Lieve Alie.
Rozen verwelken.
Bloemen vergaan.
Maar onze liefde,
blijft eeuwig bestaan.

Je Vader

Alie feels a shock go through her. 'This is the last thing he wrote before he left.' She bursts into sobs.

Gretha and Mother come to join her.

'What is it?' Gretha asks.

'He . . . even stuck pictures in my book.' Alie holds up the album.

Gretha looks at the album and reads Father's poem.

It is too much for Gretha as well.

Mother takes the album and goes back to the living room. She sits on the sofa and reads out the poem.

'Dear Alie, Roses wilt. Flowers wither. But our love will last forever.'

All three of them are silent.

'It's as if Dad himself is saying it,' says Alie, closing her eyes. 'Read it out again, will you?'

'Dear Alie, Roses wilt, flowers . . .' Mother's voice falters. She can't read on.

Gretha takes the album from her.

'Flowers wither. But our love will last forever,' Gretha says, with a lump in her throat.

'Your father loved flowers so much,' says Mother. She walks through to the bedroom. 'Especially roses, red roses.'

Alie watches as her mother hangs a sheet over the mirror in the bedroom.

'He died in December. All alone. Daddy was all alone.'

There is a knock at the door. It is Luise, the neighbour.

'I heard the news from Greet. I'm so sorry, Mrs Dias. You too, Alie,' she says.

'Thank you,' says Mother, starting to close the door.

'He was such a fine, gentle man,' the woman says, stepping inside.

Mother nods, but does not reply.

'You're going to miss him so much, aren't you?' she continues, looking at Alie.

'Yes,' Alie says, nodding quietly.

'You can call me Luise. Remember?'

Alie feels a bit uncomfortable.

'Well, we'd better be getting on,' says Mother, taking the woman's arm and trying to steer her to the door.

'Give Alie to me,' she says suddenly.

Gretha and Alie are both listening.

'Excuse me?' says Mother, shocked.

'You don't know what's going to happen to you,' says the neighbour. 'I can take care of her.'

Mother pulls her hand away and glares icily at the woman.

'Wherever I go, my daughter goes too,' she says, pushing the neighbour out of the door.

'At least think about it.'

Mother slams the door. She is trembling with fury.

'She means well, Mum,' says Gretha.

'How dare she? I feel sorry for her, because she can't have children, but . . . trying to steal my daughter?'

Alie sits on the sofa with Roosje, who wags her tail happily and gives her a lick.

'Who does that woman think she is?' Mother paces restlessly between the kitchen and the living room.

'I don't want to. I'm not going to live with the neighbour!' Alie shouts.

'Just calm down,' says Gretha. 'It's not going to happen. We're staying together.'

Mother has tears in her eyes. 'What if she's right?' she wonders. 'What then?'

She looks sadly at Gretha. 'We'll manage. We can work, but Alie . . . What is a child supposed to do in a labour camp?'

MARCH

The class is almost empty. There are only ten children left now. They are doing a test, but no one seems to be really trying. Mr Roeg is reading a book.

Alie looks outside. Rays of spring sunshine are breaking through the thick clouds. She closes her eyes and enjoys the warmth. She takes her album out of her desk and reads the poems. All the names, every poem: Annie, Mimi, Rosa, Lea, Jenny . . . She looks at Erna, who is sitting beside her, scribbling away at something. She closes the album and puts it back.

MAY

Alie is woken by a market handcart being rolled out of the garage. There are quiet voices out on the street.

Alie gets up and opens the curtain in her mother's bedroom, where she slept last night. The sun shines on the houses on the other side of the back garden, illuminating the tops of the trees. Gently, Alie opens the window a little, trying not to wake Mother. Roosje runs into the room and jumps up at Alie.

'Good morning, Rosie Posie. Did you sleep well?' she whispers.

Roosje jumps into her arms, and the fresh morning air tickles the dog's nose, making her sneeze. Alie smiles and closes the window.

'Are you hungry?' she asks Roosje, taking her into the kitchen. She finds half a loaf in the breadbin and cuts a slice. She takes the cheese from the cupboard and puts some on the bread. Then she breaks it in two, gives half to Roosje and eats the other half herself.

Mother comes sleepily into the kitchen and gives Alie a kiss on the top of her head.

'Did you manage to get some sleep?' asks Mother, yawning. 'I had a bit of a restless night. It was so quiet outside.'

She picks up the kettle and fills it with water.

'I need to go to that shop on Rijnstraat this afternoon. I can use the textile points. I'll see what they've got. I'll come and meet you after school this afternoon, alright?'

The clock in the living room rings. Alie jumps to her feet.

'It's eight o'clock already.'

She quickly gets dressed.

'Take Roosje down to the park,' says Mother. 'And bring her back too. Mrs De Vries's dog disappeared the other day.'

'Alright. Come on, Roos,' says Alie, running downstairs with Roosje.

It is chilly outside. Alie puts her collar up. Roosje runs ahead of her, barking. The park is quiet; there is no one else around.

'Go on, Roos,' Alie says. Roosje dashes into the park, still barking away.

'Ssh. Don't bark so loud,' Alie says sternly.

She looks around to see if anyone is watching. Roosje runs up to Alie. She wants to play. Alie strokes Roosje's nose through the bars.

'Come on, Roos, do your business. I have to get to school,' she says. Roosje barks and buries her nose in the grass.

'Mmm, lovely grass, eh?' She laughs at Roosje, who is sniffing at something and snorting wildly.

When she goes upstairs, her mother is sitting in her father's chair, looking deathly pale. She has a letter in her hands.

'They're coming for us.'

Alie freezes.

'Now?' she croaks.

'Tomorrow afternoon. There's a list of things you can take.'

'I have to go to school . . . Mr Roeg.' Alie runs out of the house.

'Alie, come back!' calls Mother from the top of the stairs.

But Alie does not stop. She runs outside and past the park, on her way to school.

At school she sits shivering at her desk with her coat still on.

Mr Roeg comes in and sees Alie sitting there. 'You're early,' he says in surprise, looking at his watch.

Alie is silent. Mr Roeg comes closer and is shocked to see her pale face.

'What's happened?' he asks.

Alie is unable to reply.

'I'll fetch you some water. You just sit there.'

'They . . . We . . . They're coming for us tomorrow,' she says when he gets back, the tears rolling down her cheeks. 'I don't want to go,' she whispers quietly.

Mr Roeg does not know what to say. He puts his arm around her and gives her a squeeze. They sit like that for a while.

'What should I do?' asks Alie.

Mr Roeg is lost for words.

Then he says, 'Can you manage without your mother?'

'Without Mother?' She looks at Mr Roeg and shakes her head.

'Then you need to go home and take care of things,' he says.

'What do you mean?' asks Alie.

'Your belongings. What you're allowed to take and what you'll have to leave behind. Who you want to say goodbye to. That kind of thing.'

Alie looks at the seat beside her.

'Most of them are already gone.'

Her teacher nods. 'I know.'

'Do you have to go too?' she says.

'I'll stay for as long as there are children. And then we'll see.'

Alie shakes his hand. 'Maybe I'll see you again next year, sir.'

'Keep your spirits up, Alie,' he says.

Two backpacks are waiting in the hallway.

Alie drops down onto the bed. The beds have already been stripped. The bedclothes are in the backpack. She is allowed to take one toy with her, but she has not packed one.

Her friendship album is in her wardrobe. She leafs through it and sees all her friends' names again. She quickly reads Jenny's poem one more time.

'You can't take that, sweetheart. Only what's absolutely necessary,' says Mother, who is standing in the doorway. Alie flicks through until she gets to Father's poem. Alie kisses his handwriting. Then she puts the album under some clothes that she will also be unable to take with her.

At the bottom of the wardrobe are her roller skates. She picks them up and walks to the door. Roosje follows her.

'I'm just going to take Roosje for a walk,' she says.

'You'll be back in time, won't you? It's nearly three o'clock.'

Alie walks across the road and rings Coby's doorbell.

When Coby opens the door, Alie pushes the roller skates into her hands.

'Will you look after them until I'm back?' asks Alie.

'Can't you take them with you?' asks Coby.

'I don't think we'll have time to skate in the camp,' says Alie. 'And they're too heavy. I've already filled a backpack.'

Coby comes out and gives Alie a hug.

They hear footsteps. Albertine comes downstairs, carrying a skipping rope.

'Coby, do you want to come and skip with me?'

Coby ignores her.

Albertine looks at Alie and sees the roller skates.

'Why are you giving your roller skates to Coby?' she asks.

'I'm going away this afternoon,' says Alie.

'Jews aren't allowed to travel,' sneers Albertine.

'They are if they're being sent to a camp,' Coby says angrily.

Albertine looks shocked and clearly does not know what to say.

'Oh . . . Bye then.' She glances at Alie with sad eyes, as she rushes past her and away.

'Cow,' says Coby. 'No one wants to play with her.'

They give each other one last hug.

'Come on, Roosje.' Alie quickly heads for the park.

Roosje runs to the grass and happily rolls around. Alie walks along the fence outside.

She looks at the green grass and the spring flowers. She smells the scent of the blossom. She stands still. Then she walks back along the fence. Faster and faster.

She runs to the entrance and, without hesitating for a moment, she walks with big steps into the park. She does not even look around. Roosje starts barking. Alie no longer cares.

Alie drops down onto the grass and looks up at the sky. Roosje is going crazy with excitement. Alie grabs her tightly and pulls her close. Roosje lies down and rolls onto her back too. Alie looks at the trees full of blossom waving gently above her head. She breathes in the fresh scent of springtime. Then she closes her eyes. The sounds of the city grow dimmer.

For one moment she is nowhere. Everything around her disappears. Everything except for the grass.

She enjoys it for a little longer before jumping up and running out of the park, with Roosje following her. On the corner of the street, she looks back one last time.

'Goodbye, park. So long for now.' She runs home, to her mother.

Cautiously, she pushes open the front door, which is ajar. She slowly climbs the stairs. Then she hears a man's voice.

'You're the daughter, are you?' says the man, stuffing a biscuit from the biscuit tin into his mouth. 'Grab your bag. You're coming with us.'

Alie feels herself slump.

This stranger is acting as if he lives in the house now. He has fat fingers with a gold ring, and he keeps picking up things in the living room and examining them.

Alie goes to the bedroom, where her mother is sitting on the bed. Mother is glad to see Alie.

'Why are they so early?' asks Alie.

'It's not definite that we're going yet. The other man is still looking into a few things,' says Mother loudly, so that the man in the living room can hear.

'Just pack your things, because you're coming with us. Whether you're Portuguese or not,' says the man.

Then he whistles for Roosje. 'Here, doggie.'

'Roosje!' Suddenly Alie realises Roosje can't come with them.

'What are we going to do with Roosje?' she asks in a panicky voice. 'Greet . . . ,' Alie begins, but her mother shakes her head firmly. Alie understands.

There are footsteps on the stairs. Roosje starts barking. The man's colleague comes into the bedroom.

'You have to come with us,' he says curtly.

Alie gives her mother an anxious glance. Now it is final.

'Told you, didn't I?' says the man in the living room.

'But we're on the list of people of Portuguese descent,' Mother says, making one more attempt.

'They can sort that out there,' he says bluntly.

'Mum, what about Roosje?' says Alie.

'Take her to Luise. She'll look after her.'

Alie feels tears welling up.

'We have no choice. Go on.' She pushes Alie out of the room. 'My daughter is just taking the dog to the neighbour,' Mother says to the men.

'Not a chance. She's staying here.'

Now Mother gets angry.

'She's had that dog since she was a little girl. And now she is going to take that dog to the neighbour's house and say goodbye. Otherwise we are not coming with you.'

Alie is shocked by her mother and looks anxiously at the men. The man in the living room nods at the other one.

'Quickly then. But I'm coming with you.'

'Come on, Roosje,' says Alie, her voice faltering.

Roosje comes waddling over and lets Alie pick her up. Mother gives Roosje a cuddle. Then she heaves a deep sigh.

Very slowly, Alie walks upstairs and knocks on the neighbour's door.

'Alie, you've come after all . . .' She stops speaking when she sees the man standing behind Alie.

'Can Roosje stay with you? Just until I get back?' asks Alie sadly.

The woman looks at her, full of pity. 'Do you have to leave now?' she asks.

Alie nods, hugging Roosje tightly.

'Of course, dear,' says the neighbour. 'I'll take good care of her.'

She holds out her arms to take Roosje, but Alie can't let go. She squeezes Roosje and kisses her head, again and again.

'She can take herself to the park. If you say, "Come straight back home, Roosje," then she always comes back.' Alie's voice catches, and her eyes fill with tears. The neighbour is finding it difficult now too and quickly takes Roosje from her.

Alie gives Luise a hug.

'Come along, young lady,' says the man. 'We need to get going.'

'Bye, Roosje. Bye bye, sweet, sweet Roosje. I'll come and fetch you soon,' says Alie, as she heads back downstairs. 'You be good, eh?' She blows kisses at Roosje, who barks back at her.

Alie can still hear Roosje barking through the closed door.

With heavy legs, she trudges down the stairs. Her mother is waiting with a backpack.

'Come on, grab your bag,' says Mother, trying to put a brave face on it when she sees how heartbroken Alie is.

They fetch their belongings, and the men lead them downstairs. Some of the neighbours stand and watch.

'Good luck, Mrs Dias,' a boy calls from across the street. Mother nods, but does not look around. She gives Alie a firm arm to lean on.

They follow the men, with everyone watching. Alie feels ashamed and hangs her head.

'Let's keep our dignity, Alie,' says Mother, keeping her back nice and straight.

Alie looks back and sees Luise standing at the window. She is holding Roosje in her arms. Roosje barks.

'Why do we have to go to the police station?' Alie asks Mother, as they enter the station on Stadhouderskade. Mother shrugs. She has no idea.

'Two Jewesses to be picked up,' says the man who brought them in.

'Your name?' asks the duty officer.

'Verboom. *Zentralstelle*. My colleague will be along for them later.'

'When?' asks the officer.

'Does that matter? They don't have anywhere else to go,' says Verboom with a smirk.

'Why can't they wait at home? I don't have anywhere to put them,' says the officer.

'Just put them in the cell,' says Verboom.

The officer looks at Alie and her mother. 'Is that really necessary?'

'We have to check the contents of the house,' says Verboom.

'Alright. Have them step forward for registration then,' says the officer.

'You need to hand in your key to me,' says Verboom, taking a form out of his inside pocket. 'Sign here.'

Mother looks at the form. 'What if we're allowed to go back home?' she asks.

'Then you can come and pick it up again from the *Zentralstelle*,' he says, shoving the paper under her nose. Mother reluctantly signs and hands over her key.

'You're responsible for them now,' Verboom says to the officer, giving him a hard stare. 'So keep them here. Goodbye.' He clicks his heels and leaves without looking at Alie and Mother. Alie glares at his back.

'Do you really intend to throw a child into a cell?' Mother asks indignantly.

'I'm sorry, Mrs Dias, but you'll have to come with me.' He walks ahead of Alie and Mother.

'You can wait in the interrogation room. It's not very luxurious, but it's better than a cell,' he says, opening the door of a tiny room with only a couple of chairs and a table.

'Can I offer you a drink?' the officer asks.

'Make mine a glass of champagne,' Mother tries to be light-hearted, but she can't quite force herself to laugh. 'A cup of tea, please.'

The officer leaves. Mother puts the backpacks in a corner and sits down. Alie remains standing. The room is stuffy. There are no windows and it smells of stale cigarette smoke.

'I've made some sandwiches. Are you hungry?' asks Mother.

Alie shakes her head. She can't think about food now.

The officer comes in with two mugs of tea and a couple of biscuits.

'I hope it won't take too long,' he says.

Mother thanks him for the tea.

'Do you think Roosje's missing us?' asks Alie.

'I'm more worried about Greet. I just hope she'll stay far away from the house.'

'I hope Greet will fetch Roosje though,' says Alie after a while.

'I hope your sister is smart enough to go into hiding.'

'Hello!' Mother calls through the door. 'Officer!'

After a while, the door opens. The officer brings in some more tea and some sandwiches.

'Will we have to wait much longer?' asks Mother. 'It's six o'clock. We've been here since half past three. Could you try calling?'

'Sorry. It's really busy at the station, but I'll give them a call.'

'Could we go outside for a breath of fresh air?' asks Mother.

'I'm afraid I can't allow that. I can leave the door ajar for a while though,' says the officer. Alie and Mother look down the corridor and see a woman whacking a boy with her handbag.

'It was him. He's the one who pinched my wallet from the ice-cream cart,' says the woman.

'She's lying!' the boy yells. 'The bitch is lying!'

Mother pulls Alie back into the room.

'Do we really have to stay here? We're not criminals, are we?'

An ice cream, thinks Alie. That's what I could do with right now.

After a while, it quietens down in the corridor outside.

Alie is bored and starts reading her book. She is uncomfortable, so she puts her feet up on another chair.

The door opens and the officer brings in two plates of hot food: potatoes and vegetables, with a fried egg on top.

'It's been so long since I last saw a real egg.' Alie wants to tuck in right away.

'It's seven o'clock. My shift is over. Officer Heeg is taking over now,' says the officer.

'Thank you for the food,' says Mother.

'It's the least I could do,' he replies awkwardly. 'I wish you and your daughter all the best.' He taps his cap and leaves.

After a while, the door opens again and an officer comes in with a man who has been arrested. He looks startled to see Alie and

Mother sitting there. 'I need this room,' he says, heading back out into the corridor. 'Heeg! There are people in here.'

Officer Heeg comes in and also seems surprised to see Alie and Mother.

'What are you doing in here? Oh, wait. You're the Jewesses.' He thinks for a moment.

'Alright. Up you get. We need the interrogation room.'

Before they can react, Officer Heeg takes the plates away and tells them again to stand up.

They follow him to the front desk, where he picks up a key.

'Are they coming to collect us?' asks Mother.

The officer does not reply, just tells them to follow him.

They go down to the basement – and the cells.

'You're not going to throw a child in there, are you?' asks Mother.

He still says nothing and nods at the cell door.

Mother glares at him, but has no choice. She walks into the cell. Alie follows her.

'What about our things?' asks Mother.

'You'll get them back later.' He slams the cell door and locks it.

Ah, a bed, thinks Alie. She goes to lie down.

'Wait!' Mother stops her. 'Don't lie down on it. The people who end up here are bad types. You have no idea what you might catch.'

Another officer brings their bags.

'Do you have a blanket?' asks Mother.

When the officer has brought a blanket, Mother lays it over the bed, and Alie lies down on top of it.

'Bloody police!' someone shouts.

Alie wakes up with a start. For a second, she can't remember where she is.

'I keep telling you! I didn't do it!' The man gives the door a kick as they lock him up.

'Are we leaving?' asks Alie, who is wide awake now.

'I don't know,' Mother replies.

The door opens, and an officer brings in a plate of sandwiches.

'Have you heard when they're coming to fetch us?' asks Mother.

'I'll ask again,' says the officer and he leaves.

Alie takes a sandwich.

The officer does not return.

The door opens again. Officer Heeg and another policeman are standing in the doorway, with another detainee between them. Once again, Officer Heeg looks surprised to see them.

'Haven't these Jewesses been picked up yet?' he asks the other policeman. 'I thought you were going to call the *Zentralstelle*.'

The policeman does not say anything. Officer Heeg pushes the detainee into the cell.

'You're not putting him in here with us, are you?' asks Mother.

Officer Heeg walks off, leaving the other policeman behind at the cell. He clearly does not know what to do.

'What time is it?' asks Mother.

'Almost ten o'clock,' the officer replies.

Have we been in here that long? Alie thinks. Is Roosje asleep? Does Gretha know we're gone?

'My daughter needs to sleep. You're not really going to put a man in the cell with us, are you?' Mother says angrily.

'No, I wouldn't think so, ma'am,' says the policeman, and he leaves the cell, taking the man with him.

Officer Heeg comes back. 'Give them some blankets. They won't be coming to fetch them for a while,' he says, clearly annoyed. 'Too busy apparently. As if we've got nothing better to do. This one and the other one in Cell 2 have to go to headquarters.' He slams the door.

'Are we staying here tonight?' asks Alie.

'I'm afraid so,' says Mother.

'Then they should have come for us tomorrow,' says Alie. 'I could have had a day longer with Roosje.' Her eyes fill with tears.

'Try to get a bit of sleep.'

Alie lies down. Mother sits beside her and gently strokes her head.

'Get up. Come with me!' A man's loud voice roughly wakes Alie.

She blinks in the harsh, cold light of the cell.

Mother gets up off the bed and, half asleep, gathers up their belongings.

'What time is it?' Alie asks, confused.

'Half past eleven,' the man replies.

'Do we really have to leave now?' But before she can stand up, her legs are shoved off the bed.

'Get up. Pick up your things.'

Alie, scared of the man, quickly picks up her backpack and puts on her coat. The man pushes them out into the hallway, where another man is waiting for them.

Tired, Alie leans against her mother as they wait.

'Will you sign them out?' the man asks Officer Heeg.

'Will do,' says Heeg. 'And you're Verboom?'

'Van de Kraan. Verboom just delivered them. He's more inventory. We're investigation,' says the man proudly.

'Busy night?' asks Officer Heeg.

'Fairly. About forty Jews,' says Van de Kraan. 'But there are always some that cause trouble. For the rest, it's routine.'

Alie and Mother are taken outside and put into a car. Van de Kraan gets into the back with them. There are two men in the front.

The streets are deserted. There are no lights, only the headlamps of the car to illuminate the road ahead.

'Where are we going?' asks Mother.

'You'll find out soon enough,' says Van de Kraan bluntly.

'There's an ongoing investigation into our Portuguese descent,' says Mother.

The men laugh.

'The people there know all about Portuguese Jews,' says Van de Kraan.

Mother falls silent. Alie is as quiet as a mouse.

They drive along Stadhouderskade and then Mauritskade. At the Muiderpoort, they turn left onto Plantage Middenlaan.

'Are we going to the Schouwburg?' asks Mother.

'Like he said: you'll find out. And now shut your mouth, Jewess,' says one of the other men.

Alie is scared.

'There's a little girl here, Van Keulen. Mind your manners,' says the driver.

'It'll toughen her up,' says Van Keulen.

The car stops in front of the Schouwburg. They get out.

The doors of the building open and Alie and her mother are pushed inside. In the busy hall, they are handed over to a German guard.

Van Keulen gives him a note: *Esther van Beezem-Lopes Dias und Alida Lopes Dias. Mutter und Tochter.* The guard takes it and gives him a receipt.

'Anything for the others?' asks the German.

'No, that money's mine,' says Van Keulen, quickly putting the receipt away.

Mother looks at Van Keulen, stunned.

'So that's what we're worth,' she says quietly, biting back her anger.

'Did he just get some money for us?' Alie looks at her mother in disbelief. But she can't stop to think about it for too long, as they are shoved through the door into the auditorium. They are hit by the heavy, warm air and the unbearable smell of sweat, stale air and sewers.

Alie steps back, but is immediately pushed forward into a wall of people.

At the other end of the room is the stage. In front of the stage, there is a sea of people. Everyone is trying to get somewhere. No one has any room. Children are crying. A long line of people is standing on the stairs. No one can go up. No one can go down. People are shouting and screaming. A girl cries for her father.

Alie desperately looks for her mother, and then she faints.

HOLLANDSCHE SCHOUWBURG

Alie comes to and finds herself lying on a camp bed. The heavy, suffocating air hits her again.

'Mum!' she shouts. She can't see her mother at first.

A nurse comes over and checks her eyes.

'You fainted. Are you feeling a bit better now?' she asks.

'Where's my mother?' asks Alie, anxiously looking around.

'Your mother has gone to fetch you something to eat,' says the nurse. 'You just lie there and keep calm.'

It seems like an eternity before Mother returns, with a cup of tea and some bread.

'She'll be back on her feet in no time once she's had that,' the nurse says.

'She needs fresh air. It's stifling in here. Can't someone do something about it?' says Mother angrily. She is wearing only her short-sleeved dress now.

The nurse looks at her in surprise. 'You've only just got here, haven't you?'

Mother nods.

'I hope for your sake that you get used to it,' she says in a resigned voice.

An old woman of around seventy is brought in. Alie notices that she is not wearing any shoes, only socks with holes in. The woman is laughing to herself and seems confused. 'I have no idea where my shoes are. Maybe my mother has them,' she says.

Alie can't bear to watch, so she looks away. But on the other side there is a delirious woman with a high fever. A nurse is trying to keep the woman's head cool.

The place is full of sick people. Alie stands up. 'Mum, I want to get out of here,' she says.

Another nurse comes over to her. 'How do you feel?' she asks.

'Better now,' says Alie.

The nurse checks her forehead. 'You don't have a temperature. I think you can go.'

Mother feels Alie's forehead too, just to make sure.

'Is it a good idea for her to leave the sickbay now?' she asks.

'We need the bed,' says the nurse. 'I could go and see if she can go to the crèche across the road.'

'That's for little children, isn't it?' asks Alie.

'Sometimes older children go there too,' says the nurse.

'I'd rather stay with my mother. Thank you,' says Alie.

The old woman starts sobbing uncontrollably.

'Come on, Mum. Let's go.'

A man from the Joodsche Raad walks up to Alie and Mother. 'Excuse me, you still need to register. Will you follow me?' The man walks ahead of them.

As they head downstairs, Alie feels faint again. She manages to lean on the wall just in time and rests for a moment, but she is jostled by people going up and down the stairs.

It is busy at the registration desks. They have to wait a long time. When it is finally their turn, Alie needs to go to the toilet.

'Mum, I really have to go,' she says.

'Stop fussing,' says Mother, who is tired of waiting.

'I can't. I have to go. Now.' Alie needs more than a pee.

'Excuse me, where's the toilet?' Alie asks the lady who is registering them.

'Around the corner, halfway up the stairs,' she says.

'I'll go on my own. Wait here for me,' says Alie, hurrying off.

The stairs are still packed. She manages to squeeze through and sees the entrance to the toilets. As she's about to go inside, someone stops her.

'Hey, you're not trying to push in, are you?' says a woman.

'Oh, sorry. I didn't know you were in the queue,' says Alie and she stands behind the woman.

'You need to go to the back.' The woman points to the very top of the stairs. A huge queue of woman and children is waiting.

'Then I'm not going to make it,' says Alie. She hurries back to her mother as quickly as she can.

'Excuse me, I really, really need to go,' she says to the woman on the registration desk, 'but there's a queue all the way up to the top of the building. Is there a toilet anywhere else?'

The woman barely looks up from her paperwork. 'You'll have to wait your turn.'

It all becomes too much for Alie, and she starts crying.

'Then I'll do it in my underwear, alright?'

The woman takes pity on her. 'Come with me then. But don't tell anyone else.' She leads Alie to a small room behind the registration desks, where there is a bucket.

As quickly as she can, Alie closes the door and crouches down.

She stays in there for a while, even after she has finished.

Mother knocks on the door.

'Alie, are you alright in there?' she asks in a worried voice.

'Yes. Nearly done,' says Alie.

'I'd like to go too,' says Mother.

Alie waits for her.

'What a luxury, this peace and quiet,' says Mother from behind the door. 'Let's stay for a bit longer.'

Mother comes out and they sit on the floor in the narrow corridor in front of the door.

'What's going to happen to us?' asks Alie after a while.

'I don't know,' says Mother with a sigh. 'They can't keep us here for long. So many people all crowded together – it's not right, is it?'

They cuddle up. Alie puts her head on Mother's lap. Suddenly Mother starts laughing.

'What is it?' asks Alie.

'You should have seen that woman's face when you said you were going to do it in your underwear.' Mother pulls a funny face. Alie bursts out laughing too.

'I would have done as well. I really, really had to go!'

A door opens. 'Ah, there you are,' the woman from the registration desk says. 'You need to get ready for transport.'

'Where to?' asks Mother.

'They're moving people to Westerbork at three o'clock,' says the woman. 'You're going with them.'

Alie looks at her mother with horror.

'We're not going anywhere,' says Mother fiercely. 'There's an ongoing investigation into our Portuguese descent. We want to go home.'

The woman stops to think. 'Ah, then we'll have to look into that. You'll have to come off the transport list,' she says and she leads Mother and Alie to the registration desk. She takes the transport list and crosses off their names.

'Can we go home now?' asks Alie.

'I'm going to see what I can do for you. I'll work on it,' says the woman. 'Go and find somewhere to sleep. There'll be more room when people move out to Westerbork.'

Mother and Alie return to the auditorium, where lots of people are gathering their belongings and preparing to be moved to Westerbork.

There are straw mats on the ground for people to lie on. All the lights are on.

'What time is it now?' Alie asks Mother, who is trying to make her coat into a pillow.

'We got here at around twelve. The transport is leaving at three. So I think it must be about half past two.'

'Why are the lights still on at half past two?' asks Alie.

'Maybe for the people who are going to Westerbork,' says Mother.

'The lights are always on,' says a woman who is lying next to them. 'I've been here all week and I haven't slept a wink,' she sighs.

Alie looks around, wondering how anyone can bear it.

She hears shouting in German. A large German SS officer storms into the auditorium. He is drunk and yelling orders.

'Try to not to attract his attention!' whispers the woman, turning away.

Mother pulls Alie close. The SS man is near them now. Alie is frightened and winces when he shouts again. Then he spots a man who is just standing there and, for no reason at all, he grabs him and hits him. Alie shivers.

The SS man hauls the poor man away, and Alie hears him shouting something about Westerbork.

After they have left, Alie is still shaking.

'But that man wasn't doing anything wrong, was he?' she asks her mother.

The woman, who has turned back towards them now, is very calm.

'Spend a week here and nothing will surprise you. Believe me.'

Alie gives her mother a worried look. 'Try to sleep a bit. We won't be staying here a week,' Mother says to reassure her.

Alie lies down and stares at the high ceiling. All around her she can hear constant murmuring and the shuffling of feet. How is she supposed to sleep?

Over the next few days, more and more groups of people arrive. Registration desks are placed on the stage. The newcomers have to walk down the aisle. During the daytime, all the mattresses are moved aside and there are rows of seats, as if a performance is about to begin on the stage. Alie and Mother are both on chairs. All the seats are occupied. Everyone is sitting around. Alie tries to read her book, but is distracted by a boy on the stage.

'This is what I've always dreamed of,' he says, and he starts singing a song from an opera.

Alie looks at Mother. 'He's pretty good for a child.'

When the boy has finished, a few people applaud. The boy gives an exaggerated bow. He starts singing again, but then his mother drags him to the registration desks.

'Stop that silliness now. We have to register.' She pushes his little sister into his arms. Alie goes on reading her book.

Everyone who is registered searches for a place to sit. The auditorium becomes more and more packed. Alie is finding it hard to breathe, but she cannot take off any more clothes. All she is wearing now is a thin summer dress.

'Do you think Roosje has gone to the park?' she says. 'I'd love to be there right now. It can't be much longer before we're allowed to go back home, can it?' she asks Mother, who is sewing a hem.

'I'm thirsty.'

'You'll have to go on your own or we'll lose our seats,' says Mother. 'Bring some water for me too.' She gives the cups to Alie.

Alie walks past the stage and suddenly smells fresh air, as if someone has opened a window. She walks towards the coolness and sees that a door is open. The bright daylight is shining in, but it is still nice and cool. The door opens onto a kind of roof. There is a ladder leading to a courtyard. She wants to be out there. Slowly she climbs down and suddenly she is standing outside in the courtyard in the sunshine. She closes her eyes and takes a deep breath. When she opens her eyes, she sees the houses around her. A woman is standing in a kitchen. In another house, a man is sitting in a chair.

She breathes in some more fresh air and then goes up the ladder and back inside.

When she has fetched the water, she goes back to Mother. She wants to tell her about the little courtyard, but Mother is talking to a woman.

'Lots of people have tried, but there's nothing anyone here can do to help you. I'm sorry.'

'So what do I do now?' asks Mother, disheartened.

'I can try to get you and your daughter on the list for Vught,' says the woman.

'Vught? What's that?' asks Mother.

'Vught is much better than Westerbork. It's a fairly new labour camp, not a transit camp. So at least you'll stay in the Netherlands,' says the woman. 'Maybe you'll be able to do something there about your Portuguese descent.'

'Then please put us down for that,' says Mother.

The woman leaves.

'So we're not going home?' asks Alie, disappointed.

'No, sweetheart, that's not happening. But this Vught place doesn't seem too bad,' says Mother, sounding somewhat relieved.

Alie drinks her water.

'So where is Vught?'

'I think it's near Den Bosch,' says Mother. 'Didn't you study that part of the Netherlands at school?'

'Brabant,' says Alie. 'I've never been there before.'

Alie blinks. For a moment, she does not know where she is, but then she hears the murmuring and the shuffling. Because of the light in the auditorium, she cannot tell if it is day or night. She sees her mother gathering up their belongings.

'What are you doing?' she asks sleepily, as she sits up.

'We're going to Vught,' says Mother.

'When?' she asks.

'At three o'clock,' says Mother. 'Try to get a little more sleep.'

Three o'clock in the afternoon or three in the morning? Alie wonders.

'What time is it now?'

'It's about midnight,' says Mother.

'Then we'd better pack up.' She gets up and helps Mother to pack.

'You're the first person who's ever been in a hurry to go to a labour camp,' says Mother.

'Anything is better than here,' replies Alie.

Alie and Mother are waiting in a long queue. Hundreds of people, loaded up with their backpacks, are waiting for the doors to open. Mothers with children, families. A few children of her own age.

There is more shouting in German. SS soldiers open the doors and start hitting people and pushing them outside. Alie stays close to Mother.

A line of SS men is standing outside, completely blocking the view. Everyone is shoved onto trams, and if they are not quick enough, they get kicked and beaten.

Alie tries to be brave. A soldier pushes her in the back and she quickly gets on to the tram. 'Schnell! Einsteigen!'

The tram starts moving. A long procession of trams passes through the darkness, heading for Centraal Station.

In front of the station, everyone is taken off the tram. Dutch policemen and German soldiers are waiting to lead them to the platforms. They are arranged in four lines. Then everyone has to get onto the train. Alie and Mother manage to find seats and quickly sit down. Others are less fortunate and have to stand for the entire journey.

KAMP VUGHT

Alie jerks awake as the train comes to an abrupt stop. She looks out of the window, but there are no lights outside. The only illumination is from the Germans' torches.

Soldiers with dogs flank the station. The dogs are barking.

Feeling scared, Alie takes hold of Mother's hand, but they are pulled apart.

Alie is put on a bus with the other children. Mother has to walk to the camp.

The camp is big. The children go in through the gate past a line of Dutch SS men, who shout just as loud as the Germans. They walk past barbed wire, and Alie sees men and women in a yard. They stand perfectly still as the SS men yell at them.

Alie is freezing. The children are herded into a small room, where they have to wait for their parents. The room smells new, as if it has recently been built. It is a long wait, and their parents do not arrive until it is starting to get light.

Alie immediately falls into her mother's arms.

'It's awful here,' says Alie.

Mother looks pale, but tries to comfort her.

'Be brave. At least we're together.'

Then they have to go to a different room. Everything is new. Two female German Aufseherinnen in grey uniforms come in, yelling and shouting at them to stand in rows of four. One of the female guards grabs Alie by the hair and pulls her into a row, shouting so loud in her face that Alie's eyes fill with tears.

Mother quickly goes and stands behind Alie and puts her hands on her shoulders.

Alie stands in her row, shaking. The Aufseherinnen walk along and make them hand everything over: medicine, torches, wedding rings, earrings.

They have to sit on hard benches and are given something to eat: bowls of stinking slop.

'Yuck, what on earth is this?' Alie looks at Mother, who is probably thinking the same.

'Ugh. Cabbage soup,' a woman exclaims, pushing the bowl away.

'Eat it up, Alie. You never know when we'll be fed again,' says Mother.

'But it stinks,' Alie protests.

'Then hold your nose.' Mother does the same.

After the soup, they are registered.

They stand for a really long time in the queue for the administration office. Once again, the registration is done by people from the Joodsche Raad.

'We shouldn't really be here,' says Mother, when their turn finally comes. 'We're on the list of people of Portuguese descent.'

The man on the registration desk looks up. 'Do you have the relevant documents?'

Mother takes a letter with some stamps on it out of her bag. The man examines it. Then he goes to show it to someone else. When he comes back, he has a serious look on his face.

'I'm sorry, but there's nothing we can do for you here.'

'But it's clear that we're exempted, isn't it?' says Mother angrily.

'All I can do is make a note on your card,' he says wearily.

'What good is that to me?' Mother has had enough now. 'Is there someone here I can talk to about this?'

The man leans forward to Mother.

'I'm sorry. It's just us here. We're a long way from Amsterdam. We're going to do everything we can to help you. For now you'll have to stay here.'

'Then write it on the card at least,' says Mother, despairing.

As soon as they leave the desk, they are herded into another room, where there are only women and children.

'All the women with children under four to the left. Women with children from four to sixteen to the right,' yells a female German guard.

'Are they splitting us up?'

Everyone hesitates, so the *Aufseherinnen* shout even louder. Now the group starts to move.

Alie stands with the children and watches as her mother is led outside with the other women.

'Girls aged thirteen to sixteen, come with me!' a guard yells.

Alie is thirteen, so she has to follow her. They head outside, where it is light now, and Alie sees the camp in daylight for the first time: wherever she looks there are barracks. The site is enclosed with barbed wire. They walk along a path beside the barbed wire. On the other side is a narrow ditch, and next to that ditch there are tall guard posts every few metres containing soldiers with machine guns.

This is a prison. Alie shudders.

The *Aufseherinnen* scream at them to keep walking. Alie goes as quickly as she can.

They walk past the barracks. Women are sitting out in the sunshine. She recognises a few women from her neighbourhood back home.

'Hey, Alie. Fancy seeing you here! Is your mother here too?' asks a woman.

Alie nods, but she does not dare to reply, afraid that the guards will start yelling at her.

They come to a building with a sign saying BARRACKS NUMBER 33A, and they are herded into the entrance hall. Alie peers into the laundry room. The girls in there look out curiously at the newcomers.

They are taken into a room on the right with long tables. In the corner is a cooking stove with a kettle on it. They have to pass through the dining room to the dormitory: rows of bunk beds, one after the other. Each row is actually one long bunk bed. The beds have three bunks.

All the girls who are there look up, but no one says anything.

The German guard starts yelling at them to find a bed and to hand over the rest of their belongings. They are allowed to keep only a few clothes and a couple of personal items. Alie finds an empty bottom bunk and sits down. She puts her things on the bed and looks around: the room is a mess. There are bags and other belongings lying all around. Washing is drying on many of the beds. The sun coming through the windows lights up the dust swirling out of the straw mattresses.

'What's your name?' asks a girl peering down over the edge of the bed. Alie looks up. She tries to stand, but bangs her head on the bunk above.

The girl smiles. 'Sorry, I should have warned you. It happens to me about ten times a day.'

Alie rubs her head. 'Ow! I'm Alie,' she says.

'Chellie,' the girl replies. 'Did you come from the Schouwburg?'

Alie nods.

'Then you must be tired,' says the girl, climbing down from her bunk.

'Do you know where the mothers are?' asks Alie.

'It depends. There are so many barracks. But we can go and look.'

Alie wants to set off right away.

'I'd hide your things under the blankets first. There's quite a lot of stealing,' says the girl. 'And not just by the *Aufseherinnen*.'

Alie looks around and sees some girls lying on their beds.

No one is interested in Alie. They are all focused on themselves.

'Where do I get blankets?' asks Alie.

The girl looks at her in surprise. She points at the sack on the bed. 'That's your blanket, you dope.'

Alie picks up the straw-filled sack, which is supposed to be a blanket. 'I'm supposed to sleep under that?' She looks at Chellie in disbelief.

'I'd keep an eye on it, because sometimes even your blanket gets pinched,' says Chellie wisely.

Alie quickly lifts up the sack and stashes the few belongings she has left.

Chellie takes Alie outside. The sun is shining and everything is very green.

They walk past two more barracks and come to some barbed wire. Alie can see women and younger children on the other side.

She tries to go closer to the barbed wire. Suddenly she hears someone yelling. An *Aufseherin* comes running up to her and screams in her face that she is not permitted to approach the barbed wire. Alie shrinks away and closes her eyes.

'The next time you will be punished,' the guard screams.

Alie recoils.

As Chellie pulls her back to their building, Alie starts crying.

Back in the barracks, Chellie gives her something to drink.

'You'll have to wait until Sunday. We're always allowed to see our parents then.'

Alie goes on sobbing.

'Is your father here too?'

Alie shakes her head. 'My father's dead. It's just me and my mother.'

'You can see your mother on Sunday. That's tomorrow,' she says to comfort Alie.

It does make Alie feel a bit better. She lies on her bed and listens to the other girls. Some of them are chattering away about anything and everything. One girl tells a joke. Another girl quietly hums a tune. Alie closes her eyes. She is exhausted.

'Get up! *Schnell! Los!*'

Alie is immediately wide awake. She remembers where she is: Vught.

The girls leap out of bed and pull on their clothes. Alie does not know what is expected of her. Slowly, she sits up. Immediately one of the *Aufseherinnen* knocks her out of bed with a stick.

'Ow!' she cries out.

'Shut up,' shouts the *Aufseherin*.

Alie quickly follows the example of the other girls. She gets dressed. They marched in lines out of the barracks.

It is still not quite light.

Alie looks around: women are running out of the barracks from every direction.

She wonders where they are going this early in the morning. Or is it still night?

They come to a wide open space, where they have to stand in rows of five.

There are rows of women standing on the other side of the yard. It is cold. She feels a chilly morning breeze around her legs. Everyone is standing perfectly still. The only movement is from the clouds of breath coming from the mouths and noses of the women and children.

In the distance, on the other side of the barbed wire, she can also see men in striped suits marching in lines. Some are being hit and kicked. Shocked, Alie looks away.

She desperately peers around for her mother, tears welling up in her eyes.

Then she sees someone who looks like Mother. Alie's stomach lurches. But when the woman turns around, Alie sees that it is someone else.

'What are we doing here?' Alie quietly asks a girl beside her.

The girl does not answer at once, but waits until the *Aufseherin* reaches the end of the line.

'Roll call,' says the girl quickly. 'They're counting us.'

'Counting us? What for?'

The *Aufseherin* walks along the rows and makes sure everyone is standing straight. It takes an awfully long time.

Then she starts counting. She counts extremely slowly. When she gets halfway, she curses. She walks back to the beginning and starts counting again.

Alie's legs are getting tired and she needs to pee.

The sun rises and she sees green trees in the distance. Birds are singing. It is a beautiful spring day.

She looks at the lines of women on the other side of the yard. Someone gives a tentative wave. A woman with a pale face is trying to attract her attention. She takes a closer look. An older woman. The woman is pointing at herself. It's me, she mouths.

Then Alie realises that it is her mother. She wants to shout out loud, but restrains herself. She looks around to see if anyone is watching and then quickly waves back.

Mother smiles at Alie and blows her a kiss.

Alie pretends to catch the kiss and blows one back.

They stand staring at each other, trying to look into each other's eyes. Alie blinks back her tears, because she wants to see Mother clearly.

The *Aufseherinnen* keep losing count, as if they are doing it on purpose. They laugh and start over again.

Alie is getting more and more tired. She is finding it hard to stand still. She lifts her knees a bit, as if she is walking.

Suddenly someone gives her a hard shove and she falls onto the ground. She lies there, bewildered. She does not know what she has done wrong, and she looks for her mother. She sees another woman holding Mother back.

'If I see you moving again, I'll set the dogs on you!' one of the *Aufseherinnen* snarls at her. 'Get up.'

Alie's eyes flood with tears as she makes eye contact with her mother.

She stands perfectly still throughout the rest of the roll call, hardly daring to breathe. An armed SS man with a big dog is standing by the guard post. Alie shivers.

Alie is lying on her bed, exhausted from the roll call. She is hungry, but they have not yet been given any food. She searches through the straw inside her pillow and finds a piece of bread that she saved from yesterday. Then she hears yet more shouting.

She does not want to, but she forces herself to get up when she sees the other girls leap to their feet and stand in line.

One of the *Aufseherinnen* has a list in her hands and she reads out names: Ancona, Esther. Van Baren, Betsie. Cohen, Jenny.

'Cohen, Jenny?' Alie repeats the name to herself.

Jenny? Is Jenny here? She looks around, but does not see her. All the girls are still standing by their beds.

'Why were their names called out?' Alie asks the girl beside her. But the girl does not reply.

A few more girls' names are called.

'Off you go! Now!' The girls whose names were called run to the dining room.

The *Aufseherinnen* look at the list and count the names.

'Two more needed for cleaning. Any volunteers?' No one raises their hand.

Without thinking about it, Alie puts her hand up. She knows how to clean, and maybe she will get to see Jenny. She is sent to join the girls in the dining room, where the girls who were selected are given buckets of soapy water, brushes and mops.

'Scrub the floor! And make it quick!'

The girls kneel down and start scrubbing the floor. They are each in a different area of the room. Alie regrets volunteering now. She looks for Jenny, but does not see her. When the *Aufseherin* leaves the room, she stands up and looks around at the other girls in the room.

'Jenny?' she calls quietly.

'Scrub the floor, dimwit. If they catch you, we're all for it,' hisses one of the girls.

Alie drops to her knees again. One of the girls scrubs her way over to Alie. 'Are you looking for Jenny?' she asks.

'Jenny Cohen. She is here, isn't she?' Alie asks, to make sure.

'Yes, Jenny Cohen, over there, by the door.' The girl quickly returns to her scrubbing.

Alie looks over at the door and sees Jenny from behind.

She feels a happy tingle in her stomach. Jenny, finally! She does the same as the other girl and scrubs her way over to the door.

'Jenny,' she whispers with a grin. 'It's me.' Then Jenny turns around, and the smile disappears from Alie's face. An older girl with glasses is looking back at her.

Alie gasps. 'You're not Jenny,' she says.

'Yes, I am,' the girl replies.

'Jenny Cohen?' asks Alie.

'Yes, Jenny Cohen,' the girl says.

'You're not my Jenny,' Alie says bluntly, and she sits down on the floor.

'Sorry for disappointing you,' says Jenny. She goes on scrubbing. As she is cleaning by the entrance, the two *Aufseherinnen* come in.

They have a thick layer of mud on their shoes and walk straight across the scrubbed floor.

Jenny looks up angrily. The *Aufseherin* sees her, and she starts yelling.

'Do you call this cleaning?' She kicks over the bucket of dirty water.

It goes all over Jenny. The other *Aufseherin* laughs. Together, they walk through the room with their muddy shoes. The cleaning girls glare at them.

'Come on. I'll help you,' says Alie, taking pity on Jenny. She grabs a mop and soaks up all the water. They clean their parts of the floor again. As soon as they have finished, they go to the dormitory. Jenny puts on dry clothes, and Alie helps her hang out her wet things.

'I didn't mean to be unkind,' says Alie.

'It doesn't matter,' says Jenny. 'You thought you were going to see your friend. I'd have been disappointed too.'

Jenny reaches under her mattress and pulls out a bag.

'Want some?' she says, taking out of piece of cake. Alie can't believe her eyes. This is not just some dry biscuit. It's a slice of butter cake!

'Is it real?' says Alie, snatching it from her hand. Jenny laughs.

'How on earth did you get that?' asks Alie, breathing in the scent of the delicious cake.

'I come from the countryside. You can still get all kinds of things there.' The two girls share the cake.

'So this Jenny's your friend, is she?' Jenny asks, when all the cake is gone.

'My best friend,' says Alie.

'I've got a best friend too. Her name's Rie,' says Jenny. 'She's the one who sends me all the good food. I get a parcel from her every week.'

'So she hasn't been taken away?' Alie asks in surprise.

'She's not Jewish,' says Jenny. 'I don't have any Jewish friends. There aren't even any other Jews in my village. She's keeping all my things for when I get back.'

'My Jenny's actually called Jaantje. I don't know where she is now.'

'Shall we go outside?' asks Jenny. 'My sister might be there. She's in the building behind ours.'

It is nice and warm outside. They sit on the grass beside the barracks.

It smells of outside.

If it were not for the barbed wire, this would feel like being on holiday. Roosje would love it here.

'Do you think we'll ever get to go home?' says Alie, feeling homesick.

'I think so. Why wouldn't we?' says Jenny.

'My mother and I were picked up and taken to the police station first. That was bad. Then we had to go to the Schouwburg, and that was even worse. Then we came here. And this is the worst place I've ever seen,' says Alie.

'I came here straight from home. The worst thing is not being with my family,' says Jenny with a sigh. 'Do you have any brothers and sisters?'

'My sister is nine years older than me. She's still in Amsterdam. My father died not long ago. In Germany.' Alie feels a lump in her throat. 'I'm alone here with my mother, and I'm not allowed to see her either.'

'You've got me now too,' says Jenny, putting her arm around Alie.

'Two Jennys as friends. Not bad.' Alie smiles.

A bell rings and everyone from their building runs inside.

'Why are they hurrying for that awful soup and bread?' says Jenny.

'You're lucky with your butter cake,' Alie says with a smile. She links arms with Jenny. They walk inside together, where the stench of cabbage soup comes wafting towards them.

Alie looks at a group of women stepping through a gate in the barbed-wire fence. She cranes her neck to see them better. Then she spots her mother.

'Mum!' she calls, but not too loud. She doesn't dare.

Alie runs towards the barbed wire. The guards do not react. Mother runs to meet her. They throw their arms around each other and hug. Mother showers her face with kisses. Both of them are crying.

'Oh, my sweetheart, my little love.' She holds Alie at arm's length and looks at her with a worried face. 'You *are* eating that stinky soup, aren't you?' Alie nods unconvincingly.

'Make sure you eat that rubbish. You have to stay strong.'

They go together back into Alie's barracks.

Mother looks at the chaos. There are clothes all over the place and thick layers of dust.

'Where do you sleep?' asks Mother.

Alie takes her to her bed.

'Make sure not to get your head too close to the other girls. I don't want you to catch lice. And don't share a bed with anyone either, alright? Or you'll get fleas.' Alie nods.

Mother looks at the bed and picks up the blanket. Then she tosses it back down. 'Come on, let's go outside.'

Alie and Mother sit on the grass. Mother takes a couple of slices of bread and jam out of her bag.

'Where did you get those?' Alie exclaims, eagerly taking the bread.

'Swapped something,' says Mother.

Alie sees that she is not eating anything herself. 'Don't you want some?'

'I've already eaten,' says Mother, but Alie can tell Mother was saving it for her. She holds the bread up to her mother's nose.

'Mmm, smell that. It's so good,' she says, trying to tempt her.

Mother smells the bread and jam, but quickly pushes it away.

'Go on. Have a bite.' Alie holds the bread up to her mother's face again. 'Tasty, huh?' she teases. Mother laughs and takes a bite.

Alie gives her the rest of the bread.

'You have it. I've already had some butter cake.'

Mother gives her a sceptical look.

'Honestly. Jenny gave it to me. Jenny Cohen,' Alie says with a smile.

'Are you pulling my leg?' Mother looks concerned. 'Sweetheart, Jenny isn't here.'

'Yes, she is. She's in the same building as me,' Alie says with a smile.

Mother puts her hand on Alie's forehead.

Alie bursts out laughing. 'I haven't gone mad, Mum. It's another Jenny. I was just as surprised as you. A different Jenny Cohen. She's really nice, and she comes from a village. They still have lots of good food there.'

'You're so good at making new friends,' says Mother proudly.

There is more shouting. Visiting time is over. Alie and Mother stand up. Alie walks back to the barbed wire with Mother.

'I want to go with you, Mum.' Alie has an uneasy feeling in her tummy. She is trying to be brave, but can't stop her tears. Mother wipes them from her cheeks.

'We'll see each other tomorrow at roll call,' she says.

'What good is that? All I can do is look at you.'

'Chin up, sweetheart,' says Mother, giving Alie a big hug. Then she goes back through the barbed-wire gate. Alie watches as she walks away.

Alie is sitting sadly on the bed in the barracks.

'Did you have fun with your mother?' asks Jenny, walking up to her.

Alie nods. Jenny sits down beside her.

'How about you?' asks Alie.

'I saw my mother, father, brother and sister,' says Jenny.

'You've got a brother too?' asks Alie.

'He's younger than me. He's with my father in the men's camp.' Jenny's eyes fill with tears. Alie can't take it and starts to feel teary too.

Jenny puts her arm around her. Then they hear another girl crying. They look up: a girl is lying on the bunk above, hugging her knees.

'Are you alright?' asks Alie.

The girl looks embarrassed to have been caught crying.

'Mind your own business,' she says, in a broad Amsterdam accent.

'Are you from Amsterdam?' asks Alie.

'What's it to you?' the girl says angrily, turning away. She is still crying, but a little more quietly now.

Alie stands up and tears off a bit of the slice of bread and jam that she has been saving and holds it out in front of the girl's face.

The girl sits up, snatches the bread and stuffs it into her mouth in one go. Then she lies back down and says nothing.

'Thanks to you too,' says Jenny.

Alie sits back down beside Jenny.

'My mother's really sick. She's probably going to die,' the girl blurts out. 'And I'm not allowed to go and see her.'

Alie and Jenny look at each other – how awful.

'What's wrong with her?' Alie asks.

'How should I know?' the girls snaps. 'What difference does it make?'

Alie and Jenny do not know what to say.

The girl sits up and climbs out of bed. 'It was really nice, that jam. How did you get it?' she asks.

'My mother saved it for me,' says Alie.

'You've still got your mother. Good for you,' the girl says, almost reproachfully. She sits down on the bed beside Alie and Jenny. Alie feels sorry for her.

Suddenly there is the sound of singing from one of the beds. A couple of girls are singing a beautiful two-part harmony. Alie listens breathlessly. She lies down to enjoy their voices. Jenny and the other girl come and lie beside her on the narrow bed. Exhausted, Alie shuts her eyes.

Alie sits up with a start and bangs her head on the bed above again.

'Ow! Stupid bed!'

Jenny is asleep beside her. Alie looks around: all the girls are jumping out of bed. Roll call. She shakes Jenny awake.

'Get up. It's that time again.' Jenny slowly sits up.

Alie feels under her mattress for the last bit of bread and jam, which she has hidden there. She does not want to go to roll call without breakfast. She looks, but she can't find it.

'What are you doing?' asks Jenny.

'My bread . . . ,' says Alie and she suddenly realises what has happened.

'That cow,' says Alie. 'She pinched my bread.'

She does not have much time to dwell on it though, because the

Aufseherinnen come in again and start screaming. The girls have to hurry outside.

Alie's stomach rumbles during the roll call. She thinks about what she will do when she sees the girl again. She wants to give her a good shaking. She looks around surreptitiously, but does not dare to move too much.

Then she spots her mother, who waves at her. Alie gives her a little wave back.

As soon as the roll call is over, Alie goes back to the barracks. She stops at the entrance and looks around, but can't see any sign of the girl. So she goes back to the bed where the girl was. Someone else is there now.

'Where's the girl who was here before?' she asks.

'The one with the short hair? They took her out of her bed this morning. She had to go to see her mother, because she was about to die. But this is my bed now.'

MAY

Alie is lying on her bunk. Bored, she counts the pieces of straw poking out of her blanket. Now and then she feels a tickle on her scalp and gives it a scratch.

A girl walks up to her bed. 'Hey, Alie, someone's here to see you,' she says. 'She's outside. Come on.'

Alie jumps up without banging her head and follows the girl.

'Alie!' a woman calls from behind the barracks.

The woman is standing in the shadow and Alie cannot see who it is. When she gets closer, she can't believe her eyes.

'Alie, come here, quickly.' She pulls her closer. It's Gretha.

Alie is completely overwhelmed. 'What are you doing here? Did they catch you after all?'

'Aren't you going to give me a hug first?' Gretha laughs.

Alie squeezes Gretha tight. 'Have you seen Mother yet?' she asks.

'Yes, but she wasn't very happy to see me,' says Gretha. 'She's angry with me.'

'Why?'

'Because I went to the police station and turned myself in,' says Gretha.

'Why did you do that?' Alie asks in disbelief.

Gretha is silent.

'No wonder she's angry. She said you were going to make it,' says Alie.

'What's the point of making it if I'm not with you?' says Gretha, giving Alie another hug.

'We're not allowed to be together here,' Alie says sadly.

'We'll come up with something. I'm with Mother and I'll make sure I can spend some time with you too,' says Gretha. 'I have to go back. The barracks leader only gave me fifteen minutes.'

She walks to the barbed wire. Alie watches her go. Gretha slips quickly through the open gate. They both walk together on opposite sides of the barbed wire until they cannot walk any further.

'I'll look out for you during the roll call,' says Alie. It does feel wonderful to have Gretha back.

Gretha blows her a quick kiss and heads back to her barracks.

The girls are sitting at the long dining tables. Alie is chewing on a lump of cabbage soup. It crunches between her teeth. Sand and wet cabbage. She feels sick. How is that supposed to keep you strong?

Her head is also itching like mad. She keeps scratching. Another girl is scratching too.

'Hey! What are you doing?' An *Aufseherin* throws something at Alie's head. 'Were you scratching your head?' she snarls at Alie.

'No, no,' Alie replies innocently.

The *Aufseherin* hits her on the head. 'You're lying! I saw you with my own eyes.' She pulls Alie's hair and peers at her scalp. Even though she is rough, Alie does not flinch. Then the *Aufseherin* pulls the other girl's hair.

'*Verdammt nochmal!*' she says, storming out of the dining room.

The girls look at each other.

'You've got lice,' says one of the barracks leaders.

'Lice? Ugh!' Alie feels even itchier and starts scratching like crazy. All the other girls are scratching now too and chattering away.

There is more shouting. The *Aufseherinnen* have returned. Everyone has to stand up.

'Get undressed! Clothes in a pile. Take a blanket at the door and go outside!' they scream. The girls hesitate – until the *Aufseherinnen* start hitting them. '*Los! Schnell!*'

The girls run to the dormitory and quickly get undressed and head outside. The doors of the barracks are closed. A girl who is still in her underpants is forcibly stopped: everything has to come off.

One by one, they get sprayed all over with a Flit gun. The stuff that comes out of it stinks and catches in their throats.

The girls are made to stand outside in the nude with only a blanket to wrap around themselves. Then it starts raining. They try to take shelter under the lean-to beside the barracks. But there are too many girls and not enough room.

Alie looks up into the dark sky. Can it get any worse than this?

Two hours later, the girls are allowed back inside.

All their clothes are still piled up. Alie looks for hers, but she can't find them. She quickly grabs a dress and some underwear from the pile. They are not hers, but they fit.

The mattresses have been ransacked. Alie hurries to her bunk. Luckily, her coat is still there. She puts it on over the strange clothes. She is freezing from standing outside all that time. She lies on the bed and closes her eyes. Everything stinks.

She tries to think about Roosje.

Alie wakes up in the darkness, feeling rumpled and uncomfortable. All around her, she hears coughing and sneezing.

A girl is walking around the dormitory, bumping into things. Alie hears another girl go over to her and then call for help.

A little later, the barracks leaders come in with a mechanical flashlight. Alie can see by its light that the girl is walking around in her underwear and with bare feet.

Alie hears the leaders talking anxiously. They help the girl back to her bed.

'I want to go home!' the girl screams. 'I'm too hot! It's nice and cool at home.'

Alie does not want to listen to her suffering, so she puts her fingers in her ears. She hums a tune, thinks about Gretha and Mother and does not fall back to sleep for a long time.

When Alie wakes up again, it is still not quite light.

She sees some women crying and carrying a girl to the dining room. The girl she saw last night. Alie sits up in bed.

'What happened?' she asks Jenny, who has come to climb into Alie's bunk.

'She's dead,' says Jenny sadly.

Alie lies back down, and the two girls lie together in silence.

She wants to go home – now!

'How could you be so stupid?' Mother is furious.

They are sitting in the dining room. It is raining outside.

'I'm sorry that I missed you and that I wanted to be with you,' says Gretha stubbornly. 'How was I supposed to know it was so awful here?'

'What did you think? That it was some kind of holiday resort?' says Mother.

'Could you two stop it now?' Alie has had enough.

'She could have sent us food packages. Now we don't have anything,' Mother says angrily.

'Why don't we ask Luise? She wants to help us,' says Gretha.

'Have you spoken to Luise?' asks Alie. 'Have you seen Roosje?'

'Roos is doing fine. She's being spoiled,' says Gretha.

Alie feels so homesick that her stomach hurts.

'We need to see if we can do something about our Portuguese descent,' says Gretha. 'It's our only chance of getting out of here.'

'I put in a request, but I haven't heard anything yet,' says Mother, disappointed. She looks tired.

'Then I'll chase it up,' says Gretha.

'But what if we don't get out of here? What then?' Alie asks suddenly.

Mother and Gretha look at each other as if that thought has never occurred to them.

'Don't worry about that now,' begins Mother.

'Stop it, Mum!' Alie explodes. 'I already know too much.'

'She's right, Mum. She's seen enough,' says Gretha.

Mother puts her arm around Alie. 'I know. You've seen far too much in your young life.'

'We have to stick together,' says Gretha.

'We've already been separated,' says Alie.

'Then let's make sure we get sent to the next place together, if that's what happens. None of us leave on our own. Deal?' says Gretha firmly.

'Deal,' says Alie.

Mother does not say anything. She pulls Gretha closer too.

A huge bang outside rattles the windows and shakes the ground.

Alie jerks upright, banging her head on the bunk above.

'Aargh!' Cursing, she rubs her head. Girls are jostling one another out of the way to get a spot by the window. Alie sees a red glow. She goes to the window and tries to look outside, but she is pushed out of the way by dozens of other girls who are trying to do the same.

'Fire!' Alie pushes back and finds herself by the window: the glow is lighting up the night.

'What is it?'

'Bombs!' shouts a girl. 'They've come to free us.'

'Who?' asks another girl.

'Britain, of course.'

If the British are here, she can go home. Just the thought of it makes her feel warm.

'Everyone away from the window!' comes a voice from the dining room. The barracks leaders try to get the girls away from the window.

'But the British are here!' Everyone is talking at once. A few of the girls are frightened and hide in bed under their blankets.

'We're going to die. The bombs are going to fall on us!'

'I want to go to my mother,' a girl sobs.

Alie wants to be with her mother too.

'Everyone stay inside. Put on something warm and lie in your bunks. Wait for instructions.'

They hear screams from the women's barracks.

Alie wants to take another look to see what is happening, but she does not dare.

Then there is another huge explosion. Everyone shrieks. They run to the window. An enormous fireball is rising into the air. Big flames. The girls hold their breath. It actually looks quite pretty.

'Get away from that window at once! It's far too dangerous.'

The leaders pull the girls away now.

'Have they come to free us?' asks a girl.

'Not that one in any case. It's a crashed plane,' says the leader, disappointed. 'But it could still be dangerous, so stay away from the window.'

Alie goes back to bed.

Jenny comes over to her.

'Poor pilots. They didn't make it.'

'Do you think we'll ever be freed?' asks Alie.

'I don't know. Maybe they're starting in the east and the Netherlands will be last,' says Jenny.

'That's alright, as long as they come.'

JUNE

To all camp residents.

Much to our regret, we must inform you of a terrible misfortune that has befallen us.

We have been informed that authorities at a high level have decreed that all children from the age of 0 up to 16 years old must leave the camp in order to be accommodated in a special children's camp.

The barracks leader puts down the notice. 'That means you're all leaving.'

Alie sits on the bed, frozen. Leaving? But where to? She's not going anywhere without Mother and Gretha.

All the children start to panic. Girls are crying. Some are screaming for their mothers.

Alie struggles to reach the barracks leaders, who are unable to deal with the torrent of questions.

'When are we going to see our mothers?' she shouts over the heads of the other girls. But no one hears her.

Then the *Aufseherinnen* enter the building. 'To bed! Lights out! *Schnell!*'

The girls fly in all directions, tripping over one another. Alie leaps into bed.

The shouting goes on for a while. Some girls are slapped and hit for not getting into bed quickly enough or for talking.

Finally, the girls are silent. Now and then someone looks to see if the *Aufseherinnen* have gone, but they are still on guard.

The footsteps of the *Aufseherinnen* echo around the room, but eventually they go outside. When the girls are sure they have left, they dare to talk quietly.

Jenny quickly climbs into bed with Alie.

'Can you sleep?' she asks.

'No,' Alie replies.

'Do you really think we'll be leaving with our mothers?' she asks nervously.

'We'll have to. There are little ones too – they won't cope without their mothers, will they?' says Alie.

'We have to go tomorrow or the next day,' says a girl, hanging over the side of her bed.

'Where are we going?' asks the girl in the bottom bunk next to Alie's.

Alie snuggles up close to Jenny.

'I don't want to leave without my family,' Jenny says sadly.

'I don't want to go without my mother and my sister either,' says Alie.

'Maybe we can sit together on the train,' Jenny says to Alie.

'That would be nice,' says Alie. Wherever it is that they have to go.

The roll-call yard is filled with women and children. The men are on the other side. There are lots of SS guards with big dogs standing around the outside, keeping a threatening watch on everyone.

It rained all the previous day, and the ground is muddy and cold. A guard calls out the names of all the people who have to leave. It takes a very long time.

'Lopes Dias-van Beezem, Esther! Lopes Dias, Alida!'

Alie's stomach ache is getting worse and worse. She has to go – today. She desperately searches for Mother and Gretha among the rows of women.

She does not see Mother, but finds herself looking straight into Gretha's eyes.

Gretha's name has not been called.

Alie can see the panic on Gretha's face. She feels so frustrated that there is nothing she can do or say. She feels queasy and tries not to be sick. The sour cabbage soup comes back up. She holds it in.

Calling the names takes forever. Everyone is freezing.

When they are finally allowed to leave, Alie goes back to her barracks.

Looking really anxious, Mother and Gretha come to find her.

'We have to go to the admin office right now and apply for exemption,' says Gretha.

'For what reason?' asks Alie.

'You heard them, didn't you? Anyone who has an ongoing inquiry into their descent doesn't have to go,' says Gretha, pulling Mother and Alie along with her.

They hurry to the office. There is already a long line of people, all trying to get exemptions. When it is finally their turn, the man looks at their registration cards.

'Indeed. This isn't right. You shouldn't be on the list,' he says.

Alie looks at her mother with relief.

'So are you going to get us taken off?' asks Gretha.

'I'm going to do whatever I can, miss,' says the man, and he walks over to the SS officer who is in charge.

Alie, Mother and Gretha wait anxiously to see if they will be allowed to stay. The man comes back.

'You'll have to wait. He needs to consult someone,' says the man.

'How long is that going to take?' asks Gretha.

'I'd go and start packing. Just in case,' says the man, sitting back down at his desk. More people immediately crowd around.

Alie, Mother and Gretha walk to Alie's barracks.

It is busy in there. Some of the girls have to leave today, and their mothers are helping them to pack.

'So should we pack or not?' asks Alie.

'I'd do it. In case you do have to go,' says Gretha.

'But we were going to stick together, weren't we?' says Alie anxiously.

'I'm going to pack my bag too. If you two have to go, I'm going with you,' says Gretha. She gives Alie a peck on the cheek and returns to her own barracks.

Mother stays with Alie.

'What should I take?' asks Alie. 'Where are we going?'

'We're going to Westerbork first, and then they're taking all the children to a special camp. God only knows where that is,' says Mother.

Alie takes all her things from under her mattress: a book, a few pairs of underpants, two vests, some of socks, a piece of old bread, a biscuit and her good dress.

'Is that all?' Mother exclaims. 'Where are your smart shoes and your other coat?'

'Stolen, when we came here,' says Alie.

'What a bunch of bastards, the lot of them!' says Mother, who can no longer restrain herself. 'Where's your red coat?'

Alie fetches her coat, which was hung up to dry, and feels the sleeves.

'It's still a bit damp from yesterday.'

'Keep a close eye on it, or you'll have to leave in just your dress,' says Mother, who is in a really foul mood. She pushes the mattress aside and sits down on Alie's bed.

'What a stinking hole,' she says angrily. 'Maybe it's just as well we're leaving.'

'Do you really think we'll have to go?' asks Alie.

But before Mother can reply, the *Aufseherinnen* come in and shout that everyone has to return to their own barracks. The mothers mutter and curse. A few girls cry.

Mother quickly gives Alie a kiss.

'No matter what happens, we're sticking together,' says Mother, as she leaves with the other women.

Alie piles up all her belongings and puts them into the white backpack that she brought with her to the camp. It is much emptier now.

'So you have to go after all?' says Jenny.

Alie shrugs. 'Maybe. We don't know yet.'

'My whole family has to go,' says Jenny. 'Hey, where do you live?'

Alie gives her a puzzled look.

'Then maybe we can visit each other one day,' says Jenny optimistically.

Alie has tears in her eyes when she thinks about home. She puts her arms around Jenny. 'I'd really like that. You can meet the other Jenny.'

They give each other a big hug.

'Govert Flinckstraat 265, first floor. Just behind the Albert Cuyp market. Will you remember that?'

'Forever,' says Jenny.

The barracks leaders come in. They list the names of the girls who have to go. 'Lopes Dias, Alida.'

Alie looks sadly at Jenny, who puts an arm around her and walks with her to the exit.

Outside, women and children are heading to the roll-call yard.

Mother is waiting for her. They are allowed to stand together. There is no sign of Gretha.

'Where's Gretha?' asks Alie.

'She's gone to the administration office. To ask if she can come too,' says Mother, who looks very pale.

Children are crying. It is all women and children here, and the occasional accompanying father. No one is allowed to say goodbye to those who are staying behind.

Then they have to go to the gate, and everyone tries to walk along with them. OD men help women with their luggage. They try to keep everyone calm. The SS men and Aufseherinnen stand and watch with sneering grins on their faces.

At the narrow gate, everyone starts pushing and shoving. Those who do not have to leave try to say goodbye, but are stopped by the SS men.

Alie is almost through the gate when she hears a shout. 'Alie! Mother!'

Alie looks back: Gretha! Her sister runs straight through the line of SS men.

The SS men shout at her to get back. A few other people seize their chance and run through as well.

'Alie!' screams Gretha, still running. An SS officer releases his dog. It chases after Gretha and the others.

'Greet! Look out! The dog!' Alie is terrified that it will catch her sister.

But Gretha keeps running. The dog is distracted by other people running and screaming.

'Alie! I'm not allowed to come,' Gretha sobs. 'I have to stay here!'

Alie and Mother are speechless.

'Try to stay in Westerbork. I'll keep working here to get your exemption. I'll come as soon as I can.' Gretha is out of breath.

Mother hugs Gretha. 'You're going to make it. Stay strong, sweetheart.' Mother kisses Gretha.

'Mother's right. I'll make it.' She wipes away a tear and buttons up Alie's coat.

'You are such a sweetheart, the sweetest girl there is,' she says, giving Alie a kiss.

Alie holds on tightly to Gretha. 'I love you, Greet, so, so much. You will come to us, won't you?' asks Alie.

'I promise,' says Gretha.

Alie and Mother are hurried along by the SS men. They have to go through the gate.

Alie looks back, but she can no longer see Gretha in the crowd. She holds tightly onto her mother.

At the station, the trains are waiting. It is just as busy as it was at the camp. Mothers with crying children, lost children, sick children. Each wagon has a sign indicating the disease carried by its occupants.

Alie's and Mother's names are called. They have to rush to their carriage, squeezed together by the crush of the crowd. When they get there, Alie sees that their carriage is not for humans, but for cattle.

She has no time to dwell on that before she is pushed inside.

Alie and Mother look for somewhere to sit, but there are so many mothers with younger children that they let them go ahead. Eventually they manage to find a spot on the floor. They are packed in so tightly that they can barely move.

'This is no way to treat human beings!' a woman screams. 'What do they think we are? Animals?'

The door is closed, but it is some time before the train leaves.

Alie looks up and tries to breathe.

Finally the train starts moving.

After a long journey, they arrive at Westerbork.

'Wake up, sweetheart. We're here.'

Alie peers through a crack and sees that it is still dark outside.

They stand up. The younger children start crying as soon as they wake up.

The door opens and Alie sees the shocked faces of the Jewish OD men from Westerbork.

There are no screaming SS men or *Aufseherinnen* here. The women with children are looked after well. Many of the women complain about the terrible treatment they received in Vught.

Alie is tired and cannot listen to it any longer. They are sent to a building to be registered – again. They join the queue.

People bring them food and drink. Alie accepts it gratefully. In the train, the stench and the stuffy atmosphere made it impossible to eat anything. She sits on the floor, with her backpack as a seat. It takes hours.

When it is finally their turn, Mother launches into her complaint: 'We have documents showing our Portuguese descent. It is an outrage that we were sent here. In Vught they said you'd be able to do something about it.'

The man behind the desk looks at her papers. He sighs. 'I can't do anything here other than make a note. I'll see if anything else can be done for you. For now you'll have to join the women you came from Vught with,' says the man, writing everything down neatly on a registration card.

'Are we allowed to stay together?' Alie asks in surprise.

They are taken to a barracks building. On the way there, Alie sees some people from their neighbourhood. It is good to see familiar faces. She looks for Jenny, her Jenny, but does not see her.

The big barracks is full, but they are not allowed to go outside. Here, too, there are rows of beds, three bunks high. Alie takes a bunk in the middle. She is tired and lies down. Mother comes and sits beside her.

'Will you sleep in my bed tonight?' asks Alie.

Mother strokes her hair. 'Of course.' She gives Alie a kiss on her forehead. 'I'll go and see if we can move to a different building. This one is packed.'

But she soon returns.

'We have to stay inside. Quarantine,' she say angrily.

Alie wakes up to the sound of shouting and crying. She sits up in bed. Mother is awake too.

'What's going on?' asks Alie.

'They're moving us on.' Mother looks very pale and is talking quietly.

'Moving us on? What do you mean?' Alie asks, confused.

'To Germany.'

Alie's stomach gives a huge lurch, as if someone has thumped her hard. For a moment, she can't speak.

Mother takes Alie's hand. They sit in silence.

'What about Gretha?' Alie asks, with a catch in her voice.

Mother does not reply. She shakes her head and her eyes fill with tears.

Alie stares at the window.

'What day is it today?' she asks.

'I don't know,' Mother says, uninterested. 'Do you really need to know that?'

'What's the date?' Alie insists.

'I think it's 7 June,' says Mother.

Alie thinks for a moment.

'In three months and twelve days, I'll be fourteen.'

Alie lies next to Mother in the narrow bunk. There is noise all around them: women packing, babies crying. She can also hear the snoring of those women who are actually able to sleep. She listens to her mother's regular breathing.

'Are you asleep?' she asks quietly.

'No,' says Mother. 'Who could sleep now?'

Alie moves closer to Mother, who puts her arm around her.

'I shouldn't really be lying here. I still have so much to do.'

'But what can we do now?' asks Alie.

'I have to write and tell Greet that we're being moved on. That she mustn't try to follow us. Have you got anything other than your red coat? We're only allowed to take one blanket. I don't know if that'll be warm enough for the night.'

Alie hears her mother talking, but her words do not really get through to her.

Last month she was still at school. She had a test. What was it about again? Alie can't even remember.

'Do you think we'll see everyone there again?' asks Alie. 'In Germany?'

'I don't know,' she says. 'I really don't know.'

'Can't we try to stay here? There must be someone we can ask, mustn't there? Someone who can do something to help?' Alie asks Mother.

Mother gives a deep sigh. 'We can try, sweetheart.' She hugs Alie tight. 'Maybe you should try to get a little more sleep. We need to be ready in a few hours.'

Alie desperately hopes they will be allowed to stay, that they will not be moved on.

It is four in the morning. Alie is awake. She is still lying in the bunk. Mother has brought her a bowl of semolina porridge. She takes a bite. It is warm and sweet. All around her, people are busy. Women are trying to put all the belongings they have left into their backpacks and suitcases. All their food is going with them. Children are walking and running all around. The babies are crying non-stop. It is still dark outside.

Mother talks to one of the women who are helping the people who have to leave. They are allowed to go all over the camp.

'We had a guarantee that we wouldn't have to leave Vught. Then we were told we were allowed to stay here. And now they're sending us on to Germany. Is there really no one at all who can help us? Then what's the point of these papers?' asks Mother.

The woman looks at her documents.

'I'll go and talk to someone about it right away. It might help. But you'll still have to prepare to leave,' she says. 'People do get taken off the train quite often, you know.'

Alie looks hopefully at her mother.

'Eat your porridge, and then let's get ready,' says Mother.

A long procession of mothers and children, sick people and also a few men, makes its way through the camp to the trains.

Long lines of goods carriages. Big, empty cattle trucks.

The shriek of the engine's whistle. The train building up a head of steam for departure. Clouds of smoke above the train.

Soldiers line the way. Alie accidentally looks at one of them. His cold expression scares her and she quickly turns away. Her legs feel as heavy as lead.

Mother walks slower and slower. She keeps looking back over

her shoulder. So does Alie, but all they can see is the line of people behind them. Everyone has to board the train.

They stop at a carriage. This is where they have to get on.

The door is higher than the platform. Mother pulls Alie back. They let the older people get in first, and the women with little children.

It is already quite full. There is only room for a few people to sit down. Mother looks back again to see if someone is coming to tell them they can stay. But no one comes. No one. Alie feels so terribly alone.

'You'll have to get in now,' says one of the OD men.

Alie takes Mother's hand. She looks at her. 'Come on. Let's go, Mum.'

Mother nods. Someone helps them up into the wagon.

Alie stands by the door. A barrel of water is lifted up after them, followed by an empty barrel. Don't think about it. Just don't think about it.

She looks out. The heather is in bloom. Purple flowers as far as she can see. She breathes in the fresh morning air.

The doors are closed. There is only a strip of light at the top, where the wood has been removed. Alie looks up.

The chilling screech of the engine sounds. Steam hisses as wheels start turning. Slowly the train moves along the platform.

'Goodbye, Netherlands.' Alie watches the clouds going by, faster and faster. 'See you again soon.'

Esther Lopes Dias-Van Beezem

18 November 1896
11 June 1943

1945

Gretha Waterman-Lopes Dias

14 April 1920
28 November 2010

When Alie and her mother had to leave Vught as part of the infamous 'Children's Transport' of 6 and 7 June, Gretha was not allowed to go with them and had to remain behind.

Some time later, Gretha was herself sent to Auschwitz. When she arrived there, she was put to work, as she was a young woman. She soon realised that all the old people and children were gassed upon arrival. She did not yet know that Alie and their mother had been sent to another camp, Sobibór. It was the thought of seeing them again that kept Gretha going. She had to stay alive. The work was hard, and there was little food. Women around her died of exhaustion every day.

She was faced with a choice: to keep on working and eventually starve and work herself to death, as so many others had already done – or to participate in a medical experiment. She chose the experiment, as she would be given more food and a bed in the hospital barracks.

The department was led by the infamous Dr Carl Clauberg, who became known for his cruelty. One of the experiments he performed on prisoners involved finding the most efficient way to make them sterile. Gretha and hundreds of other women were injected with formalin directly into their wombs, causing them excruciating pain and haemorrhaging. Of all the Dutch women who were in the block with Gretha and with whom she remained friends after the war, only one was later able to have a child.

As the Russians approached Auschwitz, the prisoners were evacuated and had to take part in 'death marches', walking for days without food in the cold – and sometimes snow – to other camps in Germany. Gretha survived and was liberated by the Americans at the beginning of 1945.

She wanted to return home as quickly as possible – had Alie and their mother made it? Were they on their way home too? Gretha took every available form of transport towards the Netherlands, but still walked much of the way.

When she finally arrived at Govert Flinckstraat, she was weak from exhaustion, dressed in a worn man's coat and with holes in her shoes. Her hair had still not entirely grown back, and she had a headscarf wrapped around her head. She rang the doorbell.

A strange man opened the door. He made it clear to Gretha that he lived there now and that there was nothing he could do for her. He had also taken possession of some of the furniture and house-hold goods. Gretha did not get anything back.

A neighbour took Gretha in. She had been able to save some of the family's belongings, and Gretha found Alie's friendship album among the photographs and papers.

Gretha went to Centraal Station in Amsterdam every day, where there were lists of survivors from the camps. She never found the names of Alie, their mother or Berry. The only person she found was one of Berry's brothers.

In December 1945, Gretha received an official report from the Red Cross that Alie and their mother, together with the entire children's transport, had been deported from Westerbork to Sobibór, an extermination camp in Poland: 3,017 people in total, including 1,145 children. The train had 46 carriages.

Alie, the girls' mother and all the other parents and children in that group were gassed on arrival.

Gretha wrote the last heartrending poem in the album and made a promise to keep Alie's friendship album forever. These are the words she wrote:

Dear Alie,

To my great sorrow,
this is the end of your album,
of a great destiny.
Although you are dead,
I will never, ever forget you.
You will always remain in my heart.
As long as I live, I will keep this album.
Rest in peace, my darling –
that is the wish of
your dearly loving sister,

Gretha.

GRETHA WATERMAN-LOPES DIAS

7 December 1945.

Lieve Alie.

Tot mijn groot verdriet is
dit het einde van je album,
van een groot noodlot. Je
bent wel dood, maar nooit
en nimmer zal ik jou
vergeten, jij blijft steeds
in mijn hart. Zoolang ik
leef zal ik dat album
bewaren. Rust zacht mijn

lieveling is de wens

van je innig

liefhebbende

zuster Gretha

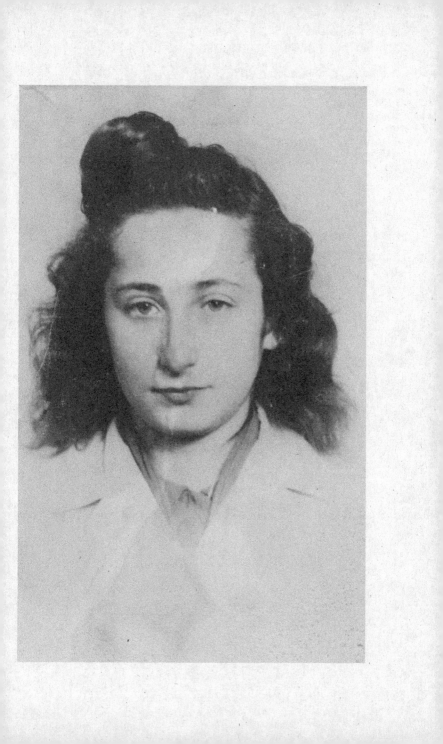

IN MEMORIAM

Annie Fransman
Agatha van Schaik
Ingeborg Frankenstein
Rosa Levie
Lena de Rood
Jenny Cohen
Lientje de Jong
Rosa Sarfatij
Liesje Aletrino
Minna Vas Nunes
Annie de Leeuw
Guta Maliniak
Erna Fleischhauer
Benjamin Roeg

Berry Waterman
Leendert Lopes Dias
Esther Lopes Dias-Van Beezem

BIOGRAPHIES OF ALIE'S FRIENDS AND FAMILY

A photograph taken on Govert Flinckstraat
in front of Coby Spaan's house.

Front right, Alie with Roosje on her lap.
Front left with roller skates, Coby Spaan, Alie's neighbour.

Annie Fransman

26 January 1930
11 December 1942

Annie's real name was Marianne. She was born in Amsterdam and lived at number 36-III President Brandstraat with:

Her mother: Esther Fransman Gosler (1898–1942).

Her father: Joseph (1893–1942).

Her sisters:

Alida (1920–1942) was a sewing machinist and needlewoman.

Anna (1923–1942) was a dressmaker.

Hendrika (1925–1942) was a clothesmaker.

Sophia (1928–1942) was a seamstress.

Betsie (1932–1942) was still at school.

Her brother Isaac (1919–1943) was married to Greta Lavino (1921–1942), and they had a child, Esther Fransman (1941–1942).

Isaac worked as a butcher's assistant. They lived at number 126-I Tugelaweg.

Her father, Joseph, had a market permit for the sale of fish. Before the war, he was allowed to sell all kinds of fish on Sundays. From 1941 he had permission to sell fish or fruit and vegetables in Amsterdam-Oost.

There is a photograph of Joseph on his market permit.

There are no known photographs of Annie, and no stories about her were recorded.

Annie wrote in Alie's album on 19 September 1941. It is the first poem in the album.

Annie reached the age of twelve.

Agatha van Schaik

1 April 1930
9 July 1943

Agatha's full name was Agatha Hendrika Klein. Van Schaik was her stepfather's surname, and Klein was the surname of her mother, Duifje Klein (1895–1942). Her father's identity is unknown. Duifje was the widow of Levie Kets de Vries. When Duifje married Cornelis Marinus van Schaik (1900–1943) in 1933, Agatha was given his surname. They lived at number 68, Eerste Oosterparkstraat. Her mother and stepfather divorced in 1941 and Agatha had to move to the Home for Jewish Working Girls on Gijsbrecht van Aemstelstraat in the Weesperzijde neighbourhood. This was a small shelter for girls who were temporarily unable to live at home. The home was run by Miss Vega. In an interview with her in the *Joodsch Weekblad* in 1941, she mentioned an eleven-year-old girl who lived at the home. That girl was Agatha.

When her mother came to live around the corner with Agatha's younger brother, Johannes Mattheus van Schaik (1935–1942), Agatha did not move back in with them. Her mother was taken away in August 1942 and sent straight to Auschwitz. Agatha remained at the home until she was taken away in June 1943. Agatha had an older sister, Cornelia Maria Klein (1927–1943), who was being taken care of in Amersfoort, but the reason is unknown. Cornelia also had a brother and sister with the surname Kets de Vries, who lived in Hilversum at the Beth Azarja van de Rudelsheimstichting, a school with a boarding section for mentally disabled Jewish children.

There are no known photographs of Agatha. She wrote in Alie's album on 2 October 1941.

Agatha reached the age of thirteen.

Inge Frankenstein

23 April 1932
7 July 1944

Inge's full name was Ingeborg Ruth Frankenstein. She was born in Berlin. Her father, Ernst Joseph (1891–1944), born in Braunschweig, Germany, was a film salesman. Her mother, Elisabete Johanna Klein (1903–1944), born in Schneidemühl, Germany, was a housewife.

In 1934, her parents fled Germany with the two-year-old Inge. The family lived first in Zandvoort but later moved to Amsterdam. They lived at number 74-I, Kromme Mijdrechtstraat.

Inge was sent to Westerbork with her parents on 28 October 1943. On 25 February 1944, they were sent to Theresienstadt. In May 1944, they were moved to Auschwitz. Her parents were murdered on 19 May.

Inge wrote in Alie's album on 2 October 1941. There are no known photographs of Inge.

Inge reached the age of twelve.

Rosa Levie

30 April 1929
15 December 1942

Rosa lived at number 56-II, Tweede Jan Steenstraat with her father, Aron Israël Levie (1896–1942), her mother, Duifje Englander (1890–1942), and her older sister, Jeannette (1924–1942).

Her father, Aron, was a cobbler by profession. Her mother was a seamstress. Jeannette was an office worker at a metal dealer's.

Her father was born in Suriname and moved to the Netherlands in 1905. At his military medical examination, his profession was given as diamond cutter. He was rejected for military service, as he was too short: 1 metre 50 (just under five foot).

The name of an uncle of Rosa's, Bernard Levie, is on the monument to war victims in Paramaribo.

Jeannette was deported in November 1942, the girls' father, Aron, in July 1943, and Rosa and her mother in August 1943. All of them were murdered in Auschwitz.

On one of the lists of names from the Herman Elteschool, the word 'opgegeven' is written beside Rosa's name in November 1942, to indicate that the school had no idea where she was and there was no point searching for her.

There are no known photographs of Rosa, only the drawing that Rosa did for Alie in her album and her poem. She wrote in the album on 6 January 1942.

Rosa reached the age of thirteen.

Lena de Rood

1 August 1930
2 July 1943

Lena was born in Amsterdam and lived at number 7-II, Eerste Boerhaavestraat, with her father, Hijman (1905–1943), her mother, Sura de Rood-Zagackier (1904–1943), her sister Sophia Rosa (1932–1943), and her brother Abraham (1934–1943).

Later they had to move to number 94-I Tugelaweg, in the Transvaalbuurt.

Lena's mother came from Mława in Poland.

Before the war, her father was a warehouse man at a hardware store. In 1924, he was exempted from military service because he was doing alternative nursing service at the NIZ, the Nederlands Israëlietisch Ziekenhuis (Dutch Jewish Hospital). He later worked as a 'funeral official' at the Nederlands Israëlitische Hoofdsynagoge at number 4, Houtmarkt. He had that position in 1941 and also worked for the Joodsche Raad. For these reasons, he obtained a Sperre.

On 21 June 1943, the whole family was sent to Westerbork. On 29 July, they were deported to Sobibór and murdered on arrival.

There are no known photographs of Lena. She wrote in Alie's album on 10 January 1942.

Lena reached the age of twelve.

Jenny Cohen

7 April 1929
12 October 1942

Jenny's name was actually Jaantje Cohen. As there was already a Jaantje in the family, she was known as Jenny. It also sounded more modern. She was born in The Hague, as were her parents, who moved to Amsterdam in 1930.

Jenny was one of Alie's best friends and she wrote in the album twice.

She lived at number 114-II, Van Woustraat, with her father, Levie Benjamin (Louis) Cohen (1894–1943), and her mother, Elisabeth (Betsie) Cohen-Kwetsie (1905–1942). Jenny was an only child.

Her father was a dealer in fabrics, buttons and haberdashery. He sold his goods at the market, but also supplied fashion houses, such as Maison de Bonneterie.

Jenny's cousin Riek kept a number of photographs of her and Jenny that were taken before the war. Riek has a Jewish father and a non-Jewish mother and made it safely through the war. Jenny's grandfather, Alexander Kwetsie, was known as the wrestling king of The Hague, and he gave shows and demonstrations during the interval at cinemas.

One of Headmaster Stibbe's lists from the Herman Elteschool says that Jenny left on 5 October 1942. On 9 October, she went with her parents to Westerbork. On 12 October, Jenny and her mother were murdered at Auschwitz. Her father, Levie, died later, in January 1943.

Jenny wrote in Alie's album on 12 January 1942 and at some point in July 1942.

Jenny reached the age of thirteen.

Lientje de Jong

3 April 1930
28 May 1943

Lientje's full name was Mendelina de Jong. She was born in Wormerveer.

Her parents, Simon (1899–1943) and Saartje de Jong-Michelson (1903–1943), had five children: Elisabeth (Lies) (1925–1943), Eva (Eef) (1927–1943), Izak (Ies) (1928–1943), Mendelina (Lientje) and Hartog (Harrie) (1933–1943).

The family was forced to move from number 1, Goudastraat, in Wormerveer, to Amsterdam in 1942. They moved in with Sara's parents at number 68, President Brandstraat. Later they moved to a house in the same street at number 56.

Her father, Simon was a cobbler. Her mother worked as a sewing machinist. Her sister was a sewing machinist. Her brother Ies also attended the Herman Elteschool and was in Class 6, Mr Stibbe's class. The list of names says that Ies and Lientje left on 23 November 1942, when Lientje was in Class 5.

Lientje is also in Class 4A's photograph at the Herman Elteschool.

She wrote in Alie's album on 12 February 1942. She also wrote in Adele Zimmer's friendship album.

Lientje reached the age of thirteen.

Roosje Sarfatij

30 September 1930
27 August 1943

Roosje's real name was Rosa, and she was born in Hamburg, Germany. In 1938, her parents moved back to Amsterdam, where they had both been born.

Roosje lived at number 9-II, Hoendiepstraat, with her mother, Francisca Sarfatij-Weening (1903–1943), and her father, Abraham Sarfatij (1899–1943).

She had two sisters: Annette (1935–1943) and Ruth Clara (1940–1943), and three brothers: Joseph (1923–1943), Israel Abraham (1932–1943) and Benjamin (1937–1943).

Rosa's father was an assistant Torah reader at the Portuguese Synagogue. He was also 'a secretarial official, religious circumciser and tends to the dead'. This made him eligible for a *Sperre* and the family's deportation was deferred.

In May 1943, the family was sent to Westerbork.

On 18 May 1943, Joseph was deported to Sobibór and murdered. The rest of the family went on the 24 August transport to Auschwitz, where they were all murdered on 27 August.

Roosje wrote in Alie's album at some point between February and May 1942, and I have been unable to find a photograph of her.

Roosje reached the age of twelve.

Liesje Aletrino

9 June 1931
2 July 1943

Liesje's full name was Elisabeth. She lived at 11-I, Eerste Boerhaavestraat.

Her father was called Benjamin (1902–1943), and her mother was Sara Aletrino-Pool (1900–1943). She had a brother, Gerson (1933–1943).

Her father was a paper merchant by profession. He was in poor health and suffered from kidney stones.

In 1942, her mother worked at the Joodsche Raad as the 'secretary of the P.I.G. Contact Committee.' (P.I.G. = Portugees Israëlitische Gemeente, or Portuguese Israelite Congregation).

On 29 June, the whole family was sent to Sobibór, where they were murdered on arrival on 2 July.

There are no known photographs of Liesje. She wrote in Alie's album at some point between February and July 1942.

Liesje reached the age of twelve.

Minna Vas Nunes

20 April 1932
11 June 1943

Minna was born in Amsterdam and lived at number 140, Amsteldijk. Her father's name was Jacob Vas Nunes (1898–1943). Her mother, Clara Vas Nunes-Wetzlar (1892–1943), originally came from Altona, Germany.

Minna had three sisters: Elisabeth (1920–1943), who was an office worker and was known as Betzy, Mary (1930–1943) and Emma (1928–1943). She also had a brother, Abraham (1923–1944), who was known as Aby. He worked as a machine operator and was a 'leader and cantor at the Dutch Jewish youth synagogue'.

Her father sold tools and was a woodworker. Minna and Mary were both at the Herman Elteschool. Headmaster Stibbe's lists say they 'left' the school on 18 November 1942.

Minna's brother, Abraham, was deported to Poland and died in March 1944. Elisabeth was sent to Auschwitz and died in October 1943. Minna's father, mother, Minna, Mary and Emma were taken to Westerbork in December 1942.

They were added to the 'children's transport' on 8 June 1943, the same as Alie and her mother. They were murdered on 11 June 1943 in Sobibór.

There are no known photographs of Minna, but there is one of her sister Emma.

She wrote in Alie's album at some point between February and July 1942.

Minna reached the age of eleven.

Annie de Leeuw

3 May 1932
22 July 1942

Annie's full name was Anna Judik de Leeuw, and she was born in Gouda.

In 1940, the family moved to number 80-I, Tweede Jan van der Heijdenstraat, in Amsterdam.

Her father, Jacob Izak de Leeuw (1904–1942), was a 'chemicals salesman'.

Her mother, Margaretha de Leeuw-Gompers (1907–1942), was a housewife.

Annie had a brother, Abraham Izak de Leeuw (1935–1942).

The list of names from the Herman Elteschool says that she will not return to school after the summer holiday in 1942. The whole family was deported to Auschwitz.

Annie, her brother and mother were murdered on 29 July 1942.

Her father died in September 1942. There are photographs of the whole family.

Annie wrote in Alie's album on 10 May 1942. She also wrote in Adele Zimmer's friendship album.

Annie reached the age of ten.

Guta Maliniak

23 April 1932
1 July 1944

Guta was born as Guta Towa Maliniak in Amsterdam and lived at number 10-II, Roerstraat.

Both of her parents came from Poland and got married in Rotterdam in 1931. They moved to Amsterdam the same year. Her father, Wolf David Maliniak (1905–1943), was a plywood salesman. Her mother, Feige Malkat Maliniak-Herschfus (1910–1944), was a shorthand typist at the Joodsche Raad. Guta had a little brother, Schalom Mordechai Maliniak (1935–1944). Her father was arrested in May 1942 because his passport had expired. He was sent as a criminal to the camp at Vught, via the house of detention on Amstelveenseweg in Amsterdam. It is not clear where he was deported to after that. Guta, her mother and brother were sent to Westerbork in November 1943 and from there to Theresienstadt in February 1944. In May 1944, they were sent to Auschwitz, where they were murdered.

There is a photograph of Guta and her brother. Guta must also be in the class photograph, but it is hard to identify her. Guta wrote in Alie's album at some point in July 1942.

Guta reached the age of twelve.

Erna Fleischhauer

24 September 1929
23 July 1943

Erna was born in Bamberg, Germany. She lived with her parents in the village of Adelsdorf. Her father, Justin Fleischhauer (1894–1942), was a cattle dealer. Her mother, Bertha Fränkel-Fleischhauer (1898–1942), helped out on the farm.

During Kristallnacht, on the night of 9 November 1938, the family's property was destroyed or stolen. Erna's parents wanted to send her away to a place where she would be safe. There was a special transport to the Netherlands for Jewish children. The family planned to emigrate to America.

Erna went on her own on the train to the Netherlands, arriving in Rotterdam on the children's transport on 16 February 1939. When they got there, it turned out that her parents had been denied a visa for America due to the high number of applicants. The Netherlands was no longer accepting adult Jewish refugees.

Erna was sent to various homes: within one year, she was moved from Rotterdam to Beverwijk, Hilversum and Groningen. In Groningen, she was taken in by the family of the author Clara Asscher-Pinkhof.

Meanwhile, Erna's parents had also been taken away from the village of Adelsdorf. Justin was sent to Dachau, while Bertha was moved to Nuremberg.

On 22 March 1942, Bertha was sent to a large ghetto, probably Izbica, in Poland. Her date and cause of death are unknown. Her archive card says: 'Cause of death: *verschollen*, missing'. After Dachau, Justin was sent back to Adelsdorf to carry out forced labour in the area. Then he was probably deported to Izbica too. His card also reports him as 'missing'.

On 18 June 1942, Erna moved to Amsterdam. In September 1942, she went to live at the Home for Jewish Working Girls, at number 27, Gijsbrecht van Aemstelstraat. She was twelve at the time. Agatha van Schaik lived in the same home. Erna also attended the Herman Elteschool, where she joined Alie's class, a year lower than she should actually have been in.

There was no further contact between Erna and her parents.

On 12 July 1943, Erna was picked up during a raid and sent to Sobibór, where she was murdered upon arrival.

Erna wrote in the album on 18 September 1942. Hers is the last poem written in the album by a friend.

Erna reached the age of thirteen.

Benjamin Roeg

2 June 1903
4 June 1943

Mr Roeg was Alie's teacher in Classes 4 and 5. He lived at number 25-II, Plantage Middenlaan.

He was married to Estera Feldstein (1909–1943), who was born in Poland. They did not have any children.

He worked as a teacher at the Herman Elteschool until the school was cleared by the Germans in spring 1943. Together with his wife, he was deported to Sobibór, where he was murdered.

Mr Roeg wrote in Alie's album on 2 October 1941.

The class photograph is the only known picture of Benjamin Roeg.

Benjamin Roeg reached the age of forty.

Berry Waterman

8 April 1920
24 January 1944

Berry's real name was Pinehas. He married Gretha at the Portuguese Synagogue in Amsterdam on 4 June 1941. After that, he moved in with the Lopes Dias family at number 265-I, Govert Flinckstraat.

He was a cheerful young man with a great sense of humour, and he worked as a milliner on Nieuwendijk in the centre of Amsterdam.

Before his wedding, he lived at 16-II, Waterlooplein.

His father sold second-hand goods at the market on Waterlooplein and on Uilenburg on Sundays. He also made reconditioned vacuum cleaners from old parts. His mother and his brothers Hatty and Moos helped him.

The Waterman family consisted of fourteen people: father Benedictus, mother Rebecca and the children: Mozes (Moos), Pinehas, Hartog (Hatty), David, the twin sisters Mietje and Duifje, Meijer, Isaac, Gretha, Johanna, Abraham and Dina.

The oldest was Mozes (b. 1918) and the youngest was Dina (b. 1937).

Hartog was the only member of the family to survive, partly because he went into hiding at Artis, Amsterdam's zoo.

Berry wrote in Alie's album on 2 October 1941.

A wedding photograph of Gretha and Berry still exists.

Berry reached the age of twenty-three.

Leendert Lopes Dias

11 April 1896
9 December 1942

The Lopes Dias family tree can be traced back to the early 1700s. Leendert was the seventh recorded generation in Amsterdam. He had seven brothers and sisters, all of whom were murdered in the war. His mother, Engelina, died in Amsterdam in 1941. His father, Jacob, was murdered at Auschwitz at the age of eighty-six, after the Portuguese Israelite old men's home at number 33, Nieuwe Herengracht, was emptied.

Leendert was born in a second-floor flat at number 40, Foeliedwarsstraat. As a young man, he worked as a butcher, and he was approved for military service in 1915, in spite of a problem with his eyes.

He married Esther van Beezem on 25 June 1919. They had two children: Gretha in 1920 and Alie in 1929. The family moved to Govert Flinckstraat, where Leendert's parents were also living by then.

Leendert sold flowers and plants. He had a permit to sell flowers from a cart or a basket at Stadionweg by the Olympic Stadium. He also sold his wares at the Monday market on Westerstraat. He was a kind and gentle man. When Gretha was a little girl and went with her friends to beg him for ten cents, he could never refuse. The family did not have much money and Leendert had to request financial support, particularly in the winter months.

He was given a market trader's permit until 1942. He did not have much work and sometimes helped out his sister and brother-in-law at the Jewish market on Joubertstraat, one of the Jewish markets that were meant only for Jewish salespeople and customers.

At the beginning of 1942, he became unemployed. He was called up for Molengoot in April 1942, a camp where unemployed people had to carry out work in order to retain their financial support. From April 1942, it became a camp exclusively for Jewish unemployed people, and this period is well documented. The residents of the camp worked for the Nederlandsche Heidemaatschappij, a land development company, and most of them had to carry out hard physical labour.

In October 1942, all the Jewish labour camps in the Netherlands were cleared, and the men were sent to Westerbork, and from there to Auschwitz. On the way to Auschwitz, a group between the ages of fifteen and fifty was removed from the trains and sent from the Polish town of Koźle (German: Kosel or Cosel), about 100 kilometres from Auschwitz, to work as forced labourers at various work camps around Auschwitz. These men became known as the Kosel Group. Leendert was sent to a labour camp at Bytom (German: Beuthen), where he was put to work, probably in the ore or coal mines. He was worked to death and passed away on 9 December 1942. He is buried in the Jewish cemetery in Bytom. Alie and her mother received the news of his death in January 1943.

He wrote in Alie's album in April 1942.

Leendert reached the age of forty-six.

Esther Lopes Dias-Van Beezem

18 November 1896
11 June 1943

Esther was one of seven children and lived at a number of different addresses in the old Jewish neighbourhood. She came from a family of street vendors and market traders.

On 25 June 1919, she married Leendert Lopes Dias.

Like Leendert, Esther had a permit to sell flowers. They had a permanent spot in the Zuid neighbourhood of Amsterdam, at Olympiaplein. Esther was a robust, resourceful woman who continued to do business after Leendert was taken away. She probably helped out her brother Joel at the Jewish market on Joubertstraat.

On 9 May 1943, she and Alie were taken from their home by H. Verboom, who worked for the Zentralstelle für jüdische Auswanderung, Abteilung Hausraterfassung. He was also from the investigation department. They were later taken to the Hollandsche Schouwburg by Van de Kraan, Bout and Van Keulen. They were admitted by Swagers, who signed their receipt.

On 14 May, they arrived at the camp in Vught. Esther was separated from Alie, who was sent to the girls' barracks. They saw each other now and then, during visiting hours or roll call.

Esther was shocked when Gretha voluntarily reported to Vught on 20 May. She had hoped that Gretha would be able to escape, although she was happy later that the three of them were together.

On 6 and 7 June, all the children had to leave Vught. Esther and Alie left together on 7 June. Gretha was not allowed to go with them, as only one parent or accompanying adult was permitted to go. They were able to say goodbye to Gretha though, when she broke through the line of soldiers and ran after them. It was a brief farewell.

This transport became known as the Vught Children's Transport.

Esther and Alie arrived at Westerbork, where their group was kept separately from the rest of the people in the camp. The very next day, they were deported to Sobibór, where they were murdered on arrival.

Esther did not write in Alie's album.

She reached the age of forty-six.

Rosa Snijders

9 July 1931

All four members of the Snijders family found a place to go into hiding in the town of Anna Paulowna in Noord-Holland with the Boonacker family, who were not well off. The father of the family worked as a postman. It was a very small house. During the summer, lots of children from the big cities came to the countryside for the fresh air, as part of a programme organised by the Dutch Reformed Church.

Rosa and her brother Marcus (Max) pretended to be part of that group of children, so they were allowed to go outside. They also had to go to church every Sunday. But then a woman from the village said that she knew they were Jewish children. After that, they did not go outside again and they no longer had to go to church. During raids for boys and men for the *Arbeitseinsatz*, they hid inside a partition wall.

When the daughter of the family became pregnant and her fiancé moved in, the Snijders family had to leave. They found new places to stay through their contacts in Enkhuizen. Rosa and her brother went to different addresses. Their parents found a place together.

Rosa was collected by a boy from the resistance and taken to an address in Blokker, where the boy himself was in hiding with the Schouten family. This was the first time Rosa had been all on her own and she found it hard. The family was very kind and she was allowed to go outside as long as she stayed at the back of the house.

After a few months, all the people who were in hiding with the Schoutens had to leave. She ended up on a farm with the Broers family. She was lucky to find herself on a farm, as it was the infamous 'hunger winter' of 1944. People from the cities were moving through the countryside of Noord-Holland, looking for food. As well as Rosa, there were two non-Jewish boys in hiding at the farm, in an attempt to avoid forced labour. The resistance used the barn as weapons stores, so two more young men came along to guard the place. Rosa could also go outside there, but again only as long as she stayed at the back of the house. If there was a raid, she had to run into the fields and hide.

After two years in hiding, on 5 May 1945, they heard that the Germans had capitulated. They went out onto the streets, where people were cheering and dancing. But a group of NSB members and Germans who did not want to surrender started shooting. This went on for a few more days.

Eventually she was taken to the address where her parents were in hiding, and they were reunited.

When they returned to Enkhuizen, they found that their house had been taken by the NSB mayor of Enkhuizen. They were allowed to move back into the house, which was full of his belongings. Rosa's father said he would rather sit on the floor than on that man's furniture – and that is exactly what they did. All the belongings they had handed over for safekeeping were returned, but they did not get back her grandparents' and aunt's property.

Rosa later moved to Amsterdam and worked at the Weesperpleinziekenhuis, a hospital. She wanted to emigrate to Israel, but then she met her husband. They married and emigrated to America. They had two daughters. Rosa still lives in the United States.

Rosa wrote in Alie's album on 10 June 1942.

Adele Zimmer

19 May 1931

Adele went into hiding with the Hofstede family in Overijssel. She stayed there until a year after liberation. She emigrated to America, where she married and had three children.

Adele wrote in Alie's album on 10 July 1942. Adele also had a friendship album of her own, which a number of the girls wrote in.

She still lives in the United States.

Members of Adele's family who did not survive the war:
Brothers
Abraham Adolf Isak Zimmer (8 August 1921–23 September 1942)
Moritz Zimmer (1 February 1923–30 September 1942)
Salli Zimmer (5 September 1928–4 June 1943)
Father
Judah Zimmer (25 November 1896–September 1942)
Mother
Malka Zimmer-Fass (5 June 1895–September 1942)

Adele's foster family
Joseph Konijn (20 May 1894–27 August 1943)
Pesia Konijn-Budzanower (28 November 1902–27 August 1943)

Salli's foster family
Joseph Reindorp (18 March 1899–4 June 1943)
Debora Reindorp-van Sister (23 May 1901–4 June 1943)

Mimi Mok

15 February 1930
21 July 1994

Mimi lived at number 21, Eerste Sweelinckstraat, with her mother, Mietje (1896–1986), and her father, Michel (1898–1943).

They had a cigar shop and lived behind the shop.

Mimi and her mother survived the war by going into hiding with relatives in Doesburg, in the eastern Netherlands, where her mother came from.

Her father died as a forced labourer at Neukirch, a camp in Poland.

Mimi wrote in Alie's album on 21 September 1941. She was one of Alie's best friends.

Mimi married after the war and had one son. She died in 1994.

Mimi de Leeuw

21 July 1930

After their narrow escape, Mimi, her mother and her sister Annie moved from Zuider Amstellaan to Hoffmeyrstraat in the Amsterdam ghetto. Life there was quite hard. She went to the Jekerschool for some time, where she taught the little children, as there was a shortage of teachers. There was also an after-school group, where she was able to do crafts and painting, and a gym where she could do gymnastics. The extended family was becoming smaller and smaller. They had to save up to send parcels to family members in Westerbork.

In September 1943, it was their turn to be taken away. Doorbells rang at four in the morning, and boots stamped up and down the stairs. Mimi had a backpack and took as much as she could with her, but she left without any warm clothes or sturdy shoes. The Germans were waiting with trucks to take people to Amstel railway station.

The whole ghetto was emptied and everyone had to wait for hours for the trains to Westerbork to leave.

Her mother had sciatica and was sent to the hospital barracks at Westerbork. Mimi helped the little children to shower, dry themselves and get dressed. Mimi was also able to do sports at Westerbork. There was a little school where she could learn and also teach a little, and they played games. Her aunt, who was in a mixed marriage, sent her parcels.

In January 1944, they finally had to leave, together with lots of family members. They were 'lucky' enough to be transported in a passenger train. The train went to Bergen-Belsen. This change came as a shock. There were not many guards at Westerbork, but at Bergen-Belsen they were met by SS men with bloodhounds.

She ended up in the women's camp with her mother and sister. Every day, they had to do roll call for hours. Every day, the bed had to be perfectly smooth. Any bumps and they were punished, beaten or given no food.

Mimi's sister Annie was soon given a job in the shoe factory. Mimi and her mother worked in the kitchen. Every day at five, hot food was delivered to the gate and Mimi took it around the barracks in mess tins. There was cabbage soup, 'coffee' and bread, and milk and porridge for the children. But the camp became more and more crowded and the food deliveries were irregular. Sometimes they were given nothing for five days, followed by coffee and raw beetroot.

Annie became sick. Because of her intestinal stricture, a raw pea had become stuck, and her body was unable to digest it. There were Jewish doctors in the camp, but no medication or any way to perform surgery. Annie weighed only twenty-five kilograms when she died. Mimi and her mother were allowed to accompany her only to the gate of the camp, where her body was collected.

Mimi tried to survive: 'just breathe'. She and her mother tried to keep each other going, to find a reason to go on living. Food, according to Mimi, was one such reason. Mimi caught typhus, but because she had always been fit, she still had enough strength to get up and move every day. Not getting up meant death.

Mimi and her mother survived the camp and were liberated by the British in April 1945. Mimi was fourteen years old at the time.

In August 1945, they returned to Amsterdam. She did not want to go back to school or to study.

Later she worked in the fabric trade. She had some health problems, suffering from rheumatism. Her doctor advised her to move to Portugal, where she immediately recovered.

Mimi married and had three children and lots of grandchildren and great-grandchildren. She now lives in the Netherlands again.

She wrote in Alie's album on 1 July 1942.

Her other sister and brother-in-law did not survive the war:
Sophia (Vicky) de Leeuw (12 October 1921–2 July 1943)
Andries (Dries) Israël de Rosa (1 February 1920–2 July 1943)

Lea Janowitz

11 April 1931
8 May 2010

At Westerbork, Lea's father Leo (1892–1983) was able to arrange for Lea, her mother, Blanka (1902–1968), and brother Harry (1929–2019) to be sent to the internees barracks, where you were allowed to live if you had a job. These were the barracks where the original refugees were housed before the war. Some of them still lived there and had the best jobs.

Lea tried to fit in and to make the best of it, 'because that was where we were living,' as she said later. She became involved with a group of girls in the Schülerkreis, a youth organisation at Westerbork set up by the German-Jewish residents. They had meetings on Shabbat and there were activities for the children on major holidays too.

When there was a reorganisation and it looked as if the family would no longer be considered internees, Lea's father was given a job as an OD man. He was accepted for the position after he said that he had fought in the First World War. This was not a lie: he had fought as a Russian soldier against the Germans. As he spoke good German, it was assumed that he had fought for Germany.

Lea, Harry and their mother ended up living in the houses reserved for the long-time camp residents, the German-speaking Jewish refugees who had been at Westerbork since 1939, while her father slept in the military barracks.

She attended the school for camp children and Harry became an assistant at the clinic, running all kinds of errands for the doctors. Lea was ill a number of times and suffered from tonsillitis. She had a very high fever, but no one was allowed to tell the doctor, because her mother was afraid of the contagious diseases in the hospital, which might result in death or deportation to an even worse camp.

Her mother did all kinds of work: she had to separate aluminium from paper that was thrown from aeroplanes to confuse radar. This was then sent to Germany for the war effort. She cleaned the camp commandant Gemmeker's office, which she did not mind, because she could take his cigarette butts. What she did not like was cleaning houses in the nearby town of Assen. The prisoners had to pay for their own lodging, and the local people could hire the prisoners to work for them. This money went to the camp management. She disliked going out to work. because it meant being confronted with the outside world and with people who didn't care about the Jews, but simply took advantage of them. She was outside the camp, but she was unable to escape.

Lea's parents never considered escaping, because they knew that for every person who escaped, ten others were deported. The punishment for fleeing was that other prisoners, often your own family, would be transported to a worse camp. So you would be risking their lives.

The family was eventually sent to Bergen-Belsen, a terrible camp in comparison to Westerbork.

The women were then sent to Vittel, France. The journey took six days. That camp was a little better, but her mother's mental state deteriorated, because she did not know where Harry and her husband were. Lea had to look after her mother.

In summer 1944, the camp was going to be emptied and the prisoners were to be sent to Auschwitz, even though the Americans were already nearby. The train was ready and waiting, but the Germans needed it to make their escape. Finally, Lea and her mother were liberated in Vittel, when Lea was fourteen years old.

Via Paris and Brussels, Lea and her mother found their way to Waalwijk in the Netherlands, where the family was reunited. They returned to Amsterdam and were able to move back into their own house. Her parents went back to their old jobs, and they never spoke about the war again.

Lea wrote in Alie's album between February and May 1942.

She married after the war and had three daughters. Lea died in 2010.

Lea Tirtsa Steinberg

28 July 1932

Lea Tirtsa Steinberg, known as Tirtsa, was born in Leipzig. Her parents were Salomon Steinberg (1900–1945), born in Berlin, and Erna Steinberg-Adler (1901–1998), born in Neustadt, Germany. They came to the Netherlands in 1939, after Kristallnacht. Tirtsa's older sister, Rachel, and her older brother, Bernard, were sent to England with the Kindertransport. Tirtsa stayed with her parents.

Her parents wanted to go to America in 1940. They had a visa, but wanted to wait until after Pesach. Then the German invasion began and they could no longer leave.

Her father was a teacher at an orphanage, teaching Hebrew and other subjects. Her mother earned some extra money by doing other people's laundry.

In September 1943, Tirtsa and her father were sent to Westerbork. Her mother was pregnant and stayed in Amsterdam at the Joodse Invalide, until she gave birth to a daughter in January 1944, Carla Ruth Sara. After that, the whole family was transported to Bergen-Belsen. Tirtsa's aunt, grandmother and cousins ended up in the same barracks.

Her father, Salomon, died in Bergen-Belsen on 5 February 1945.

In April 1945, Tirtsa was evacuated from Bergen-Belsen. She was part of what became known as the 'lost transport', which moved around without a destination until eventually being liberated by the Russians.

It was a miracle that her little sister survived. They felt that 'God chose for it to happen that way'.

Her grandmother, Fanny, did become ill though and died on one of the other transports from Bergen-Belsen.

The rest of the Adler family survived.

At the end of the war, Tirtsa's family lived at number 18, Vaalrivierstraat, in the Transvaalbuurt.

Tirtsa emigrated to England and later to Canada, where she still lives.

Tirtsa wrote in Alie's album between May and July 1942.

Tirtsa does not have any photographs of herself from this period.

NOTE FROM THE AUTHOR

The reconstruction I have created is based on Gretha's stories; interviews with Adele, Rosa, Tirtsa, her cousin Karen, and Mimi; conversations with Jenny Cohen's uncle and cousin; an interview Lea Janowitz gave for the Shoah Foundation, with additional information from her brother Harry; accounts from former students at the Herman Elteschool, the stories of Coby Spaan, Alie's former neighbour and friend, who lived in the same house on Govert Flinckstraat until her death in 2019; stories from elderly people my colleagues and I interviewed for *Oorlog in mijn Buurt* ('War in My Neighbourhood'), an educational project with the In Mijn Buurt Foundation; eyewitness accounts from people who were in the same places as the girls at around the same time, such as Vught and the crèche opposite the Hollandsche Schouwburg. And lots of research in archives and literature.

I researched everything I was able to research, such as what the weather was like on particular days. The events in the book really took place, with the exception of one incident. I invented the friendship with the 'other' Jenny in Vught. I knew Alie had friends in the camp, some from school or from her neighbourhood. In my search for Jenny (Jaantje) Cohen, I came across a Jenny Cohen from 's-Heerenberg. This Jenny could not have lived in Amsterdam, but was in the camp at Vught at the same time as Alie, in the same barracks, and was also taken away on the children's transport. It is hard to believe that they did not meet. I used Alie's friendships with other girls to construct a friendship between Alie and Jenny from 's-Heerenberg.

As previously mentioned, most of the dialogue is fictionalised. Sometimes a person could still remember a conversation word for word, but often the people I interviewed could no longer remember exactly what was said. I obtained their permission to fill in the details. Sometimes events happened in which other people were involved, whose names I was unable to discover. In such cases, I made up a name myself, usually based on the names of people who were in the same place at that time, for example, in the camp at Vught.

Rosa Snijders gave me a very special photograph: the only photograph of Class 4A with Mr Roeg. Most of the girls in the friendship album must be in that photograph, but sadly the interviewees could not put names to all the faces. I was able to find out the names of a number of the children from the list of names of pupils who had left or been placed at the school. That photograph is also special, because it was taken shortly before the star was introduced. I know of two other photographs of the Herman Elteschool during the war, in which the children are wearing stars. One photograph shows Adele Zimmer's class and the other is of the class that Harry, Lea Janowitz's brother, was in. Mimi Mok is also in that photograph.

With some events, an interviewee was certain that they had taken place on a particular date, but I had to change the date after doing research, as they turned out to have happened at a different time.

What I deeply regret – and this was also one of the driving forces behind this book – was that for some of the girls I could find nothing more than their names and dates of birth and death in an archive. No photo, no family, no stories.

At the time of publication, this is all the information I have been able to find. I hope that, after the book is published, more people will be able to provide further information about the girls.

RESEARCH

I knew that Alie lived in Govert Flinckstraat. I found the other girls' addresses at the Stadsarchief Amsterdam (Amsterdam City Archives). It soon became clear that they lived in De Pijp and the surrounding neighbourhoods: Diamantbuurt, Weesperzijde and Rivierenbuurt. Some lived in the Transvaalbuurt, where they often ended up when they had to leave their old homes, as in the case of

Mimi de Leeuw, and it was in many cases the last place they lived before deportation. This area was also known as the ghetto, an area designed to isolate the Jews from the rest of the population.

So the school they attended must have been somewhere in De Pijp or nearby. There is little archive material about schools available in the city archives.

From September 1941, Jewish students were obliged to attend one of the Jewish schools that were hastily set up. Jewish schools fell under the supervision of the Joodsche Raad, whose archive is now kept at NIOD, the Institute for War, Holocaust and Genocide Studies.

In the Joodsche Raad's archive, I found all kinds of documents from the education department. The Jewish schools were numbered and their locations were indicated. I studied lists of teachers, correspondence between the schools and the Joodsche Raad's education department, but it took me a long time to find the school attended by Alie and her friends.

Until, that is, I came across a list of teachers that included the name of B. Roeg. I knew that name from somewhere. At home, in the friendship album, I did indeed find a B. Roeg. It was the teacher who had written a poem in Alie's book. Mr B. Roeg taught Classes 4 and 5 at the Herman Elteschool.

The Herman Elteschool was a Jewish school even before the war, founded by Vereniging voor Kennis en Godsvrucht. It was a special denominational school. So the school was not given a number, but was allowed to continue under its own name. The school's address was 203, Van Ostadestraat, close to Alie's house.

Little material about the school has been preserved. I found only one notebook from the school in the NIOD archives. The book seemed fairly empty at first and I was about to put it aside, until I turned the book around and started leafing through from the back to the front – which made sense, as Hebrew is written from right to left. On the pages were lists of the names of children who had joined or left the school in the period 1940–1943.

Over the course of the war, more children left than came to join the school. Many names were followed by the words: *vertrokken Dl.*

('left for Germany'). I found nearly all the girls from Alie's album on the lists. Written in very small writing, they also mentioned that Alie had had to retake a year in 1940, together with Mimi Mok.

The headmaster of the school, Elias Stibbe, had filled in forms for the Education Inspectorate. I found lots of information about the school in those forms: the composition of the classes, who the teachers were, how the gym was equipped.

I later heard from a former student at the school that she had witnessed the school being closed down in 1943. As a precaution, she and some other children set fire to the papers that were thrown out onto the street. The children who were still left were sent to other schools. That is why Mimi de Leeuw ended up at the Jekerschool, where she taught the younger children, because there were also fewer and fewer teachers.

In 2012, I became acquainted with Mr Fleischmann, a German historian who ran a website that contained information about the history of the Jewish community in Adelsdorf, where Erna Fleischhauer was born. He put me in touch with Dr Christiane Kolbet, who has collected a number of eyewitness accounts of Kristallnacht in Adelsdorf. The Kindertransport that enabled the children from Adelsdorf and the surrounding communities to leave is also well documented. This made it possible for me to write Erna's story.

Another resource I frequently consulted was the complete collection of the *Joodsche Weekblad*. I had mixed feelings about this. I found a great deal of information there, but it was horrifying to read how people tried to make the best of things. In a 1941 edition, I found the only interview with Miss Vega, the director of the Home for Jewish Working Girls, where both Agatha and Erna lived. There is a detailed account of what the home looked like and who lived there. Her optimism is poignant. She wants to bring the girls up well: they are not allowed to have holes in their stockings.

There was some confusion about the date when Alie was given her album. On the first page, where Alie writes her details, it says:

'received in 1942'. This is strange, because the first poems were dated 19 September 1941. It appears that '1942' was added later.

For a long time, the website Joodsmonument.nl had a street photograph of children, including Alie. I could not find out who had posted it. Until we went to install commemorative brass *Stolpersteine* on the pavement outside Alie and her parents' house. The woman living across the road turned out to be Alie's childhood friend Coby Spaan. She was the one who had posted the photograph, and she still lived in the same house, opposite Alie's former home in Govert Flinckstraat.

As I have mentioned before, my research is not yet over, as archives are increasingly being digitised and made public. However, my most important sources remain the people who are still alive and whom I was able to interview.

GLOSSARY

ARBEITSEINSATZ Labour deployment, forced labour in Germany by men between the ages of 18 and 35.

AUFSEHERINNEN Female camp guards. At Kamp Vught, these were mainly Dutch women. They were infamous for their brutality and harassment.

AUSTAUSCHJUDEN Captured Jewish people who were exchanged for German prisoners of war.

GROTE SJOEL, or GROTE SYNAGOGE The oldest synagogue in Amsterdam (1671), now part of the Joods Historisch Museum (Jewish Historical Museum).

GRÜNE POLIZEI Or Ordnungspolizei, intended to keep the population in line, known as the 'Green Police' because of the colour of their uniforms.

HOLLANDSCHE SCHOUWBURG A theatre in the Plantage neighbourhood of Amsterdam, which became a temporary detention centre for Jews who had been taken from their homes before they were sent on to Westerbork. It is now a monument.

JOODSCHE INVALIDE A Jewish home for the disabled, which opened in Amsterdam in 1911.

JOODSCHE RAAD The Jewish Council, a Jewish organisation that governed the Jewish community. Established by the German occupiers as a body through which they could impose their regulations and decrees.

JOODSCHE WEEKBLAD The Jewish weekly paper. After a ban on all Jewish publications, this was the Joodsche Raad's only organ and was intended exclusively for the Jewish population. In addition to articles of a social and religious nature, all the German regulations and decrees were published here. Everything was censored by the Germans. The last edition was published in September 1943.

KINDERCOMITÉ An organisation that welcomed child refugees and allocated them to different homes.

KINDERTRANSPORT From the beginning of 1939, after Kristallnacht, Jewish children were sent on special children's transports from Germany to England and on to America. Around 500 children remained in the Netherlands.

KINDERTRANSPORT VUGHT On 6 and 7 June 1942, 1,300 children from Kamp Vught were sent from Westerbork to Sobibór. A number of children remained behind in Westerbork.

KRISTALLNACHT The night of 9 November 1938, when the SS in Germany carried out a massive pogrom against the Jews.

LECHA DODI Hymn sung in synagogues at dusk on Fridays to welcome Shabbat.

MAISON DE BONNETERIE An upmarket Dutch chain of fashion department stores.

NIZ In the first half of the twentieth century there were three Jewish hospitals in the city, the Portuguese (PIZ) on the Plantage Franschelaan (Henri Polaklaan), the Nederlands Israëlitische (NIZ) on the Nieuwe Keizersgracht and the Centraal Israëlietische Ziekenverpleging (CIZ), also on the Nieuwe Keizersgracht. In 1943 the three hospitals were evacuated by the occupying forces.

NSB Nationaal-Socialistische Beweging, the National Socialist Movement in the Netherlands.

OD Ordedienst, here, the Jewish supervisors at Westerbork.

PORTUGUESE SYNAGOGUE Completed in 1675, this beautiful Sephardic synagogue was the largest synagogue of its day. It has one of the oldest Jewish libraries in the world.

SD Sicherheitsdienst, the security and information service of the SS.

SHEITEL Wig worn by married Orthodox Jewish women.

SJEINTJE Term of endearment, from Yiddish *sheyn*, beautiful, pretty.

SJNOKKELTJE Term of endearment, from Yiddish.

SITTING SHIVA Observing the seven-day mourning period, which includes sitting at home on low stools or the floor.

SHUL (Dutch: SJOEL) Synagogue.

SPERRE A temporary exemption from deportation.

VERWALTER A non-Jewish business administrator, often appointed by the Nazis.

WA Weerbaarheidsafdeling, the paramilitary arm of the NSB.

ZENTRALSTELLE Zentralstelle für jüdische Auswanderung, the Central Office for Jewish Emigration. The logistics and execution of the deportations were carried out under the leadership of Willy Lages and Ferdinand aus der Fünten. Located in a school building on Adama van Scheltemaplein opposite the headquarters of the SD, the Sicherheitsdienst.

ACKNOWLEDGEMENTS

I would like to thank the following:

First and foremost:
    Gretha Pach-Lopes Dias, the widow of Berry Waterman,
for the album and for sharing her family's story.
    My parents, Nancy and John Philips,
John, without your efforts and support, this book would not have been written.

With special thanks to these women for sharing their stories with me, and also for their support and trust:
    Adele Zimmer, Ro Snijders, Mimi de Leeuw, Tirtsa Steinberg

The women who did not write in the album, but who were at the same school and were willing to share their memories with me:
    Karen Adler, No'omi Tal

Alie's former neighbour, who shared her memories of Alie and the street where they lived:
    Coby Spaan

The children of the women who wrote in the album and survived the war, but who had already passed away before I started writing the book:
    Michel Waterman (Mimi Mok) and Edith Andriesse (Lea Janowitz), thank you for your commitment, support and feedback on the manuscript.

The daughters of Adele and Tirtsa:
    Madeline Mendelsohn and Rachelle Silver,
thanks for all your help!

The families of the girls in the album:

Harry Janowitz (Lea Janowitz's brother)

Hartog (Hatty) Waterman (Berry's brother, Gretha's brother-in-law)

Relatives of Jenny Cohen: Alexander Kwetsie (uncle), Riet Driessen-Kwetsie (cousin), Paula Kwetsie (cousin)

Mimi de Leeuw's cousin, for providing more information about Mimi's story:

Ina Groenteman-Rosenthal

Marianne Schönbach Literary Agency:

Stijn de Vries,

thank you for your incredible support and faith in me!

Marianne Schönbach, Diana Gvozden

Uitgeverij Meulenhoff Boekerij:

Willemijn Peene,

with thanks for your expertise, support and for always making me feel that everything was going to turn out fine!

Paloma Sanchez, Ilse Delaere

And Suzan Beijer, for the beautiful and thoughtful design

Family and supporters:

Carli, Michel, John, Nancy, Rachelle, David, Rietje

Minka, Marjolijn, Marieke, Nina, Aspha, Monique, Mona, Marion, Renee, Joyce, Wil, Hedwig, Nicolien, Arnolda, Eelco, Carla

ACKNOWLEDGEMENTS

PICTURE ACKNOWLEDGEMENTS

All pictures throughout this book are from the private collection of the author, supplied courtesy of Meulenhoff Boekerij, with the exception of the following:

p. 114, 394, private collection of Rosa Snijders; p. 373, private collection of Coby Spaan; p. 379, private collection of Riet Kwetsie; p. 396, private collection of Adele Zimmer; p. 397, private collection of Mimi Mok; p. 398, private collection of Mimi de Leeuw; p. 400, private collection of Edith Andriesse.

Images on p. 384, 385 and 386 courtesy of Collection Joods Historisch Museum.

Maps, pp. ix, x and xi © Monique Wijbrands.

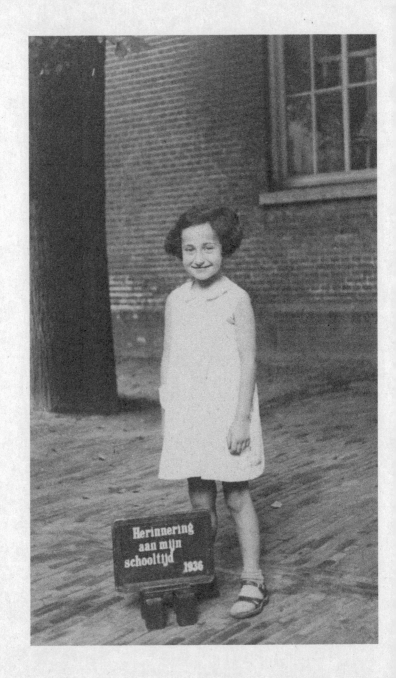